VBA Automation for Excel 2019 Cookbook

Solutions to automate routine tasks and increase productivity with Excel and other MS Office applications

Mike Van Niekerk

BIRMINGHAM—MUMBAI

VBA Automation for Excel 2019 Cookbook

Commissioning Editor: Richa Tripathi
Acquisition Editor: Karan Gupta
Senior Editor: Rohit Singh
Content Development Editor: Ruvika Rao
Technical Editor: Gaurav Gala
Copy Editor: Safis Editing
Project Coordinator: Deeksha Thakkar
Proofreader: Safis Editing
Indexer: Rekha Nair
Production Designer: Vijay Kamble

First published: September 2020

Production reference: 1180920

Published by Packt Publishing Ltd.
Livery Place
35 Livery Street
Birmingham
B3 2PB, UK.

ISBN 978-1-78961-003-1

www.packt.com

To my wife, Esmarie, for believing in me. This book would not have been written had it not been for your love and support.

– Mike Van Niekerk

`Packt.com`

Subscribe to our online digital library for full access to over 7,000 books and videos, as well as industry leading tools to help you plan your personal development and advance your career. For more information, please visit our website.

Why subscribe?

- Spend less time learning and more time coding with practical eBooks and videos from over 4,000 industry professionals

- Improve your learning with Skill Plans built especially for you

- Get a free eBook or video every month

- Fully searchable for easy access to vital information

- Copy and paste, print, and bookmark content

Did you know that Packt offers eBook versions of every book published, with PDF and ePub files available? You can upgrade to the eBook version at `packt.com` and, as a print book customer, you are entitled to a discount on the eBook copy. Get in touch with us at `customercare@packtpub.com` for more details.

At `www.packt.com`, you can also read a collection of free technical articles, sign up for a range of free newsletters, and receive exclusive discounts and offers on Packt books and eBooks.

Contributors

About the author

Mike Van Niekerk has consulted as an IT lecturer since 1995, mainly presenting project management and Microsoft Office end user application courses. With 39 years of applied experience in many industries, including language courses and the writing of manuals, he has acquired an exceptional ability to transfer knowledge. Being a Microsoft Office Specialist and Microsoft Certified Trainer, he is highly experienced in MS Word, Excel, PowerPoint, Access, MS Project, and VBA. He also works with, and trains on, Outlook, Publisher, and Visio. The training he has done includes all these applications on all levels, from beginner to advanced. He has written MS Office training manuals for several IT training companies in South Africa.

A heartfelt thank you to everyone on the VBA Automation for Excel 2019 Cookbook team. No book is ever written by just one person. There are four people that I've worked with very closely and for whom I have much appreciation. Thank you, Karan, for making me feel welcome during those first days of writing an outline and signing contracts. To Rohit, for patiently introducing me to a new style of writing, and Ruvika, for her persistence when schedules became tight. Lastly, a special word of thanks to Prajakta, the watchful Project Manager who kept us all on our toes.

About the reviewer

Belinda Loseby has been involved in IT training and development for over 20 years. During this time, she has developed software solutions specifically using VBA to adapt Microsoft applications to the needs of business users.

As a lecturer, she has had the opportunity to present on a number of IT-related topics, including VBA, C#, Microsoft Office, and business skills, to employees of corporations throughout South Africa and other countries across Africa.

She thoroughly enjoys the creative process of building software and adding value by imparting knowledge, making software easier to understand and more efficient to use.

Packt is searching for authors like you

If you're interested in becoming an author for Packt, please visit `authors.packtpub.com` and apply today. We have worked with thousands of developers and tech professionals, just like you, to help them share their insight with the global tech community. You can make a general application, apply for a specific hot topic that we are recruiting an author for, or submit your own idea.

Table of Contents

2

Working with the VBA Editor

3

The VBA Object Model

6

VBA Language Elements

7

Working with Ranges

8
Using Functions

9
Implementing Program Flow

10
Implementing Automation

11
Handling Errors

12
Debugging

13
Creating and Modifying Dialog Boxes

14
Creating UserForms

15
UserForm Controls

16

Creating Custom Functions

17

Creating Word Documents with Excel VBA

18

Working with PowerPoint in Excel VBA

Other Books You May Enjoy

Index

Preface

Visual Basic for Applications (**VBA**) has been around for decades, and was upgraded in 2010 with the introduction of VBA 7 in Microsoft Office applications. Millions of users worldwide use VBA daily, making it indispensable for streamlining work within the Office Suite.

It is probably one of the easiest coding languages to learn, and unique in the sense that it is associated with specific applications. Where other coding languages can be used to create standalone programs, VBA will function only within the MS Office environment.

VBA's main purpose is to automate tasks in Microsoft Office products, and its most outstanding feature is its simplicity. Even if you know nothing about programming, you will see results within the first day.

Starting with the macro recorder, you can create your first code by clicking a record button, and the recorder will write code for every single step you execute. Experienced coders can write more effective code, yet it enables complete novices to automate lengthy and time-consuming processes. With this recorded code as the basis, you can become adventurous by making small changes, teaching yourself as you go along.

Another useful feature is that VBA can control one application from another. You can, for example, automatically create a report in MS Word or PowerPoint, from existing Excel data.

Companies other than Microsoft also use VBA to automate some tasks. These include ArcGIS, AutoCAD, CorelDraw, LibreOffice, SolidWorks, and WordPerfect.

This book is designed to teach you the language, first on an elementary level, and later moving to more advanced terrain. We start with recording a macro, then proceed to writing your own Sub procedures. Next, we teach you the object model and language elements, program flow, error handling, user forms for capturing data, and eventually creating custom functions.

Each chapter contains code samples to explain the principles taught in each recipe. As an added bonus, there are action videos to clarify each working sample.

Who this book is for

This book is aimed at Excel users who know a bit more than the basics. If you've tried all the functions and formulas available in Excel, and you've attempted recording one or two macros, yet feel the need to automate your work further, this is the book for you.

What this book covers

Chapter 1, Getting Started with VBA, gives a general introduction to VBA, and how to go about recording and editing a macro.

Chapter 2, Working with the VBA Editor, shows us how to work with and customize the VBA Editor.

Chapter 3, The VBA Object Model, gets us familiar with objects in VBA.

Chapter 4, Working with Procedures, shows us how to write Sub procedures manually.

Chapter 5, Next Level Recording, discusses recording macros with relative or absolute referencing.

Chapter 6, VBA Language Elements, introduces us to VBA language elements.

Chapter 7, Working with Ranges, gives us an understanding of cells and named ranges, as well as referring to ranges in VBA.

Chapter 8, Using Functions, tells us the difference between Sub procedures and functions, and covers writing a simple VBA function.

Chapter 9, Implementing Program Flow, covers the implementation of program flow principles in your VBA Sub procedures.

Chapter 10, Implementing Automation, introduces us to writing event handler procedures.

Chapter 11, Handling Errors, introduces us to error handling in VBA, with practical code samples.

Chapter 12, Debugging, identifies different bugs in VBA, and uses various debugging techniques to eliminate bugs.

Chapter 13, Creating and Modifying Dialog Boxes, creates every possible type of message box and input box imaginable.

Chapter 14, Creating UserForms, introduces us to UserForms. We'll cover setting up a form, creating labels and text boxes, and using lookup fields and frames.

Chapter 15, UserForm Controls, brings life to UserForms by adding controls, namely, Combo Boxes, SpinButtons, date options, and command buttons.

Chapter 16, Creating Custom Functions, takes functions to a new level of automation, including a look at calling functions from `Sub` procedures.

Chapter 17, Creating Word Documents with Excel VBA, examines activating MS Word from within Excel VBA, opening a new document, and transferring Excel content to Word.

Chapter 18, Working with PowerPoint in Excel VBA, shows you how to activate MS PowerPoint using only Excel VBA commands, then create a new presentation and slide show with content from Excel.

To get the most out of this book

You will need the latest version of Excel installed on your PC to make the most of these recipes. The coding examples were tested on Windows 10.

All the recipes in a chapter are meant to be executed in the same order.

Software/hardware covered in the book	OS requirements
Excel 2019/365	Windows 8.1, 10

No extra installations are necessary.

If you are using the digital version of this book, we advise you to type the code yourself or access the code via the GitHub repository (link available in the next section). Doing so will help you avoid any potential errors related to copy/pasting of code.

VBA is not difficult. However, unless you apply your newly acquired knowledge diligently, you might not gain all the advantages that are there for the taking. The secret lies in spaced repetition.

Download the example code files

You can download the example code files for this book from your account at www.packt.com. If you purchased this book elsewhere, you can visit www.packtpub.com/support and register to have the files emailed directly to you.

You can download the code files by following these steps:

1. Log in or register at www.packt.com.

2. Select the **Support** tab.

3. Click on **Code Downloads**.

4. Enter the name of the book in the **Search** box and follow the onscreen instructions.

Once the file is downloaded, please make sure that you unzip or extract the folder using the latest version of the following:

- WinRAR/7-Zip for Windows

- Zipeg/iZip/UnRarX for Mac

- 7-Zip/PeaZip for Linux

The code bundle for the book is also hosted on GitHub at `https://github.com/PacktPublishing/VBA-Automation-for-Excel-2019-Cookbook`. In case there's an update to the code, it will be updated on the existing GitHub repository.

We also have other code bundles from our rich catalog of books and videos available at `https://github.com/PacktPublishing/`. Check them out!

Code in Action

Code in Action videos for this book can be viewed at (`https://bit.ly/3jQRvVk`).

Download the color images

We also provide a PDF file that has color images of the screenshots/diagrams used in this book. You can download it here: `https://static.packt-cdn.com/downloads/9781789610031_ColorImages.pdf`.

Conventions used

There are a number of text conventions used throughout this book.

`Code in text`: Indicates code words in text, database table names, folder names, filenames, file extensions, pathnames, dummy URLs, user input, and Twitter handles. Here is an example: "In the `BeforeClose` procedure, set the `BeforeClose` event's parameter to `cancel` by adding the next line."

A block of code is set as follows:

```
Private Sub Workbook_BeforeClose(Cancel As Boolean)
    MsgBox "This file cannot be closed"
    Cancel = True
End Sub
```

Bold: Indicates a new term, an important word, or words that you see onscreen. For example, words in menus or dialog boxes appear in the text like this. Here is an example: "Activate the **Developer** ribbon. In the **Code** group, click on **Macro Security** to open the **Trust Centre** dialog box."

> **Tips or important notes**
> Appear like this.

Sections

In this book, you will find several headings that appear frequently (*Getting ready*, *How to do it...*, *How it works...*, *There's more...*, and *See also*).

To give clear instructions on how to complete a recipe, use these sections as follows:

Getting ready

This section tells you what to expect in the recipe and describes how to set up any software or any preliminary settings required for the recipe.

How to do it...

This section contains the steps required to follow the recipe.

How it works...

This section usually consists of a detailed explanation of what happened in the previous section.

There's more...

This section consists of additional information about the recipe in order to make you more knowledgeable about the recipe.

See also

This section provides helpful links to other useful information for the recipe.

Get in touch

Feedback from our readers is always welcome.

General feedback: If you have questions about any aspect of this book, mention the book title in the subject of your message and email us at customercare@packtpub.com.

Errata: Although we have taken every care to ensure the accuracy of our content, mistakes do happen. If you have found a mistake in this book, we would be grateful if you would report this to us. Please visit www.packtpub.com/support/errata, selecting your book, clicking on the Errata Submission Form link, and entering the details.

Piracy: If you come across any illegal copies of our works in any form on the Internet, we would be grateful if you would provide us with the location address or website name. Please contact us at copyright@packt.com with a link to the material.

If you are interested in becoming an author: If there is a topic that you have expertise in and you are interested in either writing or contributing to a book, please visit authors.packtpub.com.

Reviews

Please leave a review. Once you have read and used this book, why not leave a review on the site that you purchased it from? Potential readers can then see and use your unbiased opinion to make purchase decisions, we at Packt can understand what you think about our products, and our authors can see your feedback on their book. Thank you!

For more information about Packt, please visit packt.com.

1
Getting Started with VBA

The recipes in this chapter will help you familiarize yourself with VBA in general, introduce you to the VBA working environment, and also help you edit and save your first working VBA subroutine. In the process, you will learn how to set up the development environment and how to edit your VBA coding.

In this chapter, we will cover the following recipes:

- Investigating VBA code
- Recording a macro
- Testing the macro
- Using the VBA Editor
- Editing the code by changing cell references
- Saving the file with an embedded macro

- Using the Trust Center for macro security
- Creating a customized ribbon

By the end of this chapter, you will be able to identify the need and use for a macro, record a macro, edit VBA code, and save the macro in an Excel Workbook.

Technical requirements

This cookbook was written and designed to be used with MS Office 2019 and MS Office 365, installed on either Windows 8, 8.1, or 10.

In the case of MS Word, MS Excel, and MS PowerPoint, the **Developer** ribbon can be activated, although this is not a prerequisite. In all the applications, on the **View** ribbon | **Macros** group, there are icons for viewing and recording macros.

Demonstration files can be downloaded from `https://github.com/ PacktPublishing/VBA-Automation-for-Excel-2019-Cookbook`.

Please visit the following link to check out the CiA videos: `https://bit. ly/3jQRvVk`.

Investigating VBA code

In this recipe, we will inspect a short VBA subroutine. Like all programming languages, VBA has a specific syntax, and the best way to understand the principles is to see what the coding looks like.

What we're going to see here will lay the foundation for the other recipes in this book, so pay close attention.

Getting ready

In order to investigate and edit VBA code in Excel, or any of the other Office applications, we first need to activate the **Developer** toolbar. Here are the steps:

1. Open MS Excel and select **Blank workbook** from the opening screen.

2. Open the `01_VBA_Code.xlsm` sample file. Click on **[Enable Content]** on the **SECURITY WARNING** ribbon.

3. If the **Developer** ribbon is not visible, activate the Backstage View by clicking on **File**, which will display the following screen:

Figure 1.1 – The Backstage View

4. From the category list on the left, select the last option, **Options**. The **Excel Options** dialog box appears:

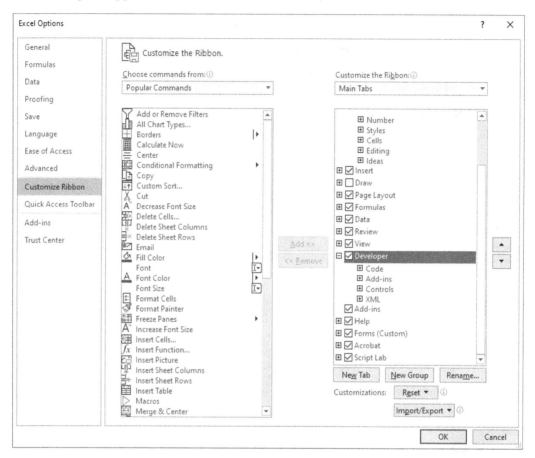

Figure 1.2 – The Excel Options dialog box

5. From the categories on the left, select **Customize Ribbon**.

6. To the far right, under the **Main Tabs** heading, look for the **Developer** option. Select the checkbox.

7. Click on **OK** to accept the change. The dialog box will close, and Excel will now display the **Developer** tab.

How to do it...

With the **Developer** tab activated, we will now proceed with the steps for this recipe:

1. With `01_VBA_Code.xlsm` open, click on the **Developer** tab:

Figure 1.3 – The Developer tab

2. In the **Code** group (the first group on the left of the ribbon), select the **Macros** icon. The **Macro** dialog box opens:

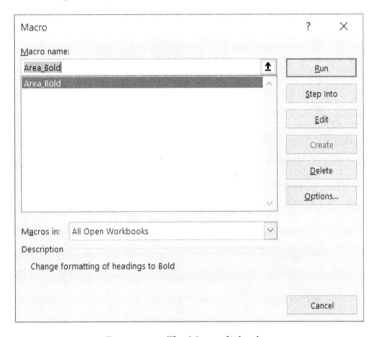

Figure 1.4 – The Macro dialog box

3. The VBA code we want to investigate is contained in the only macro: **Area_Bold**.
    Click on the **Edit** button. The **Microsoft Visual Basic for Applications** window will
    open. Maximize the window, if necessary:

Figure 1.5 – The Microsoft Visual Basic for Applications editor window

4. In the code window (the large area on the right), a short VBA subroutine
    is displayed.

How it works...

The subroutine in the VBA Editor looks like this:

```
Sub Area_Bold()
'
' Area_Bold Macro
' Change formatting of headings to Bold
'
' Keyboard Shortcut: Ctrl+Shift+B
'
    Range("B1:E1").Select
    Selection.Font.Bold = True
    Range("A1").Select
End Sub
```

Figure 1.6 – The subroutine in the VBA Editor

Let's try to understand this subroutine. Any and all subroutines in VBA start with the Sub
keyword, followed by the name of the subroutine (macro), and end with two brackets.

A single apostrophe allows you to enter a note. Comments can be added anywhere in a subroutine and will be displayed in green text, as long as it is on its own line or after a line of code (that is, it cannot be before a line of code as it would obviously comment out the code too). Indented lines without apostrophes are VBA instructions. In this case, the first instruction is when the range B1 to E1 is selected.

The selection's font style is then set to Bold. The last instruction moves the focus to cell A1. Finally, the subroutine is concluded with the End Sub keywords.

There's more...

Whether you record a macro or manually type the coding, you will always find this basic syntax structure in VBA.

In future chapters, we will be working with much longer subroutines. Before we get there, though, we are going to record a macro. With your newly acquired knowledge, you will be able to investigate the VBA code for that too.

Recording a macro

Macros are indispensable when we have to do repetitive tasks. In this recipe, we are going to create a macro in Excel. Instead of manually typing several lines of VBA code to create a subroutine, or short program, we can simply record a series of actions in Excel and then store it in the same file. The macro recorder will automatically create the VBA code, as we will see in future recipes.

These recorded steps can then be replayed, in order to execute a series of steps in a fraction of a second.

Getting ready

Like functions, macros make use of absolute and relative referencing. In this first macro, we will use absolute referencing because we have two other sheets with exactly the same layout.

Open the `02_RecordMacro.xlsx` file and confirm that **Sheet1** is active. Click on the **Developer** tab. Then, in the **Code** group, make sure that **Use Relative References** is *not* active:

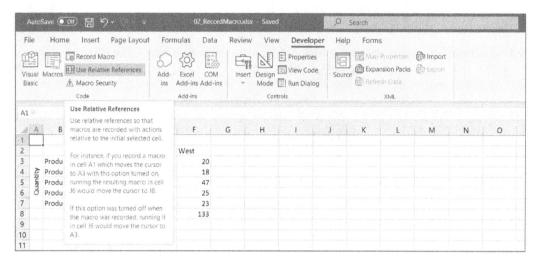

Figure 1.7 – The Relative References option

How to do it...

We will now proceed with the steps to record a macro:

1. Make sure that `02_RecordMacro.xlsx` is still open on **Sheet1**, and that cell A1 is selected. In the **Code** group of the **Developer** tab, click on **Record Macro**. The **Record Macro** dialog box appears.

2. In the first textbox, under the **Macro name** heading, type `Format_Range`. That will be the name of the macro we are going to record.

3. Press the *Tab* key, or click in the textbox under the **Shortcut key** heading to the right of **Ctrl+**:

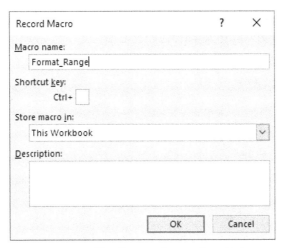

Figure 1.8 – The Shortcut key textbox, Ctrl+

4. While holding down the *Shift* key, press *F* on the keyboard.

    The shortcut key for this macro is now set to *Ctrl + Shift + F*.

5. Under **Store macro in**, make sure that **This Workbook** is selected. Other options will be discussed in later recipes.

6. Under **Description**, enter a short description of what the macro will do. Click on **OK** to start recording:

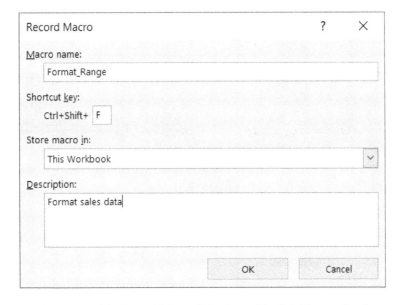

Figure 1.9 – The Record Macro dialog box with all fields completed

7. Observe the **Code** group on the **Developer** ribbon. The **Record Macro** icon has been replaced with the **Stop Recording** icon. This means you are now in recording mode, and all your actions on the keyboard and with the mouse will be recorded:

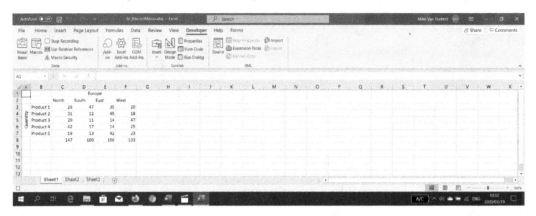

Figure 1.10 – Stop Recording is displayed when in recording mode

8. While in recording mode, click on the **Home** tab. Then, select the range C1 to F2, hold down *Ctrl*, and select the range A3 to B7:

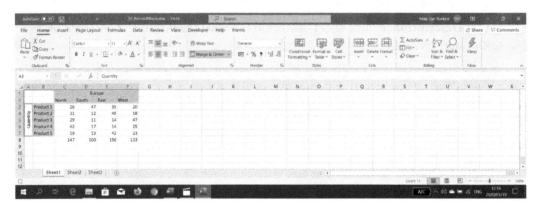

Figure 1.11 – The selected ranges

Now, change the format of the selected cells to bold.

9. Next, select the range C3 to F8:

Figure 1.12 – The selected range

Once done, center the cell content and change the format to currency (US$).

10. To finish this recording, select cell A1, navigate to the **Developer** tab | the **Code** group, and click on **Stop Recording**.

You have just successfully recorded a macro.

How it works...

Now, this was simple enough, wasn't it? Let's have a look at what just happened.

We set the referencing for the macro to absolute because we want to use the same macro on **Sheet2** and **Sheet3**, too. By starting on cell A1 on **Sheet1**, we can run the macro from cell A1 on **Sheet2** and **Sheet3** and get exactly the same results.

Macro names must start with a letter, and there should be no spaces in the name. Furthermore, VBA keywords are not allowed. Format, Copy, and Select are three examples of keywords. Special characters are also taboo.

A keyboard shortcut makes it easy to run a macro, but that's all it is – a shortcut. In the next recipe, we will run a macro from the **Macro** dialog box.

Storing the macro in **This Workbook** means it will only work in this specific workbook. To make it available for other workbooks, it must be stored in **Personal Macro Workbook**. We will find out more about that in future recipes.

Many VBA users leave the **Description** field empty. This will have no effect on the macro, but it is good practice to explain to other users what you had in mind when saving this macro.

Once you are in recording mode, all your actions are recorded, including errors. It is, therefore, a good idea to makes notes of the steps you want to record.

When you click on **Stop Recording**, the macro recorder is switched off, and you can relax. Each of your actions has been recorded and converted into VBA code in the background. By opening the **Microsoft Visual Basic for Applications** editor, you will be able to see the recording code.

There's more...

Once you understand how easy it is to record a series of actions in Excel, you will start looking for reasons to automate all your repetitive tasks.

You can, for instance, record a macro to select the entire sheet and clear it of all formatting. That is much faster than doing so manually, especially if there is more than one sheet.

Testing the macro

It's all very well to have recorded a macro, but how do we know whether it's working or not? There is only one way, and that is to test it. Sure, you can have a look at the VBA code in the VBA Editor, but unless you are a seasoned coder, it will be virtually impossible to find coding errors. Best then to do a practical test.

Getting ready

Before moving on, make sure that you have recorded the macro as per the instructions in the previous recipe. We will be using that code in this recipe.

Since we've previously used **Sheet1** to record the macro, we will have to test it on **Sheet2**. Testing on **Sheet1** will have no effect because the cells have already been formatted. **Sheet2** is still in its original form, meaning we will immediately notice any changes.

How to do it...

Let's proceed with the following steps:

1. Make sure that `02_RecordMacro.xlsx` is still open, but this time on **Sheet2**. To test how effective the Relative Reference setting is, select any cell other than cell A1.

2. Let's use the *Ctrl + Shift + F* keyboard shortcut and see what happens:

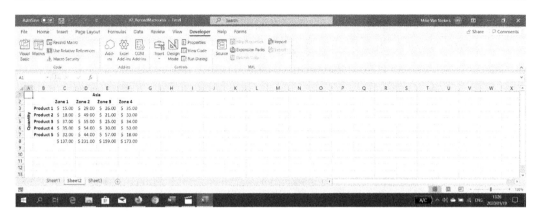

Figure 1.13 – The formatted sheet after running the macro

The content is now formatted in exactly the same way as in **Sheet 1**. Isn't that much faster than formatting each area manually?

3. Activate **Sheet3**, because there is yet another way to run a macro. Select any cell on the sheet.

4. This time, select the **Developer** tab and click on the **Macros** icon in the **Code** group:

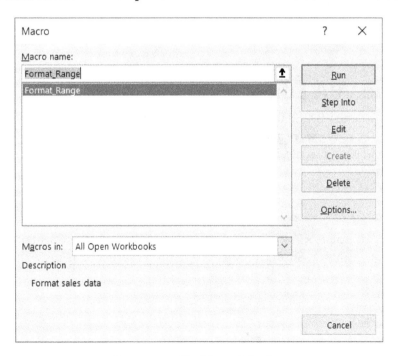

Figure 1.14 – The Macro dialog box

5.   The only available macro is the one we recorded, as you can see. To the right, there are several buttons. Click the top one, **Run**.

6.   As expected, **Sheet3** is now also formatted in the same way as **Sheet1** and **Sheet2**.

How it works...

When we first recorded the macro, the **Record Macro** dialog box gave us the option to select a keyboard shortcut. Clearly, our instructions there have worked.

A slightly longer, yet still effective, way is to run a macro from the **Macro** dialog box. Since there is only one macro, we can only execute that one. However, if there were more, we could have selected any one before clicking **Run**.

There's more...

It is good practice to always test a macro, instead of assuming that it will work. It will be exceptional for a recorded macro to fail, but when we get to more advanced subroutines – especially when you start typing your code manually – you should never assume that your coding will be flawless.

So, when everything is working the way it should, it may be a good idea to investigate the actual VBA coding.

Using the VBA Editor

We've worked with the VBA Editor before, but that was on another file, with a different Sub procedure. The recipe we're going to work with here will show you how to activate the VBA Editor in your own file. Furthermore, we're going to identify various components within the editor.

Getting ready

With `02_RecordMacro.xlsx` still open, we're going to activate the VBA Editor. Whether you are on **Sheet1**, **Sheet2**, or **Sheet3** is of no consequence, because the macro is part of the workbook.

How to do it...

Let's go through the steps for this recipe:

1. The standard way to activate the VBA Editor is to navigate to **Developer | Code | Macros**, and then select **Edit** on the **Macro** dialog box.

2. The shortcut key makes life much easier. Simply hold down the *Alt* key while pressing *F11*. This time, you bypass the dialog box by going straight to the VBA Editor:

Figure 1.15 – A Sub procedure in the VBA Editor

The evidence of what we recorded is displayed in the code window.

How it works...

Opening the VBA Editor can be done in one of two ways: with the *Alt + F11* keyboard shortcut, or by clicking on **Edit** in the **Macro** dialog box.

In the VBA Editor, you will find the following basic components:

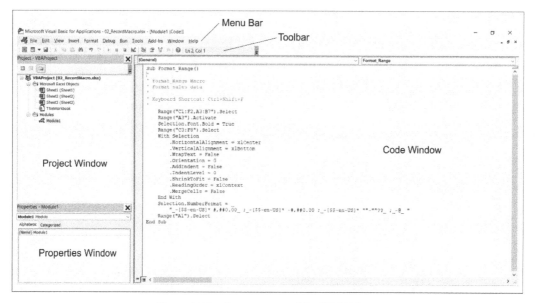

Figure 1.16 – Components of the VBA Editor

There's more...

Each element, or component, of the VBA Editor has a specific function. Up until now, we've only used the code window. In future recipes, we will be referring to and using the other elements.

Editing the code by changing cell references

This recipe shows you how to edit coding in the VBA Editor. It is more effective to make changes in the code, rather than deleting an entire macro and recording it again. We're going to start by deleting some redundant lines of code, before showing you how to edit code in order to bring about a visible change on the spreadsheet when the code is executed.

Getting ready

With `02_RecordMacro.xlsx` still open, use the keyboard shortcut, *Alt + F11*, to activate the VBA Editor.

How to do it...

For this recipe, the steps are as follows:

1. In the VBA Editor, double-click on **Module1** to open the code window.

2. In the code window, select the second line of the executable code. Delete the line of code, as well as the empty line:

Figure 1.17 – Selected code to be deleted

3. Switch back to Excel, clear all formatting on the data and run the macro. The result is the same as with the first test.

4. Next, select all the lines after `.HorizontalAlignment = xlCenter`. Press *Del*:

Figure 1.18 – Selected code to be deleted

5. Once again, switch back to Excel, clear all formatting on the data, and run the macro. The result is still the same as with the first test.

6. Finally, change the cell reference in the last line from A1 to G2:

Figure 1.19 – Cell reference to be changed

7. For the last time, switch back to Excel, clear all formatting on the data in the spreadsheet, and run the macro. The formatting is done as before, but the focus is on cell G2 and not on A1 this time.

How it works...

Let's understand what just happened.

The `Range("A3").Activate` line can be deleted because the C1:F2, A3:B7 range is already selected. It is that selection that will be formatted to bold.

When the C3:F8 range is selected, we only want it to be centered. The other lines are automatically added but are redundant, and can, therefore, be deleted.

Instead of ending on cell A1, we change the focus to cell G2.

There's more...

The macro has been recorded, tested, and edited, but we have not saved the file yet. As simple as it may sound, there is a trick to it. Refer to the next recipe to take care of that.

Saving the file with an embedded macro

This recipe will show you how to save a file with an embedded macro. You might think that saving a file cannot be that difficult, and it isn't. The point is a normal Excel file will not allow you to save the macro you've just recorded, at least not with the normal file extension.

Getting ready

With `02_RecordMacro.xlsx` still open, close the VBA Editor.

How to do it...

Now, proceed with the following steps:

1. In Excel, click on the **Save** button. The following message box appears:

Figure 1.20 – Message box warning

2. Since we want to save the file together with the newly recorded macro, click **No**.

3. Select the folder where you want to save the file in the **Save As** dialog box.

4. At the bottom, below the **File name** textbox, to the right of the **Save as type** textbox, click on the arrow. From the list of options, select the second one from the top, **Excel Macro-Enabled Workbook (*.xlsm)**:

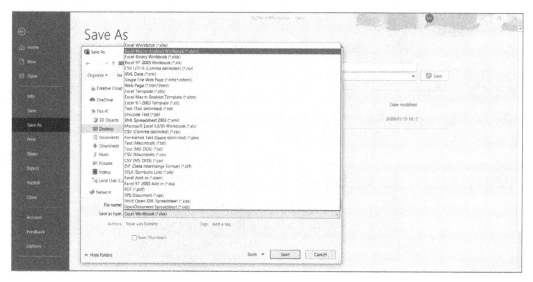

Figure 1.21 – Choosing the macro-enabled file option from the Save As dialog box

5. Click on **Save**. In the title bar, the file extension has changed to `.xlsm`:

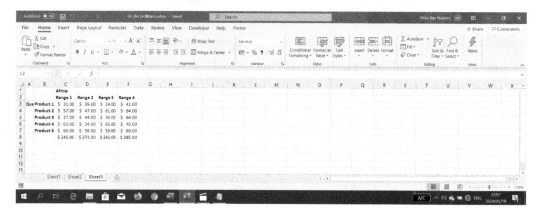

Figure 1.22 – Altered file extension visible in the title bar

How it works...

There are a couple of things to notice:

- The standard `.xlsx` file extension will not allow a macro to be saved with the file.

- Only files with the `.xlsm` file extension will allow you to save a file with an embedded macro.

There's more...

File extensions allow you to distinguish between files with or without macros.

Using the Trust Center for macro security

This recipe is all about security, at least as far as macros are concerned. We will show you where to find the Trust Center in Excel, and after that, how to choose between four levels of macro security.

Getting ready

We've successfully created and tested our macro. We've even made some changes to the code by editing it in the VBA Editor. The final step is to have `02_RecordMacro.xlsm` open in order to set the macro security.

How to do it...

Proceed with the following steps for this recipe:

1. Activate the backstage view by clicking on **File**:

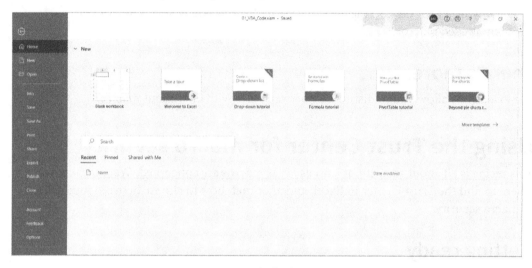

Figure 1.23 – The backstage view

2. From the category list on the left, select the last one, **Options**. The **Excel Options** dialog box appears:

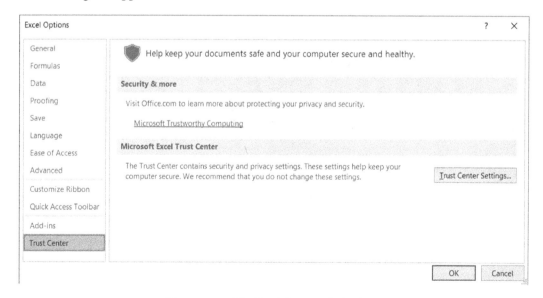

Figure 1.24 – The Excel Options dialog box

3. Select the last category on the left, **Trust Center**, and then click on the **Trust Center Settings** button on the right:

Figure 1.25 – Macro Settings in the Trust Center dialog box

4. Select the **Macro Settings** category on the left. The details will be displayed on the right.

5. Click the second radio button from the top, **Disable all macros with notification**.

6. Click on **OK** to close the **Trust Center** dialog box.

7. In the **Excel Options** dialog box, click on **OK**.

How it works...

Macro Settings has four levels of security in order to prevent viruses from entering your system. These options are as follows:

- **Disable all macros without notification**: Choosing this option will enable all macros. It is safe but defeats the purpose of creating macros.

- **Disable all macros with notification**: This is the standard setting, selected by most users. A yellow message bar will appear when you open a file with an embedded macro. If you know and trust the person that sent the file, go ahead and disable the macros. If not, do not enable the macros.

- **Disable all macros except digitally signed macros**: Only macros that have a digital signature are allowed to run. However, you will still receive a security warning for signatures that haven't been marked as trusted.

- **Enable all macros**: This setting is not recommended because potentially dangerous code can run. Unless you are not connected to the internet, or any other computers in a LAN, never choose this option.

There's more...

The keyword here is vigilance. In this day and age, computer security is vital. A good starting point would be to always have an anti-virus application running on your PC. It is better to be safe than sorry.

Creating a customized ribbon

This recipe is optional, though very useful.

There are several ways that you can invoke a macro. After activating the **Developer** ribbon, it is relatively easy to click on the **Developer** tab, and then to choose the **Macros** button in the **Code** group. But what if you don't want to do it that way? Shortcuts may help, but only up to a point because macros have a way of proliferating quickly.

This recipe will show you how to create a new ribbon, group, and icons.

Getting ready

Open Excel, with a new sheet active.

How to do it...

1. Before starting with customization, there is an important yet simple way to manipulate the ribbon in Excel. This is not really a customization, but it is still important to know how to control the interface. If you double-click any of the tabs on the ribbon, the ribbon will collapse. By double-clicking the tab again, the ribbon will expand, showing the standard, full view:

Figure 1.26 – The Developer ribbon in the expanded view

The tabs are collapsed as shown:

Figure 1.27 – Collapsed ribbons

The standard tabs normally provide all the functionality you need. However, if you have a series of functions you want to use regularly, or even a series of macros, it will help a lot if you could display the shortcuts to those items on a ribbon.

2. To add a new tab to the ribbon, right-click on any existing tab. Choose **Customize the Ribbon**:

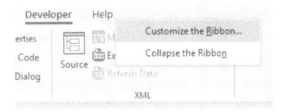

Figure 1.28 – Right-clicking on the Help tab

3. You could also right-click anywhere to the right of an existing ribbon, in the gray area, and choose **Customize the Ribbon,** or you can click on **File | Options | Customize Ribbon**.

The **Excel Options** dialog box will appear:

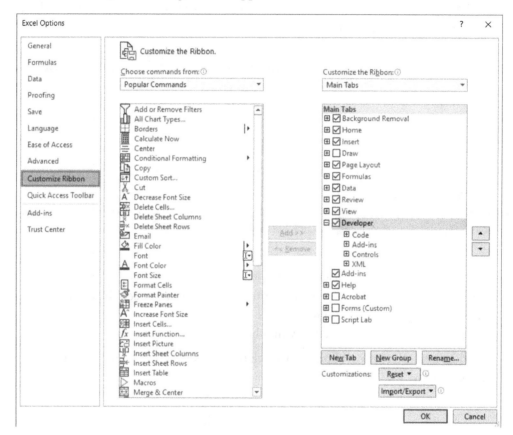

Figure 1.29 – The Excel Options dialog box

There are two columns in the **Excel Options** dialog box. We will be working on the right side, under the **Customize the Ribbon** heading.

4. Make sure that all the main tabs are collapsed. If any of these are expanded, click on - to collapse them.

5. Select the **Help** tab without expanding it, because we want the new tab to appear to the right of the **Help** tab:

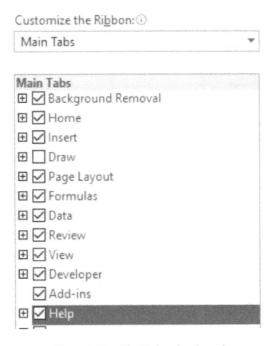

Figure 1.30 – The Help tab selected

6.   At the bottom of that column, click on **New Tab**:

Figure 1.31 – The Help tab selected

7. A new entry will appear on the list – **New Tab (Custom)** – and under that is **New Group (Custom)**:

Figure 1.32 – The New Tab option inserted

8. Select the **New Tab (Custom)** listing, then click on **Rename** at the bottom:

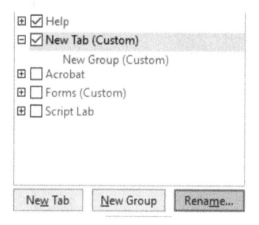

Figure 1.33 – Renaming the new tab

9. In the **Rename** dialog box, enter an appropriate name for the tab. Click **OK**:

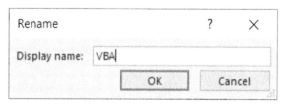

Figure 1.34 – Typing a new name

10. Select the **New Group (Custom)** listing:

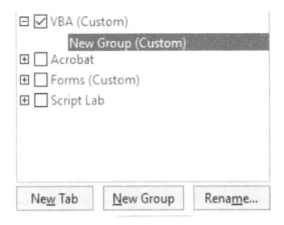

Figure 1.35 – Selecting the new group

11. Click on **Rename** at the bottom, then enter a name for the new group. Click **OK**:

Figure 1.36 – The Rename dialog box for groups

12. In the left column, select **Macros** from the commands list:

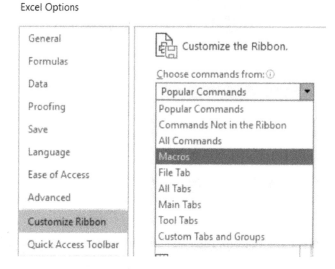

Figure 1.37 – Selecting Macros

A list of the available macros in this Excel file will appear:

Excel Options

General

Formulas

Data

Proofing

Save

Language

Ease of Access

Advanced

Customize the Ribbon.

Choose commands from: ⓘ

Macros

FormatFunction
Function_Samples
StringFunction
TimeLapse
WorksheetFunctions

Figure 1.38 – List of recorded macros

13. Select the macro you want to add to the group, then click **Add**:

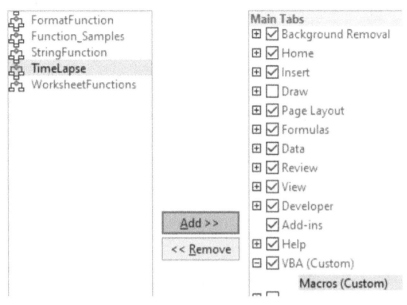

Figure 1.39 – Click Add to add a macro to the group

14. Select the newly inserted icon and click on **Rename**. Type a more descriptive name for the macro, and choose a fitting icon. Click **OK**, and **OK** again:

Figure 1.40 – Name and icon selection

You will have a new tab with a new group, and one icon in the group:

Figure 1.41 – The new ribbon with the new group

15. Click the new icon to run the macro associated with it. You can insert more macros to the same group by repeating the steps from *Step 12* on this list.

This recipe should enable you to create an easy access point for all recorder macros in a workbook.

2
Working with the VBA Editor

The recipes in this chapter will familiarize you with the working environment of the **Visual Basic for Applications** (**VBA**) Editor. It is an integral part of all applications in the MS Office suite. In order to use the Editor effectively, we need to investigate all of its elements, features, and characteristics. Getting to know the VBA Editor components is vitally important for any potential VBA coder.

In this chapter, we will cover the following recipes:

- Identifying, activating, and manipulating components in the VBA Editor
- Creating a module for storing a Sub procedure
- Creating a basic procedure in the code window of the Editor
- Creating VBA code in the code window in three different ways
- Customizing the Editor to suit your preferences

By the end of this chapter, you will be familiar with the working environment of the VBA Editor.

Technical requirements

This cookbook was written and designed to be used with MS Office 2019 and MS Office 365, installed on either Windows 8, 8.1, or 10.

In the case of MS Word, MS Excel, and MS PowerPoint, the VBA Editor can be activated by using the *Alt + F11* keyboard shortcut. By pressing *Alt + F11* a second time, you can switch between the Editor and the application you are working in.

Demonstration files can be downloaded from `https://github.com/PacktPublishing/VBA-Automation-for-Excel-2019-Cookbook`.

Please visit the following link to check out the CiA videos: `https://bit.ly/3jQRvVk`.

Identifying, activating, and closing components in the VBA Editor

The VBA Editor is the heart and soul of writing your code. In this recipe, we will examine the VBA Editor in detail in order to understand the layout and location of components. There are several components in the Editor, each with a specific function and purpose.

Getting ready

All applications in the MS Office Suite contain the VBA Editor as an integral part of the application. In this recipe, we will be working with Excel. If you do not have Excel installed on your PC or laptop, please install it now.

How to do it...

Let's take a look at the steps for this recipe:

1. To get to the Editor, we first need to open Excel.

2. With the home screen visible, also referred to as the welcome screen, select the first option, **Blank workbook**:

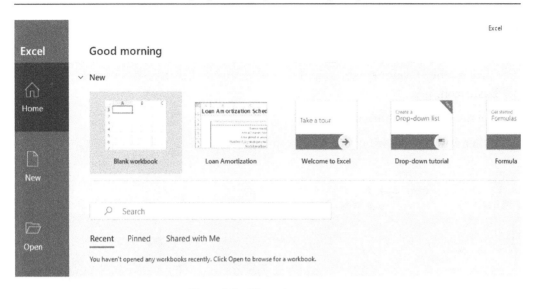

Figure 2.1 – The welcome screen

A new Excel spreadsheet named **Sheet1** is displayed. Since the file has not been saved, the workbook name, as displayed in the title bar, is **Book1 - Excel**:

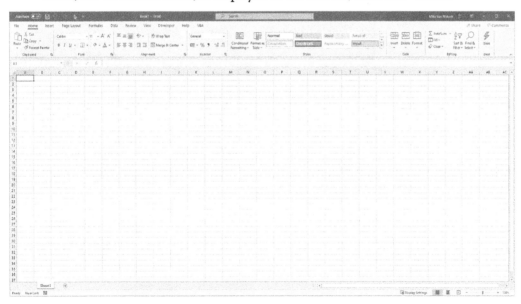

Figure 2.2 – Book1, Sheet1

3. With **Sheet1** active, the next step is to open the VBA Editor. This can be done in one of two ways:

    Click on the **Developer** tab, go to the **Code** group, and click on the **Visual Basic** icon.

    Use the keyboard shortcut, *Alt + F11*.

    Either way, the following screen will appear:

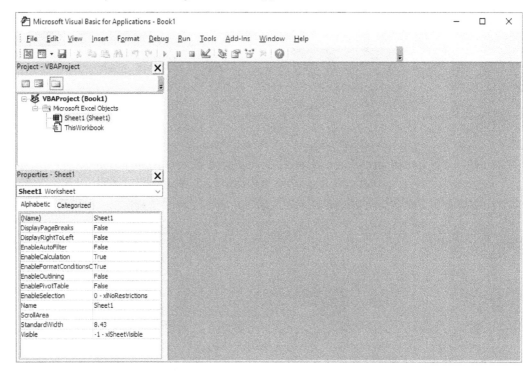

Figure 2.3 – The VBA Editor

4. Since there was no recorded macro, the code window will not be available. Press *F7* to open a new code window or, if you want, click **View** on the menu bar, then select the first option, **Code**:

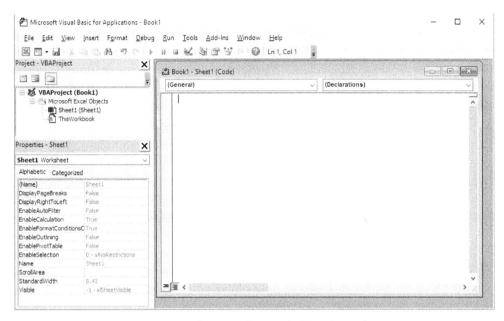

Figure 2.4 – The VBA Editor with the code window

5.   With the VBA Editor open, we can now identify the different components:

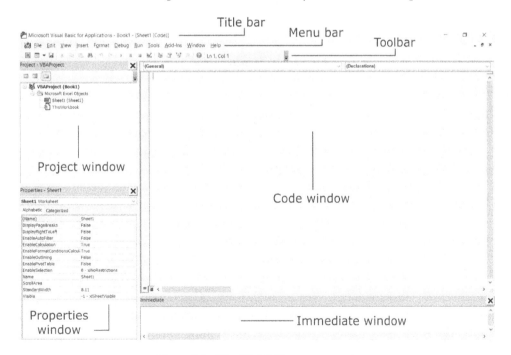

Figure 2.5 – The VBA Editor components

How it works...

Figure 2.5 shows the VBA Editor and its components. Let's look at each component in detail.

The title bar

All applications in the Microsoft environment have a title bar. As the name suggests, it identifies the application you are working in. It also displays the familiar minimize, maximize/restore, and close buttons on the rightmost end:

Figure 2.6 – The title bar

The menu bar

All the latest Microsoft applications make use of ribbons to categorize icons and commands. Menu bars are, therefore, not all that common anymore. However, in the case of the VBA Editor, the menu bar has survived the test of time. It contains all the commands you need to work within the various components of the VBA Editor. Drop-down menus will also show shortcut keys for some of the commands:

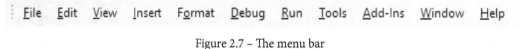

Figure 2.7 – The menu bar

The toolbar

The standard toolbar is displayed directly under the menu bar. There are three other toolbars, which can be activated by using the **View | Toolbars** command, or by right-clicking on the toolbar. All these toolbars can be customized and moved around, although most users leave the toolbars as they are:

Figure 2.8 - The toolbar

The Project window

The Project window displays a tree diagram of the objects currently available in Excel. In this case, only one workbook with one sheet is open in Excel, meaning that only **Sheet1** and **ThisWorkbook** will be displayed under **Microsoft Excel Objects**. To expand and collapse the objects under **Microsoft Excel Objects**, you can either double-click on the folder icon or click on the minus sign to the left of the folder icon.

To close the Project window, click on the close button on its title bar, and to open it, press *Ctrl* + *R* or **View** | **Project Explorer**:

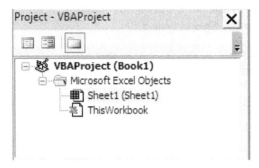

Figure 2.9 – The Project window

The Properties window

The Properties window is displayed directly below the Project window. It does exactly what it says: it displays the properties of objects. When you click on the **Sheet1** object in the Project window, the Properties window will display the related properties. The same happens when you select the **ThisWorkbook** object:

Figure 2.10 – The Properties window

The code window

The code window is the place where the VBA code is stored. Every object in a project has its own code window. To view the code window for **ThisWorkbook**, double-click on the object. The same applies for the **Sheet1** object.

Because we have not saved a macro or typed any code for any of these objects, the code window for both objects will be empty:

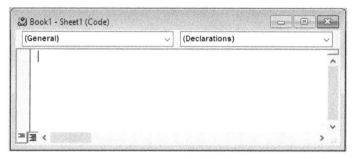

Figure 2.11 – The code window

Like all windows, the code window can be restored (and maximized). By restoring both the code windows, you can either tile or cascade them:

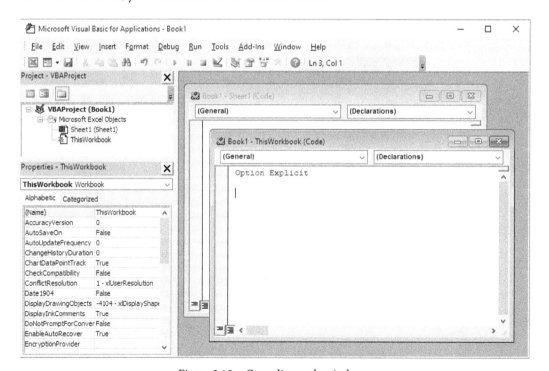

Figure 2.12 – Cascading code windows

The Immediate window

When you open the VBA Editor the first time, the **Immediate** window is normally not visible. Use the **View | Immediate Window** command, or press *Ctrl + G* to display the **Immediate** window. Closing it requires clicking on the close button on the title bar.

If you are new to VBA, the **Immediate** window will not be of much use to you, since it is used to execute VBA statements directly, as well as for debugging your code. Until you have a bit more experience, feel free to close this window:

Figure 2.13 – The Immediate window

Creating a module for storing a Sub procedure

In this recipe, we will be creating a new module, which is yet another object, in the Project window. So far, we've seen only two objects in the Project window: **Sheet1** and **ThisWorkbook**. It is possible to create a code window for each, but Sub procedures must be created and stored in a module in the Project window. This is where coding for all objects can be created and saved.

Getting ready

Make sure that Excel is open and that the VBA Editor is visible.

How to do it...

The steps for this recipe are as follows:

1. With Excel open on a new sheet, select the **Developer** tab. In the **Code** group, select the Visual Basic icon to activate the VBA Editor. If you prefer using the shortcut key, simply press *Alt + F11*.

    In the VBA Editor, observe the Project window. Under **Microsoft Excel Objects**, only two objects are visible: **Sheet1 (Sheet1)** and **ThisWorkbook**.

2. On the menu bar, select **Insert**. From the drop-down menu, select **Module**, as shown:

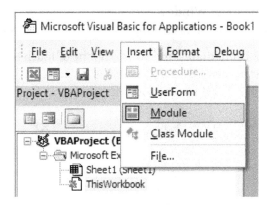

Figure 2.14 – The Insert menu's Module option

Once you've made your selection, the VBA Editor adds a new module – visible in the Project window – and a new code window appears on the right:

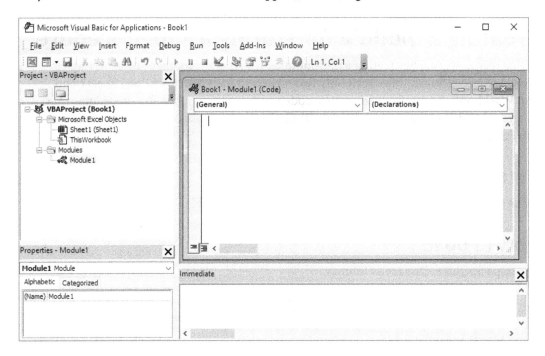

Figure 2.15 – Newly inserted module

How it works...

When you open a new spreadsheet in Excel and then activate the VBA Editor, no modules will be visible in the Project window.

However, should you record a macro and then activate the VBA Editor, that macro will be stored in a module.

Finally, if you choose not to record a macro, but to insert the code yourself, you have to create a module yourself.

Creating a basic procedure in the code window of the Editor

In this recipe, we will create a basic procedure in the code window of the Editor. We're at the point where everything is coming together now; you know the different components, and you know how to create a module. All that's left is to create code – a simple Sub procedure – in the newly created module.

Getting ready

Make sure that you've created a module in the VBA Editor. The module should be visible as an object in the Project window, and the title bar of the code window should display the name **Module1 (Code)**. If you cannot see the title bar, click on the restore window button to make the window smaller.

How to do it...

Let's go through the steps for this recipe:

1. In the code window, type the following code:

```
Sub MyName()
    MsgBox "My name is Yourname" (Replace Yourname _
    with your first name.)
End Sub
```

2. Press *Alt + F11* to switch to Excel.

3. Click on any cell of the active sheet. Go to **Developer | Code,** and click on the **Macros** icon. The **Macro** dialog box appears:

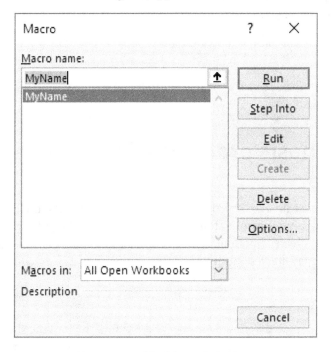

Figure 2.16 – The Macro dialog box

The only available macro is the one that you've just created; **MyName**. Click on the **Run** button.

A message box will appear with the words **My name Mike,** as shown:

Figure 2.17 – Message box from a basic procedure

A much shorter way to execute the code is to press *F5* while in the VBA Editor. You will automatically switch to Excel, where the message box will be displayed.

How it works...

Entering code in the VBA Editor is relatively simple, on the condition that you have a basic understanding of VBA coding. Looking at a few code samples online before going solo is advisable, and will save you many hours of frustration.

As a bonus, the Editor will make adjustments to the text you enter. The first example of this is when you type the Sub statement and the name of your procedure. When you press *Enter*, the Editor automatically inserts the End Sub statement. As we progress, you will see how spaces are inserted, and how capitalization and text colors are changed.

Once your code is error-free, the code can be run. In this case, the outcome is a message box, displaying the words **My name Mike**.

Creating VBA code in the code window in three different ways

Our first Sub procedure was as simple as it gets. It wouldn't take much imagination to understand that coding can become more complex than that. If that's the case, it makes you wonder how long it would take to manually type the coding for super-long Sub procedures.

All depending on the situation, there is more than one option to create coding. In this recipe, we will investigate the different methods to create code.

Getting ready

With Excel open, activate a worksheet in the workbook.

How to do it...

We will now go through the steps of working with each method to create code.

Recording a macro and then opening the VBA Editor to view the code

When using this method, you'll need to perform the following steps:

1. Fill the range A1:A10 with any numerical value. In this case, I filled the range with the value **100**. Once done, click on cell A1:

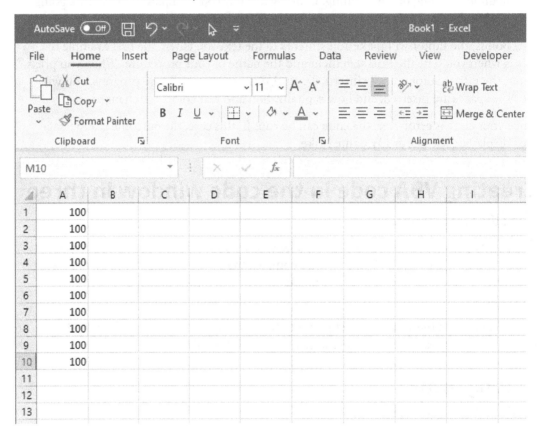

Figure 2.18 – Fill the range A1:A10

2. Navigate to **Developer | Code** and click on **Record Macro**. The **Record Macro** dialog box appears. Give the macro a name and shortcut key, and type a short description, as shown:

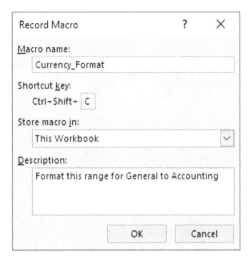

Figure 2.19 – The Macro dialog box

3. Click on **OK** to start recording the macro. The first step is to highlight the range A1:A10. Then, format the range as **Accounting** by using the drop-down list from **Home | Number**, as shown:

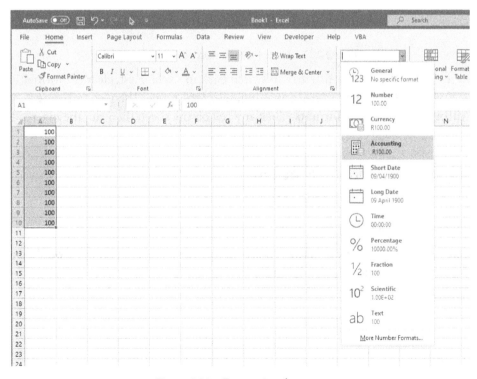

Figure 2.20 – Formatting the range

4. Once the formatting is done, stop the recording from **Developer | Code** by clicking on **Stop Recording**.

5. Now, view the code. Press *Alt + F11* to display the VBA Editor. Double-click on **Module1** to open the code window:

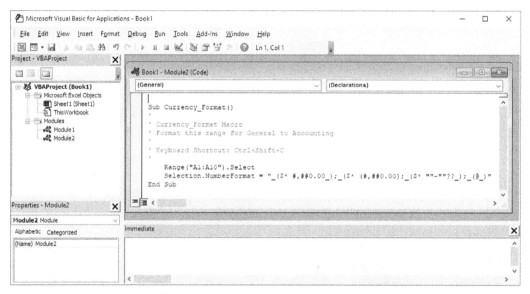

Figure 2.21 – Code for the recorded macro

6. To test the macro, press *Alt + F11* to switch back to Excel. First, clear the formatting on range A1:A10. To clear the formatting, select the range. Then, go to **Home | Editing | Clear | Clear formats**. Click any cell on the sheet, then run the macro. The range A1:A10 will be formatted as **Accounting**.

Entering the code manually by typing

In this method, we will be typing the code manually using the following steps:

1. While still in the VBA Editor, click on **Insert**, then select **Module**.

2. A new module will appear in the Project window. Double-click on the **Module** icon to open the corresponding code window.

3. Type the following code:

```
Sub MsgBoxOKCancel()
    MsgBox "Do you want to continue?", vbOKCancel
End Sub
```

4. To run the code, press *F5*. The Excel spreadsheet will appear, with a message box on the screen. When you click on **OK**, you will switch back to the VBA Editor.

Copying and pasting

When you work in MS Word and want to copy text from one document to the other, you need both pages to be open. The same applies for code in VBA.

Open the module with the code you want to copy, as well as the one where you want to paste it. Select the code in the first module – use *Ctrl + C*, or right-click and **Copy** – then switch to the new module. *Ctrl + V* will paste it, or you can right-click and select **Paste**.

How it works...

Now let's see how each method works.

Recording a macro, and then opening the VBA Editor to view the code

Many Excel users are introduced to the world of VBA coding after recording a macro or two. Looking at the recorded steps and starting to understand how VBA works is quite exciting.

If you have to record a series of steps in Excel, there is no better or faster way to create the code than with a macro.

Entering the code manually by typing

It normally comes as a shock when you realize that not all coding can be done with the macro recorder.

Take, for instance, the message box we created with the sample code. There is no way to create that message box other than manually typing the code.

If you are new to VBA, typing code manually might sound like a challenge. However, with a little bit of experience, you will soon be able to type lines of code like a professional.

Like with any other typing, you can cut, copy, paste, and delete text in the Editor. To make the code easier to read, indent some of the lines with the *Tab* key. Don't forget that undo and redo can also be used!

If a single line becomes too long to read on one screen, use a space and an underscore (_) to break to a new line.

Copying and pasting

This sounds like the lazy man's escape, but there are many good reasons for copying code. Firstly, if you created a Sub procedure for another project that can be used in your current project, it would be a waste of time to retype it.

You will also find many examples of VBA code on the internet. This is a very good way of learning from people with experience.

There's more...

To make the macro we recorded a bit more useful, do the following:

1. In the VBA Editor, copy the `Currency_Format` Sub procedure and paste it directly below the last line.

2. Still in the Editor, rename it to `Range_Format`.

3. Now, delete all the notes in the `Range_Format` procedure.

4. Finally, delete the line that selects the range A1:A10.

Your code should now look like this:

```
Sub Currency_Format()
'
' Currency_Format Macro
' This macro formats a range to currency
'
' Keyboard Shortcut: Ctrl+Shift+C
'
    Range("A1:A10").Select
    Selection.NumberFormat = _
        "_-[$$-en-US]* #,##0.00_ ;_-[$$-en-US]* -#,##0.00 ;_-[$$-en-US]* ""-""??_ ;_-@_ "
End Sub

Sub Range_Format()

    Selection.NumberFormat = _
        "_-[$$-en-US]* #,##0.00_ ;_-[$$-en-US]* -#,##0.00 ;_-[$$-en-US]* ""-""??_ ;_-@_ "
End Sub
```

Figure 2.22 – Altered code

If you switch back to Excel, you can now use the second macro to highlight any range and format it to accounting.

Customizing the Editor tab to suit your preferences

In this recipe, we will change settings in the **Editor** tab to suit your preferences.

Getting ready

Make sure that the VBA Editor is visible.

How to do it...

In order to proceed with executing this recipe, you need to go through the following steps:

1. With the VBA Editor active, choose **Tools | Options** from the menu bar. The **Options** dialog box will appear as shown here:

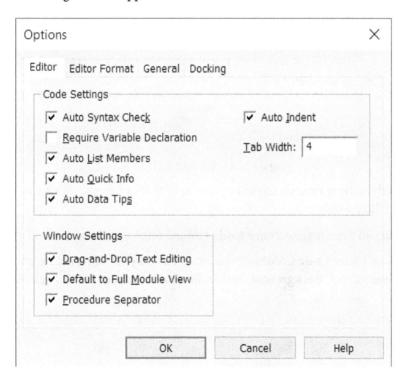

Figure 2.23 – The Options dialog box

2. In the **Options** dialog box, click on the **Editor** tab, if it is not already selected.

    There are two sections: **Code Settings** and **Window Settings**. In each of these sections, you will find several boxes, some with tick marks and others empty.

3. Click in any of these tick boxes to select or deselect the option, as described to the right of the tick box:

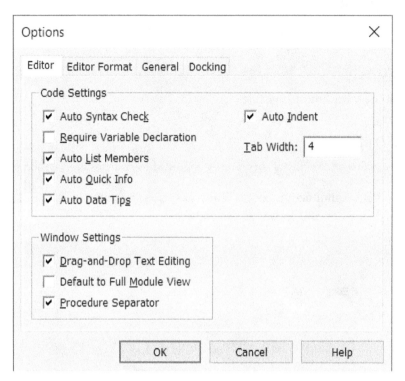

Figure 2.24 – The Editor tab

4. Click on the **Editor Format** tab to activate it. With this tab, you can customize the way the Editor looks.

Here, you will find three sections: **Code Colors, Font,** and **Sample.**

The options under **Code Colors** can be customized by selecting a different color under **Foreground, Background,** and **Indicator** for each of the code elements.

The font and size can be changed by selecting either **Font** or **Size**, while a sample will display the effect of your choices in the **Sample** section, as shown:

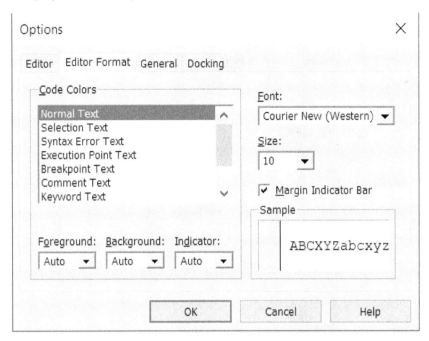

Figure 2.25 – The Editor Format tab

5. Click on the **General** tab to activate it. This is where the less dedicated settings can be made.

    In this area, you will find four sections: **Form Grid Settings**, **Edit and Continue**, **Error Trapping**, and **Compile**.

Once again, changes can be made by either selecting or unselecting tick boxes, as shown:

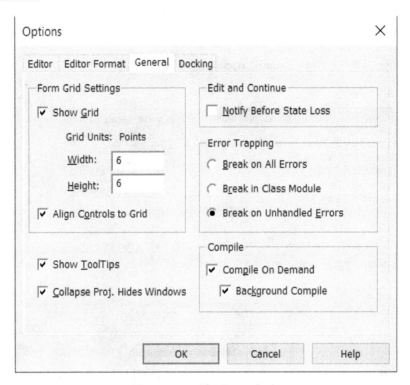

Figure 2.26 – The General tab

6. Click on the **Docking** tab to activate it. The only purpose of this tab is to set the behavior of the different windows in the VBA Editor.

There is only one section with a list of tick boxes, each with a description:

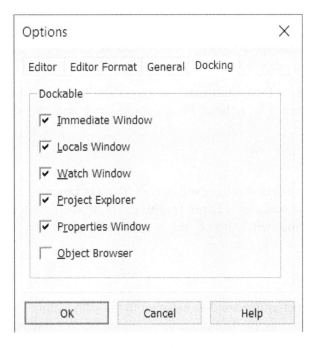

Figure 2.27 – The Docking tab

How it works...

We will now have a quick look at what customizing these tabs entails.

The Editor tab

The default settings are default for good reasons and speak for themselves, in most cases. There are two possible changes I would suggest, which are as follows:

- **The Auto Syntax Check**: For novice users, this option is indispensable, so keep it as it is. For people with more experience, the pop-up dialog box that appears when it discovers a syntax error in the code can be irritating. You choose what you prefer.

- **Default to Full Module View**: Many coders prefer to see a maximized code window. However, if you know that you're going to work in multiple modules, it is sometimes nice to have the code window in restore down mode so that you can easily select and move between them.

The Editor Format tab

With this tab, you can customize the way the Editor looks. Once again, these settings are the default because they've been tried and tested.

So, unless you are working for a multi-national company where the project managers have developed their own color settings, I would strongly advise that you stick to the factory settings.

The General tab

In almost every case, the default setting will be best. There is, however, one setting that must be mentioned, and that is **Error Trapping**. The default setting is **Break On Unhandled Errors**. If you switch this off, your error handling code will not work. More on this will be covered later in the book.

The Docking tab

As said, these settings determine window behavior in the VBA Editor. When a window is docked, it is fixed in place in the VBA program window, meaning that your environment is fixed and familiar.

If you turn off all docking, windows in the VBA Editor can potentially become a confusing mess of floating screens. In this case, I would strongly advise against undocking windows.

3
The VBA Object Model

VBA is essentially object driven. Excel, for example, provides dozens of objects that can be manipulated. This includes workbooks, worksheets, ranges, charts and images, and shapes. These objects are arranged in a hierarchical structure. If you want to do anything in VBA, understanding the VBA object model is essential. The recipes in this chapter will be your reference to understanding and working with objects in VBA.

In this chapter, we will cover the following recipes:

- Understanding and identifying objects in VBA
- Objects as a collection, and changing the attributes of the entire collection
- Modifying object properties
- Associating methods with objects
- Using events to activate objects
- Using the Object Browser in the VBA Editor

By the end of this chapter, you will be able to work with objects in VBA.

Technical requirements

This cookbook was written and designed to be used with MS Office 2019 and MS Office 365, installed on either Windows 8, 8.1, or 10.

Demonstration files can be downloaded from `https://github.com/ PacktPublishing/VBA-Automation-for-Excel-2019-Cookbook`.

Please visit the following link to check out the CiA videos: `https://bit. ly/3jQRvVk`.

Other than the aforementioned requirements, you have everything you need.

Understanding and identifying objects in VBA

In this recipe, we will learn how to identify objects. Whether you record a macro or manually enter code, you will be working with objects. In essence, the Excel object model is a hierarchy of objects contained in Excel. Each object has certain properties and can be manipulated to perform certain actions in Excel.

Once you understand this hierarchical structure, you will have a good understanding of **object-oriented programming (OOP)**.

Getting ready

As long as you have Excel installed on your system, you have everything you need. You may not have been aware of it, but every time you've used Excel in the past, you've been using objects.

How to do it...

The steps for this recipe are as follows:

1. Open a blank workbook in Excel. The first object we're looking at here is the application itself. That's the familiar Excel interface we deal with every time we work in Excel.

2. Next, contained in Excel, the main object, there are other objects such as workbooks. The default workbook will be Book1, and every new workbook after that – Book2, Book3, and so on – are all separate objects.

3. Each workbook, in turn, contains its own set of objects such as worksheets. By inserting new worksheets into workbooks, the number of objects increases accordingly.

4. On a lower level, worksheets also contain objects such as names, comments, and ranges.

How it works...

The best way to explain the hierarchical structure of objects is with a diagram, as follows:

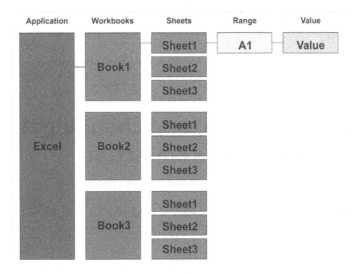

Figure 3.1 – The object hierarchy

In this scenario, the application is the main object on the left. It contains three Book objects, while each of the Book objects contains three Sheet objects. **Sheet1** of **Book1** contains a range object with a specific value.

If we had to refer to these objects in VBA, the syntax used would be vitally important. Similar to *Figure 3.1*, where the **Application** object is on the left, followed by the rest of the objects, typing the code also flows from left to right.

If we had to type code to describe the objects in *Figure 3.1*, it would be done as follows:

```
Application.Workbooks("Book1.xlsx").Worksheets(1).  _
Range("A1").Value
```

This code example is known as a fully qualified reference of the preceding diagram. The syntax dictates that each object is separated from the next by a dot (.).

Notice that the book name is in quotation marks. This is necessary for Excel to identify it as an object, instead of a variable name. For the worksheet, the number is not in quotation marks. That is because we refer to the object by its index number. The range name is in quotation marks again, and the value is just the value.

A simplified object reference for the same object would be the following:

```
Range("A1").Value
```

The reason for this much simpler reference is because the application object is always assumed. Further, if you're sure that `Book1.xlsx` is the active workbook, you can omit that too. Similarly, if you know that **Sheet1** is the currently active worksheet, Excel will assume that reference.

Note that Excel does not have a cell object. A cell is simply a range object consisting of a single element.

Objects as a collection, and changing the attributes of the entire collection

This recipe will take us one step further down the path of discovering objects.

It is common knowledge that a workbook is made up of any number of worksheets. These worksheet objects are of the same type and form a collection. Collections are objects in themselves.

There are, of course, more objects that form collections than just worksheets. Here is a list of other commonly used workbook objects:

- **Workbooks**: All currently open workbook objects form a collection.
- **Worksheets**: All worksheet objects contained in a particular workbook object constitute another collection.
- **Charts**: All chart objects/chart sheets contained in a particular workbook object are yet another collection.
- **Sheets**: All sheets, regardless of type, contained in a particular workbook object also form a collection.

Having this understanding of collections will be useful for all future recipes.

Getting ready

Open Excel and make sure that **Book1** is active.

How to do it...

Now let's proceed with the following steps:

1. With **Book1** open, insert three more sheets by clicking on the add button (+) to the right of **Sheet1**. We need a total of four sheets in **Book1**.

2. Now, create a new workbook – **Book2**. Leave it with only one worksheet.

3. Once done, activate the VBA Editor by pressing *Alt + F11*.

4. The **Project** window displays all the recently created objects. It is important to take note of the collections. **Book1** and **Book2** are in bold because they belong to the same collection. Similarly, all the sheets belong to another collection:

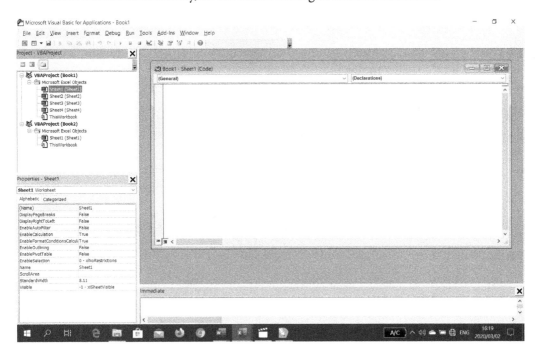

Figure 3.2 – Objects in the Project window

5. While still in the VBA Editor, select **Book1**. Then, on the menu bar, click **Insert | Module**.

6. In the code window for `Module1`, type the following code:

```
Sub ChangeFont()
        Sheets(Array("Sheet1", "Sheet2", "Sheet3", _
        "Sheet4")).Select
        Sheets("Sheet1").Activate
        Cells.Select
        With Selection.Font
                .Name = "Arial"
                .Size = 12
        End With
        Selection.Font.Size = 11
        Range("A1").Select
End Sub
```

7. Once done, run the macro. (To do this, press *F5* and then *Alt + F11* to switch back to Excel. Alternatively, press *Alt + F11* to switch back to Excel, and then click **Developer Tab | Code Window | Macros | Run Macro | ChangeFont**).

8. Observe that all four sheets on **Book1** have been selected, and that the font for each sheet is now Arial set to size 11.

How it works...

When we run the **ChangeFont** macro, the following happens:

1. Line one of the code selects and groups all four sheets in **Book1**. At the same time, **Book1** is activated. Because these sheets are grouped, any action taken on **Sheet1** will also be applied to the rest of the group.

2. Next, all cells on the sheets are selected.

3. The font is changed to Arial, while the font size stays at 12 points for the moment.

4. Now, the size is reduced to 11 points.

5. Finally, cell A1 is selected.

You can check any of the four sheets to confirm that the font has been changed to Arial, size 11.

Modifying object properties

Knowing how to refer to objects is only the first step in working with them. In this recipe, we will be learning how to modify the properties of objects. You can think of properties as attributes that describe an object. In order to use them to do something of value, you must be able to do the following:

- Read an object's properties and then modify them.
- Specify a method of action to be used with that object (more about this in the next recipe).

Getting ready

Make sure that a blank workbook is active in Excel.

How to do it...

Let's see the steps for this recipe:

1. With Excel open, press *Alt + F11* to activate the VBA Editor.
2. In the **Project** window of Explorer, double-click on **Sheet1** under **Book1**. The corresponding code window will appear:

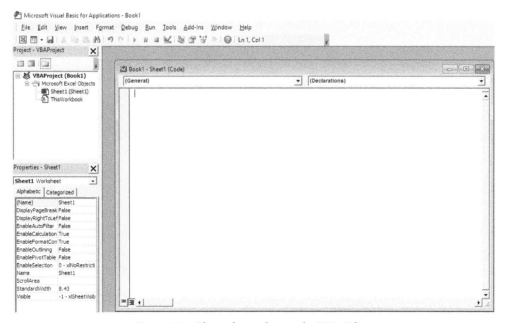

Figure 3.3 – The code window in the VBA Editor

3. Type the following code:

```
Sub ChangeValue()
        Worksheets("Sheet1").Range("A1").Value = 555
End Sub
```

4. Press *F5* to run the code, and then press *Alt + F11* to switch back to Excel.

5. The cell A1 of **Sheet1** now contains the value **555**.

How it works...

Here's how the preceding steps worked out:

1. Cell A1 was empty. In other words, its value property was zero.

2. The ChangeValue Sub procedure first activated **Sheet1**, then cell A1, and finally set the value of cell A1 to **555**.

3. By running the macro, we changed the value property of cell A1 from empty to **555**:

Figure 3.4 – The new value property in cell A1

There's more...

With the preceding sample, we've only scratched the surface. Other properties, such as bold or italic, font color, font size, alignment, and many more, can be set in the same way.

The following code sample is extremely clumsy, but I need to make a point here.

First, clear cell A1. Then type any value into cells B1 and C1 of **Sheet1**. When done, activate the VBA Editor, and add the following lines to the existing Sub procedure:

```
Sub ChangeValue()
      Range("A1").Value = 555
      Range("B1").Font.Color = -16776961
      Range("C1").Font.Bold = True
End Sub
```

Run the macro.

Cell A1's value is once again set to 555, while cell B1's font color has changed to red. Similarly, cell C1's font weight is set to bold.

Associating methods with objects

So, what is a method, and what is its connection with objects? Objects have properties, as we have seen, while a method is something an object does. A method is a specific piece of code you type after an object. It's like an instruction to the object: copy (the cell object), print (the sheet object), or select (the range object). In this recipe, we will use three basic methods: Activate, Copy, and ClearContents. In this recipe, we will copy content from one selection to another.

Getting ready

Make sure that a blank workbook is active in Excel. Type the words Monday, Tuesday, and Wednesday into cells A1, B1, and C1, respectively.

How to do it...

1. Press *Alt + F11* to activate the VBA Editor.

2. In the **Project** window of Explorer, double-click **Sheet1** under **Book1**. The corresponding code window will appear.

3. Type the following code into the code window:

```
Sub CopyCell()
    Worksheets("Sheet1").Activate
    Range("A1:C1").Copy Range("A2")
End Sub
```

Run the macro, and then press *Alt + F11* to switch back to Excel. Observe how the content of the three cells has been copied to the following row.

4. Press *Alt + F11* to activate the VBA Editor again.

5. Under the CopyCell Sub procedure, press *Enter* to create a new line. Type the following code:

```
Sub RangeClear()
    Range("A1:C1").ClearContents
End Sub
```

6. Press *F5* to run the code, and then press *Alt + F11* to switch back to Excel.

7. Whatever values you had in the range A1 to C1 have been cleared.

How it works...

Cells A1 to C1 each contained a value. The CopyCell Sub procedure first activated Sheet1, and then used the Copy method to copy the contents of cells A1, B1, and C1 to cells A2, B2, and C2.

Following this, we also saw how we can use the RangeClear Sub procedure to clear the content from cells A1, B1, and C1.

Using events to activate objects

The last element in relation to objects that we need to discuss is events. In simple English, an event is what happens when an object does something, such as *open* a workbook, *close* a sheet, or *print* a file. Events are initiated by a user, for example, by clicking a mouse or pressing a key.

In this recipe, we're going to cover only the most basic principles, since an entire chapter is dedicated to events later in this book.

Getting ready

With Excel open, ensure that a blank workbook is available and active.

How to do it...

The first thing to remember about events is that the code is not stored in a module object, but in the workbook object. Place the code anywhere else and it will simply not work.

The steps for this recipe are as follows:

1. Press *Alt + F11* to activate the VBA Editor.

2. In the **Project** window, double-click on the **ThisWorkbook** object to open the code window.

3. At the top left of the code window, from the drop-down list, select the object that you're coding for; in this case, a workbook:

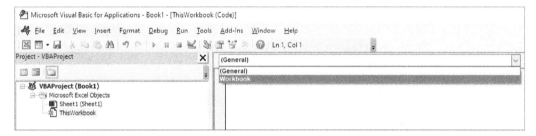

Figure 3.5 – The object drop-down list in the VBA Editor

4. The default event inserted will be Open. If you want to code for another event, select from the drop-down list at the top right of the window:

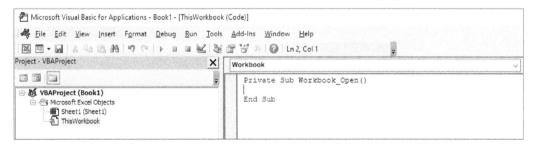

Figure 3.6 – The Open event code

5. Between the opening and closing statements of the Sub procedure, type the following code:

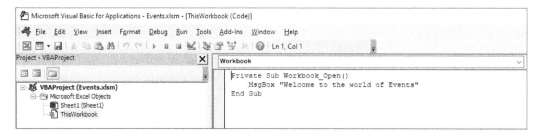

Figure 3.7 – Completed Sub procedure

6. Once done, don't just run the code by pressing *F5*. You need to trigger the event that the Sub procedure is attached to, meaning that you have to save the file and then open it. The event will only be activated when the file is opened.

7. Press *Alt + F11* to switch back to Excel.

8. Save the file as a macro-enabled workbook and close it.

9. When you open it now, click on **Enable Macros**. The event will be initiated, and a message box will be displayed. Click on the **OK** button to close the message box:

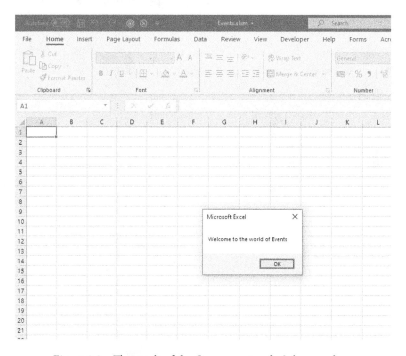

Figure 3.8 – The result of the Open event code Sub procedure

Take note that the message box must be closed before you can do any work on the spreadsheet.

How it works...

Events are initiated by objects that do something. In this case, the event is linked to the opening of a specific workbook. When the workbook is opened, the event is triggered, and as per the instructions in the code, a message box is displayed.

Using the Object Browser in the VBA Editor

This recipe covers usage of the Object Browser in the VBA Editor. The name says it all; the Object Browser lets you browse through the objects available to you.

In later recipes, we will look into the autocompletion of our code. For instance, when you type the name of an object in the code window and type a dot, a context menu appears with a list of actions you can choose from:

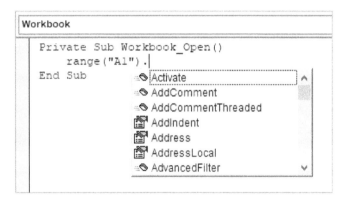

Figure 3.9 – The context menu with available library options

The green icons are methods, including cutting, pasting, and clearing contents. The other icons are properties. You can, in other words, choose methods or properties here, or use the Object Browser, as described hereafter.

Getting ready

Make sure that a blank workbook is active in Excel.

How to do it...

1. Activate the VBA Editor by pressing *Alt + F11*.

2. With the Editor active, press *F2* to activate the Object Browser. You can also do this by clicking on **View | Object Browser**:

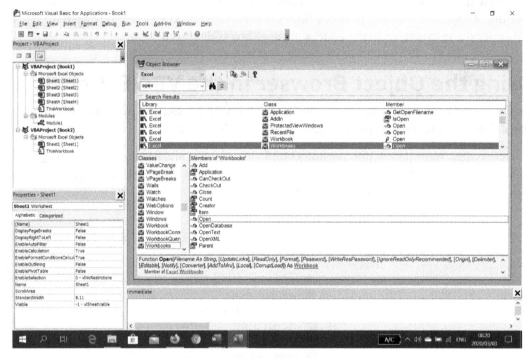

Figure 3.10 – The Object Browser

3. The drop-down list in the top left-hand corner, just under the title bar, contains a list of all the object libraries that are currently available. *Figure 3.10* displays the Excel libraries.

4. Just below that, a second drop-down list lets you enter a search string. In this example, I searched for all Excel objects that deal with *open*.

5. The object library now displays everything that contains the text *open*. If you want to know more about *Close*, for instance, click on that object and press *F1* for more information.

6. There is also the Auto List Members feature. It provides a list of properties and methods as you type. *Figure 3.11* shows an example of this for the worksheets collection:

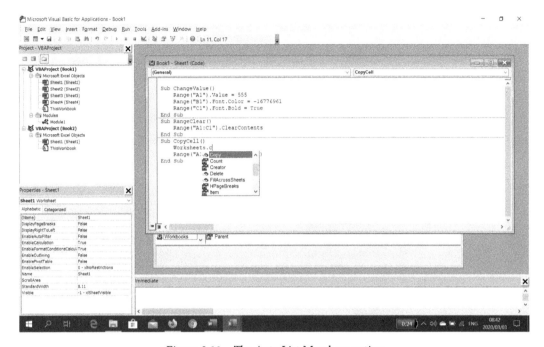

Figure 3.11 – The Auto List Members option

How it works...

The Object Browser is a tool in the VBA Editor that lets you browse through the objects available to you.

The Auto List Members feature provides a list of properties and methods as you type. It eliminates some typing, and also ensures that the property or method is spelled correctly.

4
Working with Procedures

A good starting point for this chapter would be to help you understand what a procedure is.

When recording a macro, Excel captures every action you take. Each step is stored in the VBA Editor in a specific text form, or a little *program*. The correct term for these recorded lines of code is a **procedure**. When recording a macro, your actions in Excel are stored in a VBA procedure.

A procedure, therefore, is a block of statements. It starts with a particular declaration statement and ends with an End declaration. When you then run the macro, the procedure carries out whatever task you recorded.

Macros are useful on an elementary level. To make the most of VBA, you need to know how to write procedures manually.

VBA distinguishes between Sub procedures and Function procedures. We will investigate both procedures to help you understand the difference, role, and function of each. Naming conventions become important here and are explained in detail. To make things crystal clear, we make use of practical examples to explain the difference in executing a Sub procedure and a Function procedure.

In this chapter, we will cover the following recipes:

- Creating Sub and Function procedures
- Executing Sub procedures directly
- Executing Sub procedures from the **Macro** dialog box
- Executing Sub procedures using buttons
- Executing Sub procedures using a shortcut key
- Executing Function procedures using a worksheet formula
- Executing Function procedures by calling from a Sub procedure

By the end of this chapter, you will be able to write a Sub procedure manually.

Technical requirements

This cookbook was written and designed to be used with MS Office 2019 and MS Office 365, installed on either Windows 8, 8.1, or 10.

If your hardware and software meet these requirements, you're good to go.

Demonstration files can be downloaded from `https://github.com/PacktPublishing/VBA-Automation-for-Excel-2019-Cookbook`.

Please visit the following link to check out the CiA videos: `https://bit.ly/3jQRvVk`.

Creating Sub and Function procedures

In this recipe, we will be creating the two most common types of procedures; **Sub** and **Function** procedures.

A Sub procedure is, in essence, a series of VBA statements, with the purpose of performing an action within Excel. The simplest Sub procedures can be as short as a single line of code (between the Sub and End Sub statements), while complex Sub procedures can become quite long. It is, however, advisable to divide huge Sub procedures into a series of shorter Sub procedures.

Another procedure often used in VBA is the Function procedure. The purpose and use of this type of procedure differs from the Sub procedure in the sense that it performs a calculation and returns a single value.

It can happen that you want to do a complex calculation, like a nested If statement, or a nested And/Or statement. By incorporating these functions into a **User-Defined Function** (**UDF**), you can simplify the process considerably.

Function procedures can also be used for very simple calculations, such as finding the exponent of a value.

So, watch closely as we show you how to create a Sub and a Function procedure.

Getting ready

Open Excel and make sure that **Book1** is active.

How to do it...

Sub procedures are a series of steps or instructions that we can apply in Excel.

Let's say you have to create a new data table every day. The layout and headings must be exactly the same for each new table. Instead of creating the table manually, you can write a Sub procedure to automate the work for you. The table headings we want to create should look like this:

	A	B	C
1	First Name	Last Name	City
2			
3			

Figure 4.1 – The table headings we want to create

Let's create a simple Sub procedure by taking the following steps:

1. Activate the VBA Editor with *Alt + F11* or click on **Developer** | **Code** | **Visual Basic**.

2. In the Editor, click **Insert** | **Module** to create a new module in **Book1**.

3. In the code window for **Module1**, type the following code:

```
Sub TableData()
    Range("A1").Value = "First Name"
    Range("B1").Value = "Last Name"
    Range("C1").Value = "City"
    Range("D1").Select
End Sub
```

4. Save the procedure by clicking on **File** | **Save**.

Next, we will be creating a simple Function procedure:

1. Under the existing Sub procedure, type the following code:

```
Function Exponent(x As Integer, y As Integer) As Integer
    Exponent = x ^ y
End Function
```

2. Save the Function procedure by clicking on **File | Save**.

How it works...

Sub procedures are a series of steps or instructions that we can apply in Excel:

1. In the code window of **Module1**, we first typed the word Sub, then the name of the procedure, TableData, and then pressed *Enter*. The End Sub statement, as well as the parentheses, were inserted automatically.

2. In this case, we want the heading First Name to appear in cell A1. By typing in the range, and then setting the value of that range to First Name, we've assigned the text value to cell A1.

3. The values Last Name and City were assigned to cells B1 and C1, respectively.

4. Finally, after placing the three headings, we want cell D1 to be selected.

Function procedures return a single value. In this example, we want to calculate the value of a base number and any exponent. There is no existing function in Excel that does this. Let's see how we did it:

1. In the code window, we typed the word Function and then the name we wanted to assign to that function. By pressing *Enter*, the End Function statement as well as the parentheses were inserted automatically.

2. We then clicked between the parentheses and declared two variables, x and y, as integers. We ended off by setting the result to an integer as well.

3. In the next line, we typed the name of the function again, and made sure that it was exactly the same as in the first line.

4. Next, we set the function name to the calculation. In this case, we wanted the first value as the base value, and the second value as the exponent. The ^ (caret) character is used to set the second value as the exponent.

There's more...

In the Microsoft environment, there are at least two (sometimes three) different ways of getting things done. Writing a Sub or Function procedure is no different.

If typing is not your thing, you can always use the VBA Editor to help you create procedures:

1. In the VBA Editor, in the Menu bar, click on **Insert | Procedure**.

2. The **Add Procedure** dialog box appears:

Figure 4.2 – The Add Procedure dialog box

3. Type the name of your Sub or Function procedure in the **Name** box.

4. Next, select the **Type** of procedure: **Sub**, **Function**, or **Property**. (The **Property** function will be discussed at a later stage.)

5. Under **Scope**, select **Public**.

6. Click **OK**.

7. In the code window, the opening and closing statements will automatically appear. All you have to do is type the rest of the code.

> **Important note**
> A public procedure has no access restrictions, meaning that it can be accessed by any Sub procedure in any other module. Private procedures can only be accessed from Subs stored in the same VBA module.

Executing Sub procedures directly

Having created a Sub procedure is a waste of time if it doesn't make your life easier. Instead of creating a table manually, you want the Sub procedure to do the work automatically.

So, how do you get the Sub procedure to work? You run it, or execute it. Whether you call it by running the code or executing the code makes no difference. All you want to do is to get the code to do what it was supposed to do.

In this recipe, we will be investigating one specific way of executing a Sub procedure. It is not better or faster, it's just one of about ten different ways in which we can run a Sub procedure.

Getting ready

Make sure that you are still in the code window that contains the procedure we created in the previous section.

How to do it...

To execute a Sub procedure directly, do the following:

1. Click anywhere in the code window of the procedure you want to run.
2. Press **Run | Run Sub/Userform**. (The keyboard shortcut is *F5*.)
3. Press *Alt + F11* to switch back to Excel.
4. Cells A1, B1, and C1 will display the values `First Name`, `Last Name`, and `City`, respectively.

How it works...

Lines of code in the code window are nothing more than a set of instructions for Excel to follow. When we run a macro, these text values will be inserted in the required cells. Because the macro was created in a module, it can be used on any worksheet.

Executing Sub procedures from the Macro dialog box

This recipe will show us how to execute a Sub procedure from within Excel. Once again, there is no right or wrong, no better or faster method; it is just another way of getting the macro to do what it is supposed to do.

Getting ready

If you are not already in **Sheet1**, press *Alt + F11* to switch back from the code window to Excel and clear cells *A1*, *B1*, and *C1*.

How to do it...

To run the macro from the Macro dialog box, do the following:

1. Click **Developer | Code | Macros** to activate the **Macro** dialog box:

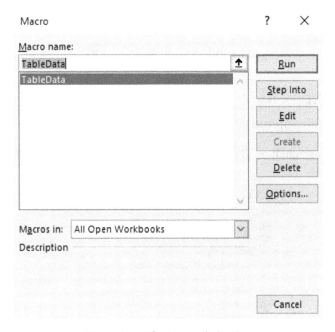

Figure 4.3 – The Macro dialog box

2. The only available macro is the one you've just created: `TableData`. Click on **Run**.

3. As per the coding instructions for the Sub procedure, you will find the text inserted into cells A1, B1, and C1. Cell D1 will be selected, yet empty.

How it works...

We executed exactly the same Sub procedure as before. The only difference is the method: instead of running it directly from the code window, we selected the macro from the **Macro** dialog box.

The results were also exactly the same. The principle behind this is that the executing method is not what is important, but rather the underlying coding.

Executing Sub procedures using buttons

In this recipe, we're going to take the running of macros one step further by executing them when clicking on a button.

There is a very good reason for creating buttons on a spreadsheet. Some users may not be familiar with the VBA Editor, meaning that they wouldn't know how to run a macro from there. Even the **Macro** dialog box can be a challenge. That's when buttons become very useful, because even a novice will know that clicking on a button normally makes something happen.

Getting ready

Ensure that Excel is open on the same workbook that we've been working with so far.

How to do it...

The following steps will help you complete this recipe:

1. In any worksheet, click on **Developer | Controls | Insert | Button (Form Control)**:

Figure 4.4 – Inserting the Button form control

2. Now click and drag anywhere on the worksheet to create a button. Size is not important, but remember that a very small button would make it difficult to see button text, and a very large button would obscure data on the spreadsheet. A button called **Button 1** will now be visible:

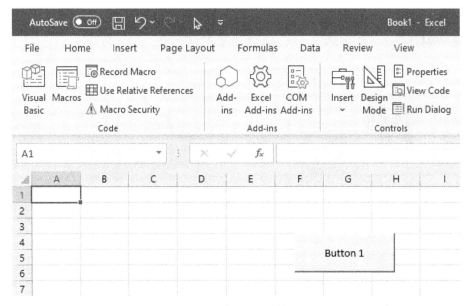

Figure 4.5 – The inserted button

3.   The **Assign Macro** dialog box appears:

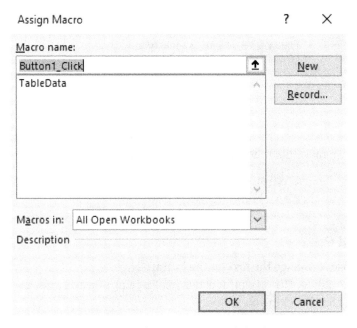

Figure 4.6 – The Assign Macro dialog box

4. To override the default name, click on the **TableData** macro. Observe how **Button1_Click** is replaced:

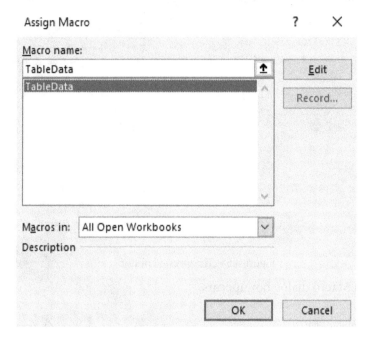

Figure 4.7 – Assigning a macro to the button

5. Click **OK**.

How it works...

Assigning a macro to a button means that we've associated the code in Explorer with the button. That way, we make life much easier for users in general.

Instead of running the macro from the VBA Editor or from the Developer toolbar, users can now conveniently click on a button to insert headings into cells A1, B1, and C1.

There's more...

It would make sense to change the text on the button. No one would have any idea what **Button1** can or should do. However, if it is named Insert Headings, users would be much more comfortable clicking on it.

Do the following to change the text on **Button1**:

1. Right-click on **Button1** and select **Edit Text**:

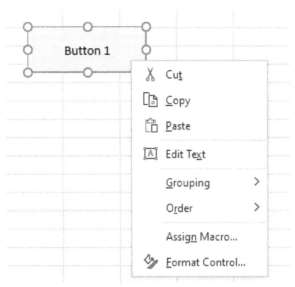

Figure 4.8 – Editing the button name

2. The menu disappears, while the text on the button can now be edited. Change it to `Insert Headings`.
3. Once done, click anywhere on the spreadsheet to accept the change.

Executing Sub procedures using a shortcut key

Another very popular way of executing a macro is to press a shortcut key. If you assign that shortcut key when you record a macro, it's quite simple. But what if you entered your code directly in the code window? How do you assign a shortcut key from there?

In this recipe, we are going to assign a shortcut key to a macro and execute it that way.

Getting ready

Excel is still open in the same workbook that we've been working with so far. The VBA Editor is active.

How to do it...

The following steps will show you how to assign a keyboard shortcut to an existing macro:

1. In the VBA Editor, choose **Developer | Code | Macros**.

2. The **Macro** dialog box appears:

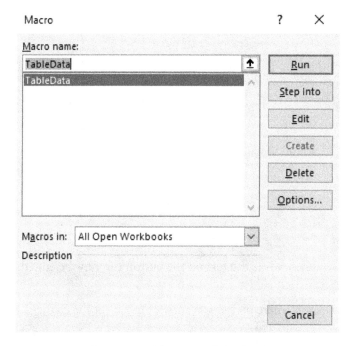

Figure 4.9 – The Macro dialog box

3. The only available macro is already selected. Click the **Options** button. The **Macro Options** dialog box appears:

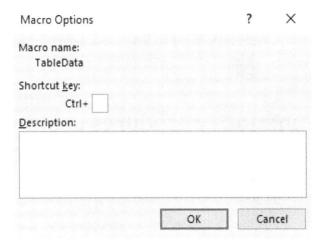

Figure 4.10 – The Macro Options dialog box

4. Enter a shortcut key in the **Ctrl+Shift+** box. For this shortcut, we are going to hold down *Shift*, and then press T. The keyboard shortcut has now been set to *Ctrl + Shift + T*:

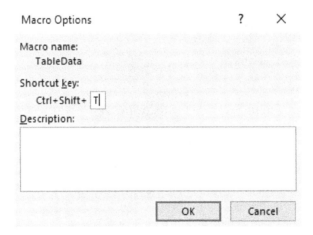

Figure 4.11 – Creating a shortcut key

5. Click **OK** to close the dialog box.

6. Clear all data from **Sheet1** and press the shortcut key *Ctrl + Shift + T* .

7. The headings will once again appear in cells A1, B1, and C1, since it is the same macro that has been executed.

How it works...

Whether you run the macro directly from the code window, from the **Macro** dialog box, or with a keyboard shortcut, it boils down to the same thing; the code must somehow be executed. The method doesn't matter, as long as the result is agreeable.

Executing Function procedures using a worksheet formula

Unlike Sub procedures, Function procedures cannot be executed directly. In fact, they can be executed only in two ways: by another procedure, or with a worksheet formula.

In this recipe, we will be executing the Exponent Function procedure from within Excel. It is done in exactly the same way as any of the other worksheet functions in Excel; you click on a cell, type the = (equals) sign, and move on from there.

Let's go through the steps and see how it's done.

Getting ready

Make sure that Excel is still open in the same workbook that we've been working with so far.

How to do it...

To execute, or call a function in Excel, do the following:

1. Click on any open cell on **Sheet1**. As with any other function, press =.

2. Now type exponent to call up the function we created earlier.

3. Press *Tab* to activate the function. After the first parenthesis, type 5 , 2 and press *Enter*.

4. The result, **25**, will be displayed in the active cell.

How it works...

1. By typing = in any cell, a list of available functions, starting with **exp,** will appear.

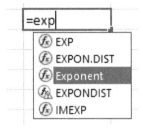

Figure 4.12 – Selecting the Exponent function

2. By selecting **Exponent** and pressing *Tab*, the function was inserted, waiting for us to provide the arguments.

3. By typing the base value as the first argument, followed by a comma, and then exponent as the second argument, the function was completed.

4. By pressing *Enter*, the result appeared in the active cell.

Executing Function procedures by calling from a Sub procedure

In this last recipe, we will be calling the Function procedure from a Sub procedure. Once again, unless we call a Function procedure directly in Excel, the only other way to execute it is to call it from a Sub procedure.

Getting ready

Press *Alt + F11* to activate the VBA Editor.

How to do it...

Follow these steps to create a Sub procedure to call the Exponent Function procedure:

1. Under the last procedure in the code window, type the following code:

```
Sub CallSample()
    Result = Exponent(5, 2)
    MsgBox Result
End Sub
```

2. Save the file, and then press *F5* to run the procedure.

How it works...

Function procedures cannot be executed like standard procedures. You cannot even execute it by running it as a macro. The only way to run a function is to use it in the Excel spreadsheet like a built-in function, or to call it from another procedure. That is why we had to create the `CallSample` procedure.

In this procedure, we set the `Result` variable as equal to the Exponent function, with 5 as the base value and 2 as the exponent. The expected result would therefore be 25 (5 x 5 = 25).

By pressing *F5*, the `CallSample` procedure is executed. It calls the `Exponent` function and displays the value 25 in a message box in Excel.

5
Next Level Recording

Doing a basic recording is simple. There is, however, more to recording a macro than meets the eye. Planning plays a role, and so does relativity. Understanding and using absolute or relative references when recording a macro can make or break your procedure. It is also useful to understand that macro recordings are limited to direct actions taken in a worksheet. Functions, IF statements, loops, and custom dialog boxes, to name a few, cannot be recorded.

Relative referencing in macros opens up a new world of functionality. Most importantly, it allows you to run a macro on specific, chosen cells, instead of being limited to one location. You can, in other words, record a macro starting in cell A1, but when it comes to executing, you can choose the starting cell to be any other cell on the sheet.

In this chapter, we will cover the following recipes:

- Setting the macro recorder for absolute or relative reference
- Recording options

By the end of this chapter, you will be able to record macros with relative or absolute referencing.

Technical requirements

This cookbook was written and designed to be used with MS Office 2019 and MS Office 365, installed on either Windows 8, 8.1, or 10.

If your hardware and software meet these requirements, you have everything you need.

Demonstration files can be downloaded from `https://github.com/ PacktPublishing/VBA-Automation-for-Excel-2019-Cookbook`.

Please visit the following link to check out the CiA videos: `https://bit. ly/3jQRvVk`.

Setting the macro recorder for absolute or relative reference

In this recipe, we will be working with relative macro recordings.

The default setting for a macro recording is absolute. In simple English, this means that the execution of your macro will always start on the same cell where the recording was done.

With a relative setting, you can record a macro and choose a different starting point when executing the macro. Unlike the absolute reference macro, you are not restricted to a specific range or starting point.

Getting ready

Open Excel and make sure that **Book1** is active.

How to do it...

To record a macro in relative mode, do the following:

1. Click in cell A1. Activate the **Developer** ribbon.
2. In the **Code** group, select the **Use Relative References** option:

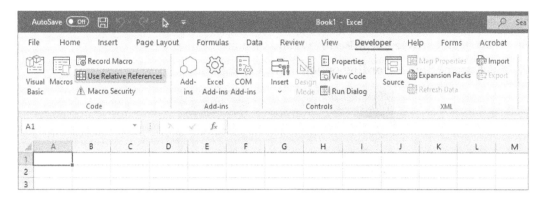

Figure 5.1 – The Use Relative Refences option

3. Still in the **Code** group, click on **Record Macro**. The **Record Macro** dialog box appears:

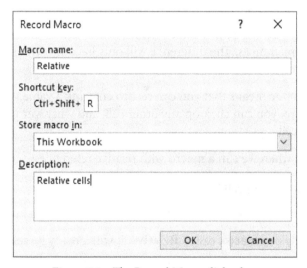

Figure 5.2 – The Record Macro dialog box

4. In the **Macro name** textbox, type `Relative`. Set the shortcut key to *Ctrl + Shift + R*, store the macro in this workbook, and add a short description in the bottom textbox.

5. Click on **OK**. You are now in recording mode.

6. With cell A1 selected, type Heading and then press *Enter*.

7. Click on the **Stop Recording** option in the **Code** group:

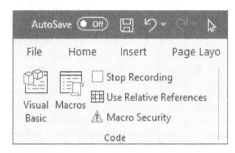

Figure 5.3 – The Stop Recording button in the Code group

How it works...

The steps for recording a macro with relative references are exactly the same as those for a macro with absolute references. The difference will only become evident when we run or execute the macro.

Recording in relative mode means that you can record entering a value in cell A1, but when you run the macro, you can click on any other cell, and whatever you recorded will appear in the selected cell.

Let's see what happens when we run a macro with relative references:

1. With Excel open, click in cell D10.

2. In the **Code** group, click on **Macros**. The familiar **Macro** dialog box appears.

    Since there is only one macro, called **Relative**, it will already be selected. Click on **Run**.

3. Observe how **Heading** now appears in cell D10. If the recording was done as an absolute reference, the text would have appeared on A1 again, where it was recorded:

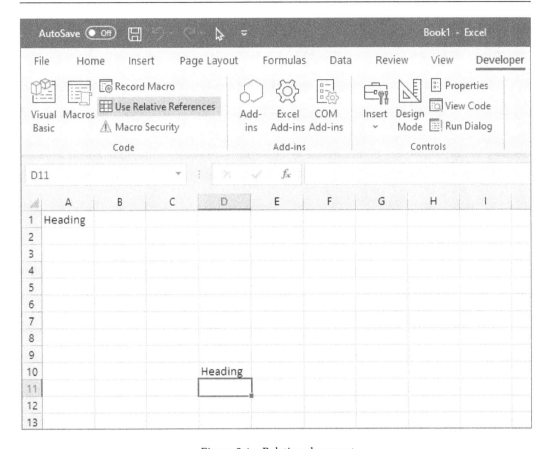

Figure 5.4 – Relative placement

There are many more possible ways of using relative referencing when recording a macro. As long as you understand the principles, you should be able to apply and use it effectively.

Recording options

Whenever we record a macro, there are a number of options to consider. Beyond the choice between absolute and relative references, there are other settings we need to take note of.

In this recipe, we will be looking at different options when recording a macro.

Getting ready

Open Excel and make sure that **Book1** is active.

How to do it...

Here are the steps to set options for recording a macro:

1. With **Sheet1** active, click on **Developer | Code | Record Macro**. The **Record Macro** dialog box appears:

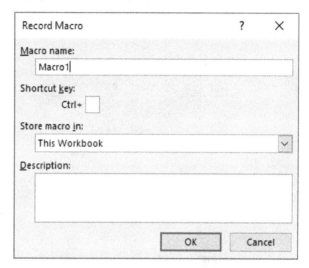

Figure 5.5 – The Record Macro dialog box

2. The **Macro name, Shortcut key, Store macro in**, and **Description** options can all be changed, based on personal choice and need.

How it works...

The details of each option will now be discussed in the following subsections.

Macro name

All macros must have a name. There is, however, a specific naming convention that we need to follow. Macro names follow these conventions:

-   Must begin with a letter
-   Must contain only letters, numbers, and underscores
-   Cannot contain any spaces
-   Should not be the same as cell references, to avoid errors
-   Cannot be the same as existing Excel functions or keywords, such as `Sum`, `Average`, `Copy`, and `Paste`

Shortcut key

You can use any combination of keys in this section. There are certain constraints you should be aware of:

- Try to use unique keyboard shortcuts, such as *Ctrl + Q*.

- If you use an existing keyboard shortcut for a macro – for example, *Ctrl + C* – it will override the *Copy* shortcut in Excel (for that specific worksheet).

- If you run out of keyboard shortcut options using *Ctrl*, combine it with *Shift*. *Ctrl + Shift + C* will not influence any existing shortcuts.

Where to store the macro

You can store the macro in one of three places:

- **Personal Macro Workbook**: Storing a macro in this location will make it available to multiple Excel workbooks on your PC. The Personal Macro Workbook is a hidden workbook named `Personal.xlsb`.

- **New Workbook**: If you select this option, Excel will open a new, blank workbook for you to record and save the macro in.

- **This Workbook**: Excel will store your macro, by default, in a module in the active workbook. It will be available on all sheets of that workbook, but not for any other Excel workbooks.

Description

The **Description** box is a good starting point to save comments. You can, of course, also store comments directly in the recorded macro.

The point is that comments are an important and often ignored element in code. You might think that you will remember what you did in a specific procedure, but believe me when I tell you that you do not always remember. You sometimes create complex sequences for a client, save the file, and move on. When you later see that macro again and need to make adjustments, you will be shocked to realize how little you remember of the thinking process you went through to create that macro. Comments will save you a lot of time and frustration.

Finally, if you don't want to leave comments for yourself, think about the possibility of someone else having to amend your coding. Once again, comments would make a world of difference for that person.

6
VBA Language Elements

Visual Basic for Applications (**VBA**) has its origins in Visual Basic, a programming language developed by Microsoft. It is important to understand that VBA is not a standalone program, meaning that you cannot compile code and run it as a separate program outside the MS Office environment.

Its main reason for existence is the customization of the MS Office host applications in which it runs: Word, Excel, Access, PowerPoint, Visio, and Publisher. Companies such as Corel also make use of VBA to allow customization of their applications.

Customization involves the recording and creating of macros to automate repetitive tasks. It is also used to generate custom forms, including event-driven buttons and fields.

Like any language, you need to understand the structure of VBA, which is a programming language. It starts with vocabulary. From there, you learn what effects certain words, also known as commands, will have. The more you use the language, the better you understand it. So, if you want to use VBA to its full potential, this chapter will empower you, in every sense of the word, in doing the following:

- Adding comments
- Declaring variables
- Declaring constants
- Working with data types in variables and constants
- Scoping variables
- Declaring arrays

By the end of this chapter, you will be able to use VBA language elements.

Technical requirements

This cookbook was written and designed to be used with MS Office 2019 and MS Office 365, installed on either Windows 8, 8.1, or 10. If your hardware and software meet these requirements, you have everything you need.

Demonstration files can be downloaded from `https://github.com/ PacktPublishing/VBA-Automation-for-Excel-2019-Cookbook`.

Please visit the following link to check out the CiA videos: `https://bit. ly/3jQRvVk`.

Adding comments

In this recipe, we will be working with comments. Before we start, you need to understand three important principles about comments:

- VBA code does not depend on comments, meaning that macros will run flawlessly without a single comment.
- At the same time, comments are an important and often-ignored element in code.

- The most important reason why you need to leave comments in code is two-fold.

  Comments, or notes, serve as a *reminder to yourself*. You sometimes create complex sequences for a client, save the file, and move on. When you later see that macro again and need to make adjustments, you will be shocked to realize how little you remember of the thinking process you went through to create that macro.

  Comments also serve as an *explanation for someone else* that might have to amend your coding. Instead of trying to waste time on trying to figure out your thought process, comments make a world of difference for that person.

- Finally, when you record a macro, certain comments will be inserted automatically, courtesy of the VBA recorder. However, nothing prevents you from adding extra comments.

Getting ready

Open Excel and make sure that **Book1** is active. Save the file as `Comments.xlsm`.

How to do it...

Let's start with the steps:

1. Enter the following data in **Book1**, **Sheet1**:

◢	A	B	C	D	E
1	Mon	Tue	Wed	Thu	Fri
2	100	100	100	100	100
3	100	100	100	100	100
4	100	100	100	100	100
5	100	100	100	100	100
6	100	100	100	100	100
7	500	500	500	500	500
8					

Figure 6.1 – Sample data

2. Next, record a new macro with the following specifications:

   a. Call the macro `Comments`.

   b. Add a shortcut key: *Ctrl + Shift + Q*.

   c. In the **Comments** section, type `Demonstrate the use of comments`.

d. Format cells A1:E1 as bold, 12pt, and center.

e. Format cells A2:E7 as **Accounting**.

f. For cells A7:E7, add a single line to the top and a double line at the bottom.

g. Select cell F1 before stopping the recording.

3.   Switch to the VBA Editor to view the code. After deleting the redundant lines, your code should look like this:

```
(General)                                                        ∨   Comments

Sub Comments()
'
' Comments Macro
' Demonstrate the use of comments
'
' Keyboard Shortcut: Ctrl+Shift+Q
'
    Range("A1:E1").Select
    Selection.Font.Bold = True
    Selection.Font.Size = 12
    With Selection
        .HorizontalAlignment = xlCenter
    End With
    Range("A2:E7").Select
    Selection.NumberFormat = _
        "_-[$$-en-US]* #,##0.00_ ;_-[$$-en-US]* -#,##0.00 ;_-[$$-en-US]* ""-""??_ ;_-@_ "
    Range("A7:E7").Select
    With Selection.Borders(xlEdgeTop)
        .LineStyle = xlContinuous
        .ColorIndex = xlAutomatic
        .Weight = xlThin
    End With
    With Selection.Borders(xlEdgeBottom)
        .LineStyle = xlDouble
        .ColorIndex = xlAutomatic
        .Weight = xlThick
    End With
    Range("F1").Select
End Sub
```

Figure 6.2 – Auto-inserted comments

The first six comments were automatically added during the recording of the macro.

4.   Add extra comments, as per the following example:

```
(General)                                              ∨    Comments

  Sub Comments()
  '
  ' Comments Macro
  ' Demonstrate the use of comments
  '
  ' Keyboard Shortcut: Ctrl+Shift+Q
  '
      Range("A1:E1").Select    'Format the headings
      Selection.Font.Bold = True
      Selection.Font.Size = 12
      With Selection
          .HorizontalAlignment = xlCenter
      End With
      Range("A2:E7").Select    'Format the data as ACCOUNTING
      Selection.NumberFormat = _
          "_-[$$-en-US]* #,##0.00_ ;_-[$$-en-US]* -#,##0.00 ;_-[$$-en-US]* ""-""??_ ;_-@_ "
      Range("A7:E7").Select
      With Selection.Borders(xlEdgeTop)    'Add a single line above the totals
          .LineStyle = xlContinuous
          .ColorIndex = xlAutomatic
          .Weight = xlThin
      End With
      With Selection.Borders(xlEdgeBottom)    'Add a double line below the totals
          .LineStyle = xlDouble
          .ColorIndex = xlAutomatic
          .Weight = xlThick
      End With
      Range("F1").Select
  End Sub
```

Figure 6.3 – Manually inserted comments

How it works...

When recording a macro, the VBA Editor will insert some comments automatically. Extra comments can be added manually. Start a comment by first inserting the single apostrophe symbol ('). The VBA Editor will not interpret text following the apostrophe as code.

Comments can be inserted anywhere you want in either of the following ways:

- As a line of text before the VBA code
- As an added comment after a line of code
- After the last line of code

There is an exception to this rule, however. You cannot insert a comment in the middle of a line of code, because the apostrophe will cancel out all the code following it.

Declaring variables

Before confusing you with the definition of what a variable is, it helps a lot to first understand where and how variables can be used. Let's use the following example.

Imagine you are capturing data on a standard Excel spreadsheet. The fields expect users to enter their name, the department they work in, and age, all on **Sheet1** of a workbook. The captured data must then be stored on a separate sheet, most likely **Sheet2** of the same workbook.

The longest, most difficult way of doing that would be to copy the data from **Sheet1** and paste it manually into **Sheet2**. It is quite clear that automation would save a lot of time.

The question is how to achieve this automation. Without some way of automatically copying and then storing that data somehow, somewhere, and then pasting it in the new position, you will never get around to doing any other work than just that.

Automation would be something like the following. You enter your details on **Sheet1**, and then run a macro to copy the details in order to automatically populate the table on **Sheet2**. Enter data, copy and store, then paste—all in one action!

The problem here is how to copy and store the entries from **Sheet1**. That is where variables come in. A variable is simply a line of VBA coding with the purpose of storing information on a temporary basis. This stored information can be accessed repeatedly while the Excel file is open, but is not stored when the application is closed.

There is a lot more to be said about variables, such as naming conventions, data types, and scope, but more about that later.

In this recipe, we will be declaring and using variables.

Getting ready

Open Excel and make sure that **Book1** is active.

How to do it...

The steps to create or declare a variable are as follows:

1. With **Sheet1** active, enter the following data:

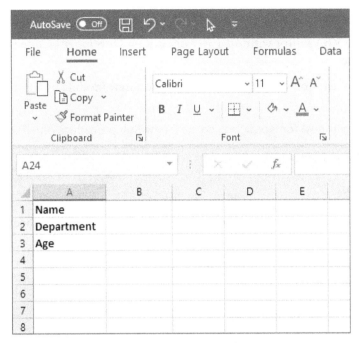

Figure 6.4 – Headings on Sheet1

2. Insert a new sheet, **Sheet2**, then enter the following data:

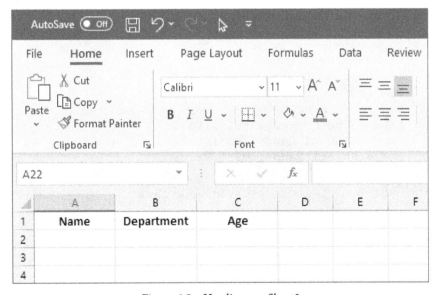

Figure 6.5 – Headings on Sheet2

3. Save the workbook as a macro-enabled file. Call it `Variables.xlsm`.

4. Activate the VBA Editor with *Alt + F11* or click on **Developer | Code | Visual Basic**.

5. In the editor, click on **Insert | Module** to create a new module in `Variables.xlsm`.

6. In the code window for `Module1`, create a new Sub procedure called `Form_Data`:

```
Sub Form_Data()

End Sub
```

7. Next, declare variables for the three values that will be entered on **Sheet1** in cells B1, B2, and B3:

```
Sub Form_Data()
    Dim Name As String
    Dim Dept As String
    Dim Age As Integer
End Sub
```

We will discuss data types in the next recipe.

8. The variables have been named, but are still empty. Let's assign a value to each by setting it equal to the values in cells B1, B2, and B3:

```
Sub Form_Data()
    Dim Name As String
    Dim Dept As String
    Dim Age As Integer

    Name = Sheet1.Range("B1").Value
    Dept = Sheet1.Range("B2").Value
    Age = Sheet1.Range("B3").Value

End Sub
```

9. The final step is to transfer the captured data from **Sheet1** to **Sheet2**. Type the following code:

```
Sub Form_Data()
    Dim Name As String
    Dim Dept As String
    Dim Age As Integer

    Name = Sheet1.Range("B1").Value
    Dept = Sheet1.Range("B2").Value
    Age = Sheet1.Range("B3").Value

    Sheet2.Range("A2").Value = Name
    Sheet2.Range("B2").Value = Dept
    Sheet2.Range("C2").Value = Age

End Sub
```

10. To test the macro, enter data on **Sheet1**, in cells B1, B2, and B3. You can type any values you want, but for the purpose of this exercise, I am adding the following:

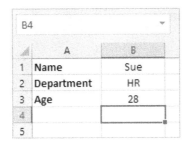

Figure 6.6 – Data on Sheet1

11. Run the macro by clicking **Developer** | **Code** | **Macros**. From the **Macro** dialog box, select the only macro, **Form_Data**, then click on **Run**.

12. Switch to **Sheet2** and confirm that the values from **Sheet1** have been placed on **Sheet2**.

How it works...

Let's have a look at what happened in the background for these variables to work the way they did:

1. Press *Alt + F11* to activate the VBA Editor.

2. With the VBA Editor open, click **View | Locals Window**:

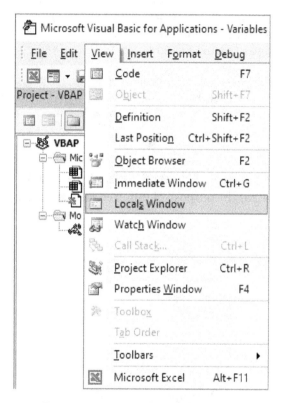

Figure 6.7 – Activate the Locals window

The **Locals** window will be visible at the bottom of the application:

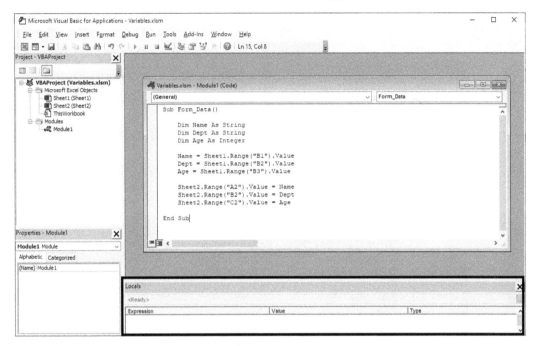

Figure 6.8 - The Locals window

3. We're going to use the **Step Into** functionality in the VBA Editor to see how each line is executed. Click on the first line of code in the code window, then click **Debug | Step Into** (note that the keyboard shortcut is *F8*).

4.   The first line of code is now highlighted in yellow. At the same time, in the **Locals** window at the bottom, the three variables are displayed. Only the names and data types are displayed because we have not assigned any values to them:

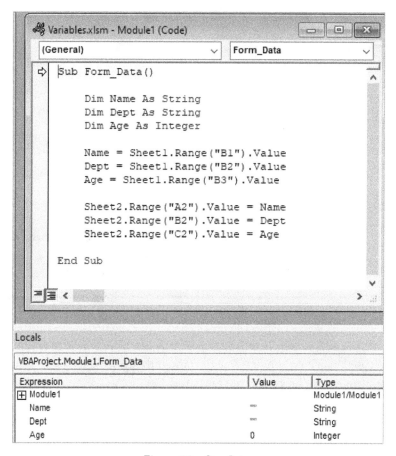

Figure 6.9 – Step Into

5.   By pressing *F8*, the next line of code is highlighted:

```
Name = Sheet1.Range("B1").Value.
```

Take note that variables are not executable code but containers for data. There are no changes in the **Locals** window either because the highlighted line has not been executed yet.

6.   Press *F8* again. This time, the first line of code is executed. Proof of that can be found in the **Locals** window, where the Sue text value, found in cell B1, is displayed after the Name variable.

7. At the same time, the next line of code is highlighted:

```
Dept = Sheet1.Range("B2").Value
```

8. When you press *F8* again, the value in cell B2 is assigned to the Dept variable, and the next line of code is highlighted:

```
Age = Sheet1.Range("B3").Value
```

9. Pressing *F8* will execute this line, assigning the value in cell B3 to the Age variable:

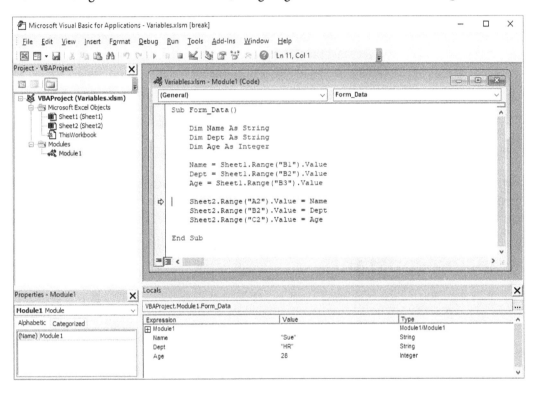

Figure 6.10 – Values assigned to variables

10. The following line is now selected:

```
Sheet2.Range("A2").Value = Name
```

When we press *F8* next, it will take the value Sue, which has been assigned to the Name variable, and place it in cell A2 of **Sheet2**.

11. The next line is now selected:

```
Sheet2.Range("B2").Value = Dept
```

As with the previous line, the next variable, Dept, with the value HR assigned to it, will be placed on cell B2 of **Sheet2**.

12. The last line is now selected:

```
Sheet2.Range("C2").Value = Age
```

The last variable, Age, with the value 28 assigned to it, will be placed in cell C2 of **Sheet2**.

13. By pressing *F8* for the very last time, the procedure is ended, and the **Locals** window is cleared of all variable data. That is in line with the definition of a variable being a temporary storage space.

14. If you go back to **Sheet1** now, you can type different values into cells B1, B2, and B3. By running the macro again, these new values will be assigned to the variables and placed on **Sheet2**.

The coding in this example can be improved upon because the macro will simply overwrite the values on **Sheet2**. In later recipes, we will write code to find the first open line under the data in **Sheet2** and place it there.

Declaring constants

If a variable is a line of VBA coding with the purpose of storing information on a temporary basis, a constant is a line of coding that stores information on a *permanent basis*.

Let's work with a practical example again.

Doing calculations in Excel is easy; you use a function or a formula and the problem is solved. But let's say you have to calculate the tax for products sold in a store on a daily basis. The data is not only on one spreadsheet, and people often randomly ask you to do these tax calculations.

As simple as it is to add a short formula, this is a waste of time. If you could click on a button with a macro assigned to it to do the calculation for you automatically, it would make your life much easier.

The tax rate can be stored as a permanent value in a constant and, depending on the VBA code, you can click on a cell and run the macro to calculate the tax for that specific item.

Getting ready

Open Excel and make sure that **Book1** is active.

How to do it...

The steps to declare a constant are the following:

1. With **Sheet1** active, enter the following data:

S1

	A	B	C
1	Price	Sales Tax	
2	$ 100.00		
3	$ 200.00		
4	$ 300.00		
5	$ 400.00		
6	$ 500.00		

Figure 6.11 – Entries on Sheet1

2. Save the workbook as a macro-enabled file. Call it `Constants.xlsm`.
3. Activate the VBA Editor with *Alt* + *F11* or click **Developer** | **Code** | **Visual Basic**.
4. In the Editor, click **Insert** | **Module** to create a new module in **Book1**.
5. In the code window for `Module1`, create a new Sub procedure called `Tax`:

```
Sub Tax()

End Sub
```

6. Next, declare a constant for the tax percentage that must be added to a price:

```
Sub Tax()
Const Tax As Double = 0.1

End Sub
```

By typing `Const`, VBA will treat this line of code as a constant. After this keyword, we type the name of the constant – in this case, `Tax`. The data type is `Double`. Most importantly, the value for the constant is added in the same line.

7.   Once done, enter the last line of code:

```
Sub Tax()
Const Tax As Double = 0.1

    ActiveCell.Value = ActiveCell.Offset(0, -1) * Tax

End Sub
```

8.   To test the macro, switch back to **Sheet1** by pressing *Alt + F11*.

9.   Click on cell B2 on **Sheet1**.

10. Run the macro by clicking **Developer | Code | Macros**.

11. There is only one macro available: **Tax**. Click **Run**.

The calculated value appears in cell B2.

How it works...

Here is an explanation for each step as the macro was executed:

1.   Press *Alt + F11* to activate the VBA Editor.

2.   Make sure that the **Locals** window is still active in the VBA Editor.

3.   The **Step Into** function will take us through the execution process again. Click on the first line of code and press *F8*:

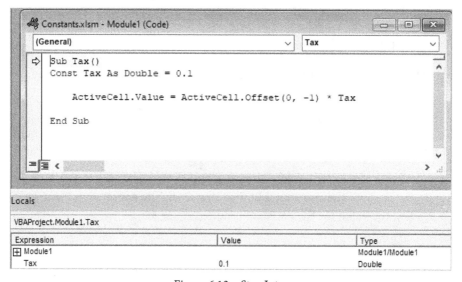

Figure 6.12 – Step Into

4. The first line of code is active and highlighted in yellow. The **Locals** window shows us that the value `0.1` has been assigned to the `Tax` constant. Press *F8* again.

5. The constant is not highlighted, but the next line is. This line of code is what will make things happen on **Sheet1**.

6. Cell B2 is the active cell on **Sheet1**. The value we want to appear in that cell must be equal to the cell directly to the left, multiplied by *0.1*, or *10%* – the constant. The `Offset` values, `(0,-1)`, mean move 0 rows down and one column to the left.

7. By pressing *F8*, the code is executed and the calculated value appears in the active cell, cell B2.

There's more...

By clicking on another open cell, cell B3, you can run the macro again, this time without using **Step Into**:

1. Activate **Sheet1** and click on cell B3.

2. Run the `Tax` macro and observe the calculated value appear in B3.

To speed things up, you can add a button to **Sheet1** and assign the `Tax` macro to it:

◢	A	B	C	D
1	Price	Sales Tax		
2	$ 100.00	$ 10.00		
3	$ 200.00	$ 20.00		Calculate
4	$ 300.00			
5	$ 400.00			
6	$ 500.00			
7				
8				

Figure 6.13 – Button with assigned macro

This way, it will be much easier to run the macro in order to do the calculations.

Working with data types in variables and constants

In this recipe, we will be investigating the different data types you can assign to variables and constants.

Getting ready

Open Excel and make sure that **Book1** is active, and save the file as `DatTypes.xlsm`. Open the VBA Editor by pressing *Alt + F11*. In the VBA editor, click **Insert | Module** to create a new module in **Book1**. On the menu bar, click **View | Locals Window**, if the **Locals** window is not already active.

How to do it...

1. In the code window for `Module1`, create a new Sub procedure called `Data_Types`:

```
Sub Data_Types()

End Sub
```

2. Once done, declare the following variables. Ensure that the data types are added exactly as per the example:

```
Sub Data_Types()

Dim Small As Byte
Small = 75

Dim Big As Integer
Big = 3333

Dim Large As Long
Large = 800011100

Dim Yes As Boolean
Yes = True

Dim Dec As Double
Dec = 3.14159

Dim Text As String
Text = "MyName"

Dim DOB As Date
DOB = #12/25/1990#

Dim Price As Currency
Price = 24.55
```

```
'Variant
Dim Name
Name = Range("A1")

End Sub
```

3. With everything done, press *F8* to step into the procedure.

4. The first line is highlighted, and all the variables are recognized in the **Locals** window.

5. Press *F8* repeatedly to step through each variable declaration. Observe how each variable's value is assigned, and how the data type affects the value.

How it works...

It is important to assign data types to variables because it helps your code run faster, and also because memory is allocated more efficiently. In simple English, it means that you will be wasting memory if, for instance, you assign a Long data type if you could get away with an integer.

The following table explains the size of data types:

Data Type	Memory Used	Range
Byte	1 byte	0 to 255
Integer	2 bytes	-32,768 to 32,768
Long	4 bytes	-2,147,483,648 to 2,147,483,647
Boolean	2 bytes	True/false
Double	8 bytes	Very large negative-to-positive range with high precision (also used for %)
String	1 byte per char	Depends on length
Object	4 bytes	Any object

Data Type	Memory Used	Memory Used
Date	8 bytes	01/01/100 to 12/31/9999
Currency	8 bytes	Very large negative-to-positive range up to 4 decimal places
Variant	16 bytes (more with char)	Any value – can also hold values such as Empty, Nothing, and Null

Table 6.1 – Data types and sizes

As a final remark, you need to understand that you can declare a variable without a data type. However, by doing that, VBA will automatically assign the Variant data type to that variable. An integer would have used 2 bytes of memory, while a variant would grab a minimum of 16 bytes per entry.

Make sure that you have a good understanding of this table and get into the good habit of always assigning data types.

Scoping variables

In this recipe, we will be working with the range of effect, or scope, of variables.

Whenever you declare a variable in a module, you would expect that variable to at least have an effect within that module. You can also say you would expect your macro to work on the sheet where you created the macro, at the very least.

What has not been said before is that a workbook can accommodate any number of VBA modules and a module can accommodate any number of Sub and Function procedures. This information is merely academic.

This knowledge becomes important when you have more than one procedure in a module, several modules in the workbook, and more than just one worksheet in a workbook. The questions are: which macro will have an effect in which module, and is it possible for one macro to work in more than one module, or even in several sheets?

All depending on what you want to achieve with your macro, you can set the scope of a procedure with certain keywords. Let's see what those keywords are.

Getting ready

Open Excel and make sure that **Book1** is active. Save the file as Scope.xlsm. Open the VBA Editor by pressing *Alt + F11*. In the VBA editor, click **Insert | Module** to create a new module in **Book1**.

How to do it...

1. In the code window, declare the following procedure-only variables:

```
Sub Proc_Level()
    Dim Distance As Integer
    Dim Number As Long
    Dim Fraction As Double
    Dim Name As String
End Sub
```

2. Take note that more than one variable, as in the following example, can be declared with a single `Dim` statement:

```
Sub Proc_Level2()
    Dim Distance As Integer, Number As Long, _
    Fraction As Double, Name As String
End Sub
```

3. If a line of code is too long, you can insert a line continuation character, which is an underscore (_). A line continuation character will only work if you insert a space immediately before it and press *Enter* immediately afterward.

4. Insert a new module. To declare module-level variables, make sure that you declare all variables before the module's first Sub or Function statement:

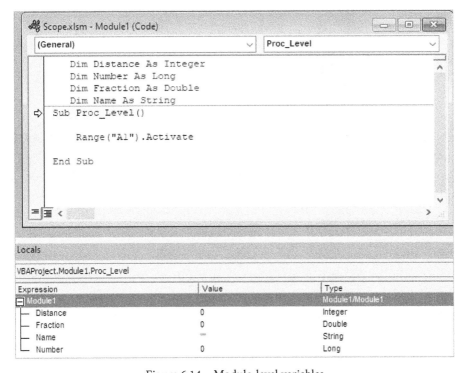

Figure 6.14 – Module-level variables

5. To check the scope of these variables, click on the Sub procedure and press *F8*. The declared variables do not appear in the **Locals** window in the usual way; you have to click on the + sign to the left of **Module1** to expand the contents. This is an indication that these variables are available in every procedure throughout the module.

6. Insert yet another module. Public variables, also referred to as global variables, are declared by using the `Public` keyword:

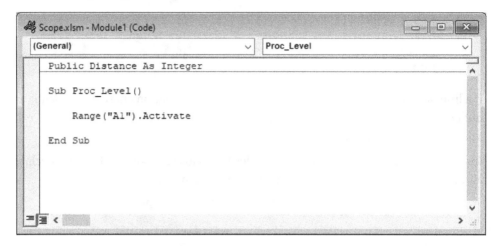

Figure 6.15 – A public-level variable

This variable will be available in all procedures and all modules of the workbook.

How it works...

1. Procedure-only variables have the lowest level of scope for a variable. In other words, they can only be used in the procedure that they were declared. It is also important to understand that this type of variable will no longer exist once the procedure ends. However, when you execute the procedure again, it will become active again but with a new value, because the previous value was cleared from memory.

2. Module-only variables are used in a situation where you want one or more variables to be available to all procedures in a module. It saves a lot of coding to declare variables this way. The alternative would be to declare the same variables repeatedly in every procedure of that specific module.

3. Public variables are also known as global variables, indicating their scope. Like module-level variables, they must be declared before the first Sub procedure. The difference is that you need to use the `Public` keyword to indicate its status and the `Dim` keyword is not used.

Declaring arrays

Arrays are variables of a specific type. While a variable can store only one value at a time, arrays store multiple values, or elements. An array is therefore a group of variables sharing a common name. One example of an array would be the days of the week typed in a single column in Excel.

Like variables, arrays are also declared with a `Dim` statement. The rest of the line of code differs in the sense that with arrays, you have to specify the number of elements in the array.

In its simplest form, the elements consist of a first and last index number, separated with the `To` keyword, all in parentheses. This is known as a one-dimensional array, which stores a single line of values. Multidimensional arrays stores multiple rows and columns of values.

In this recipe, we will be discussing three types of arrays:

- One-dimensional arrays
- Multidimensional arrays
- Dynamic arrays

Getting ready

Open Excel and make sure that **Book1** is active. Save the file as `Arrays.xlsm`.

On **Sheet1**, enter the days of the week in cells *A1* to *A7*.

Open the VBA Editor by pressing *Alt + F11*. In the VBA editor, click **Insert | Module** to create a new module in **Book1**.

How to do it...

To create a one-dimensional array, do the following:

1. Start by creating a new Sub procedure called `StatArray`:

```
Sub StatArray()

End Sub
```

2. Next, declare a variable and call it `WeekArray`:

```
Sub StatArray()
    Dim WeekArray(0 To 2) As String
End Sub
```

When you declare a variable, it is not always necessary to declare both the upper and lower index of the elements. The following declaration would mean exactly the same as the preceding one:

```
    Dim WeekArray(2) As String
```

In this case, VBA assumes that 0 is the lower index. It must be mentioned that it is more reliable to declare both elements, though.

3. Let's now populate the array:

```
Sub StatArray()
    Dim WeekArray(0 To 2) As String

    WeekArray(0) = Range("A1").Value
    WeekArray(1) = Range("A2").Value
    WeekArray(2) = Range("A3").Value

End Sub
```

4. To demonstrate how to read from an array and write values to cells, add code to create a new worksheet. Then, pass the array values to cells *A1* to *A3* on the new sheet. Type the following code:

```
Sub StatArray()
    Dim WeekArray(0 To 2) As String

    WeekArray(0) = Range("A1").Value
    WeekArray(1) = Range("A2").Value
    WeekArray(2) = Range("A3").Value

    Worksheets.Add.Activate

    Range("A1").Value = WeekArray(0)
    Range("A2").Value = WeekArray(1)
    Range("A3").Value = WeekArray(2)

End Sub
```

Populating an array like this, with only three values in it, can easily be done manually. However, when you want to work with an array with hundreds, or even thousands, of values, this technique will clearly not be effective.

In a future recipe, where we will be explaining loops, this problem will be addressed. With loops, you can write code that can handle any number of elements in an array.

For a multidimensional array, do the following:

1. Switch to Excel. Insert a new sheet, then enter the following data:

◢	A	B	C	
1	1	Monday	20-Apr	
2	2	Tuesday	21-Apr	
3	3	Wednesday	22-Apr	
4	4	Thursday	23-Apr	
5	5	Friday	24-Apr	
6	6	Saturday	25-Apr	
7	7	Sunday	26-Apr	
8				

Figure 6.16 – Multidimensional array

2. Switch back to the VBA Editor by pressing *Alt + F11*. In the VBA editor, create a new Sub procedure under the existing one:

```
Sub MultiArray()

End Sub
```

3. Declare a multidimensional array:

```
Sub MultiArray()

    Dim TableArray(0 To 6, 0 To 2) As Variant

End Sub
```

4. We are only going to populate the first row. Type the following code:

```
Sub MultiArray()

    Dim TableArray(0 To 6, 0 To 2) As Variant

    TableArray(0, 0) = Range("A1").Value
    TableArray(0, 1) = Range("B1").Value
    TableArray(0, 2) = Range("C1").Value

End Sub
```

5. Open the **Locals** window by selecting **View | Locals**. Press *F8* to step into the procedure. Observe how only the values in row one are assigned.

Populating the rest of the rows can be done in the same manual way, but creating loops would once again be much more effective.

Declaring dynamic arrays

So far, we've been working with static or fixed arrays. In other words, we knew how many rows and columns there were in the Excel sheet and did not expect it to change. But what do we do if the data is not fixed? Let's say users have access to the data and have to add details. The ideal would be to use an array where the size can be changed while a program is running. That, by definition, is what a dynamic array is.

To declare a dynamic array, you simply leave the parentheses empty:

```
Dim MyDynamic () as Integer
```

Take the following steps:

1. Create a new Sub procedure and declare a dynamic array:

```
Sub DynamicArray()
    Dim Days() As String
End Sub
```

2. To define the number of elements in the array, use the ReDim statement. In this case, use the value 6 to include all 7 entries in the column:

```
Sub DynamicArray()
    Dim Days() As String
    ReDim Days(6)
End Sub
```

How it works...

By going through the steps for a one-dimensional array as they are executed in the VBA Editor, the process will become clear:

1. With the VBA Editor open, press *F8*. The three elements of the array will be displayed in the **Locals** window, although without values:

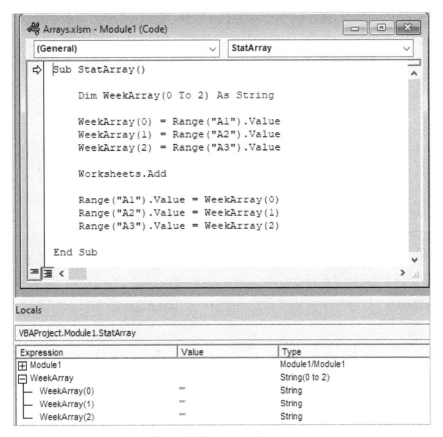

Figure 6.17 – Array elements

2. Press *F8* another four times, and observe how the values on cells *A1* to *A3* are assigned to the array elements:

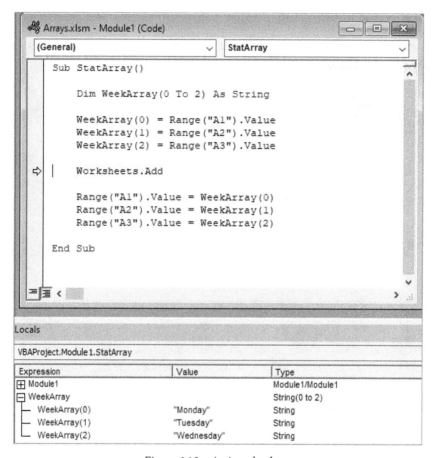

```
Arrays.xlsm - Module1 (Code)

(General)                              StatArray

    Sub StatArray()

        Dim WeekArray(0 To 2) As String

        WeekArray(0) = Range("A1").Value
        WeekArray(1) = Range("A2").Value
        WeekArray(2) = Range("A3").Value

  ⇨ |   Worksheets.Add

        Range("A1").Value = WeekArray(0)
        Range("A2").Value = WeekArray(1)
        Range("A3").Value = WeekArray(2)

    End Sub
```

Locals		
VBAProject.Module1.StatArray		
Expression	Value	Type
⊞ Module1		Module1/Module1
⊟ WeekArray		String(0 to 2)
— WeekArray(0)	"Monday"	String
— WeekArray(1)	"Tuesday"	String
— WeekArray(2)	"Wednesday"	String

Figure 6.18 – Assigned values

3. Press *F8* yet again to add a new worksheet. Then, press it another three times to write the values of elements WeekArray(0) to WeekArray(2) to cells *A1* to *A3* on the newly inserted worksheet.

4. By pressing *F8* one last time, the Sub procedure will end, and all the values of the array will be cleared.

The steps for a multidimensional array can also be observed in the **Locals** window:

1. While you are still working in the VBA Editor, and with the **Locals** window active, press *F8*. In the **Locals** window, expand the first two objects – `TableArray` and `TableArray(0)`:

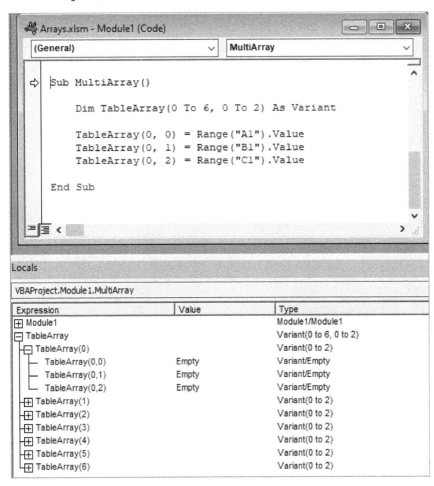

Figure 6.19 – Multiple arrays

2. Press *F8* four times until the first elements of the array have been populated.

    Once again, populating the rest of the row manually will become more and more laborious and time-wasting. In the *Using Loops* recipe in *Chapter 9, Implementing Program Flow*, we will show you how to populate multiple rows with great efficiency.

Dynamic arrays

As with the two fixed arrays, it is best to see how it works in the **Locals** window:

1. When a dynamic array is declared, no values are assigned to the elements.

2. Press *F8* to step through the code until you get to the End statement:

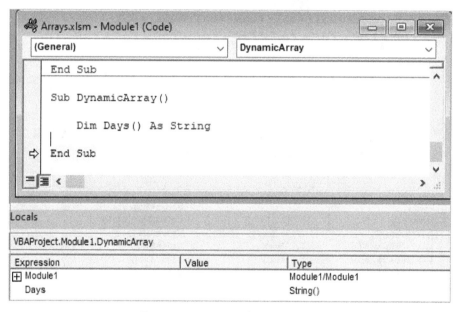

Figure 6.20 – Empty dynamic array

3. By using the ReDim statement, you create the requested number of elements:

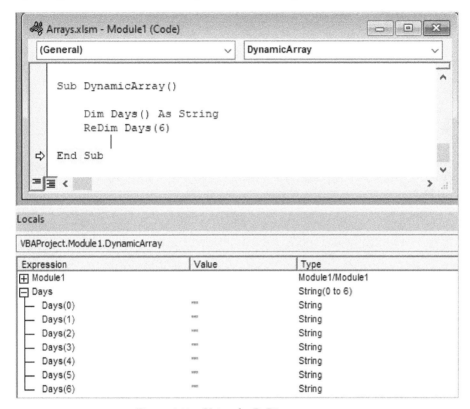

Figure 6.21 – Using the ReDim statement

Where the Days array was previously empty, there are now seven elements added.

We are not going to populate the values because it will be easier to do so with a Loop statement.

7
Working with Ranges

Ranges are used in Excel because Excel is all about cells, and the Range object is a container for cells. Without a solid understanding of ranges, working in Excel is virtually impossible. It's all about moving around on the spreadsheet, assigning values, changing properties, and using methods. Although less important in Word and PowerPoint, the principles of working with ranges are still essential.

In this chapter, we will cover the following recipes:

- Referring to ranges
- Using the Range object properties
- Adding the Range object's methods
- Making ranges work

By the end of this chapter, you will be able to work effectively with ranges in VBA.

Technical requirements

This cookbook was written and designed to be used with MS Office 2019 and MS Office 365, installed on either Windows 8, 8.1, or 10.

If your hardware and software meet these requirements, you have everything you need.

Demonstration files can be downloaded from `https://github.com/PacktPublishing/VBA-Automation-for-Excel-2019-Cookbook`.

Please visit the following link to check out the CiA videos: `https://bit.ly/3jQRvVk`.

Referring to ranges

In this recipe, we will be working with `Range` objects, with specific instructions on how to refer to ranges. Keep in mind that the `Range` objects have properties and methods, like all other VBA objects. Range properties can be examined and changed, while methods perform certain actions on the object.

To eliminate any misunderstandings, let's first define the word *range* within the Excel environment.

A **range** can be a single cell, a group of cells, or a column or a row, or even the entire worksheet. Clicking on a cell – in other words, selecting a range – in any worksheet, or selecting a group of cells, is normal. That's what you do whenever you work in Excel.

Things change when you start working in the VBA Editor, though. There are no cells to click on, yet you still need to instruct Excel to select cells or assign values to cells. And what do you do when you need to retrieve values from cells and use them in calculations?

As if that is not enough, how do you refer to a range in another worksheet, or even in a different workbook?

The simple answer is that you refer to any range or ranges by making use of cell references, according to the VBA language rules.

Let's have a look at these language rules.

Getting ready

This recipe covers the theoretical aspects of range references. Making notes might be a good idea!

Before digging in, let's quickly create a named range, because we're going to need that for *Step 3*:

1. Open Excel and activate a new workbook. In **Sheet1**, select range A1:C10:

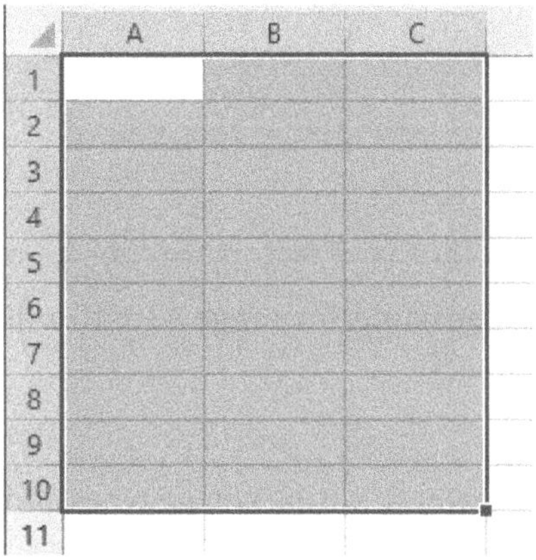

Figure 7.1 – Selected range

2. In the Name Box, type Data and press *Enter*. That will be the name of the selected range of cells:

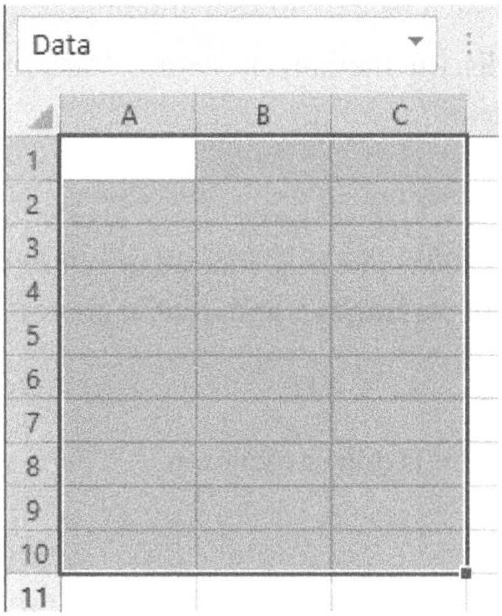

Figure 7.2 – Name of the range typed in the Name Box

3.   Click on any cell outside the range to deselect it.

4.   Now, click on the drop-down arrow on the right side of the Name Box to see the named range:

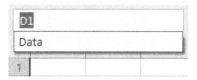

Figure 7.3 – The named range in the drop-down list

5.   The moment you click on the name, the range A1:C10 will be selected again.

How to do it...

The following steps show how to refer to various range types and sizes:

1.   Let's start with a single cell. The correct way to refer to a single cell is as follows:

```
Range("B1")
```

First, there is the `Range` keyword, followed by the address. Take note that the address is always surrounded by parentheses and double quotes.

2.   To refer to a group of cells, use the same keyword. The address will include the first and last cells in the range:

```
Range("A1:C10")
```

3.   A named range reference looks like this. Instead of cell references, the name of the saved range is enclosed by parentheses and double quotes:

```
Range("Data")
```

4.   Referring to a single column is done as follows:

```
Range("C:C")
```

You can refer to more than one column in the following manner:

```
Range("A:D")
```

5. A row reference looks like this:

```
Range("5:5")
```

To refer to multiple rows, use the following reference:

```
Range("1:5")
```

6. Non-contiguous ranges are referred to in the following way:

```
Range("A1:D6,D8:E12")
```

7. Referring to a specific worksheet in the same workbook is done like this:

```
Worksheets("Sheet2").Range("B1:B10")
```

8. Referring to a different workbook should be done like this:

```
Workbooks("Admin.xlsx").Worksheets("Sheet1"). _
Range("A1:D10")
```

How it works...

Referring to range objects in VBA has a specific syntax. Keywords such as `Range`, `Worksheets`, and `Workbooks` indicate which objects you are referring to. Range references or range addresses will set a focus on the specified cell range.

Take note that these code snippets are not executable. In other words, if you want to run any of these references, you will have to place it in a Sub procedure first, and then add a method such as `activate` or `select`.

The following two recipes will help you understand how all these elements fit together.

Using the Range object properties

In this recipe, we will be working with the `Range` object's properties. Ranges are objects, and all VBA objects have properties – some are read-only, while others can be edited.

A `Range` object has many properties, much more than we normally use. Once you understand the principle, you can apply it to all objects.

Getting ready

Open Excel and activate **Book1**. Make sure **Sheet1** is active. Save the file as Ranges. xlsm, and then press *Alt + F11* to activate the VBA Editor. Insert a new module in the Explorer.

How to do it...

1. In the code window, create the following Sub procedure:

    ```
    Sub RangeProperties()

    End Sub
    ```

2. Add the following lines of code:

    ```
    Sub RangeProperties()
        MsgBox Range("A1:B4").Address
        Range("A1").Value = 10
        MsgBox Range("A1:C1").Count
        Range("A1").Font.Bold = True
    End Sub
    ```

3. Press *F8* to step into the code and execute it line by line. Observe how the properties are displayed.

How it works...

1. The first property, Address, is read-only, meaning you cannot edit it. When the line is run, the address will be displayed in a message box:

Figure 7.4 – Message box showing the address property

The `Value` property can be changed. In this case, you assigned the value `10` to cell *A1*. In the next run, you can assign a different value:

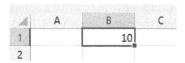

Figure 7.5 – Value assigned to cell B1

2. The `Count` property is also read-only because it simply tells you how many cells there are in the indicated range:

Figure 7.6 – Message box showing the count of cells

3. The `Font` property has to be set to bold, or regular, or whatever option you chose. The effect of the changed property will be visible on the selected range, based on your instructions:

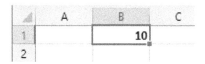

Figure 7.7 – The Font property set to bold

That should take care of properties. Adding methods is the next logical step.

Adding the Range object's methods

This recipe covers methods. Properties need to be activated. We call these actions methods. Think of giving commands; you've told VBA to refer to a range, but VBA has no idea what to do with the range. Should it select the range, activate it, or do something else? Should it assign a value to the range, or should it copy the content and paste it in another location?

There is a method for every action you can imagine doing with a range. The four methods we will cover in this recipe are the tip of the iceberg. The principle, however, is always the same.

Getting ready

With `Ranges.xlsm` still open in **Sheet1**, clear the value in cell A1. Now type your first name in cell A1, your last name in cell B1, and the word `Test` in cell A6.

Press *Alt + F11* to activate the VBA Editor. Insert a new module in the Explorer and change its name to `Prop_Methods`.

How to do it...

This is how to add methods to references with properties:

1. In the code window, create the following Sub procedure:

```
Sub RangeMethods()


End Sub
```

2. Add the following lines of code:

```
Sub RangeMethods()
    Range("A1").Select
    Range("A1").Copy Range("A5")
    Range("B1").Clear
    Range("A5").Delete xlUp
End Sub
```

3. Press *F8* to step into the code and execute it line by line. Observe how the methods are acted upon in the Excel sheet.

How it works...

The following explains what happens when a method is executed:

1. The `Select` method will go to the indicated range. Our instructions in the Editor refer to range `A1`, while the next instruction is to select the mentioned range.

2. This method will first copy range `A1`, and then paste the value in range `A5`. The code can be somewhat confusing, so let's dissect this. The first part is simple; the code refers to cell A1, and then the copy method is applied. The second part, to paste the copied value, does not use the word *paste*. The VBA syntax just works like that; when you copy something and then refer to another cell in the same line of code, VBA knows that it should paste the value in the referred cell.

    If this is still not clear, you are welcome to use another longer method. The code for this copy-and-paste routine reads as follows:

    ```
    Sub CopyPasteSample()

          Range("A1").Select
          ActiveCell.Copy

          Range("A5").Select
          ActiveCell.PasteSpecial

    End Sub
    ```

3. Whatever value or formatting is in range `B1` will be cleared. Please note that not only will formatting be cleared but also the contents of the cell.

4. The value in cell `A5` will be deleted, and cells will shift up from below.

Making ranges work

In this last recipe, we're going to create and add data to a short list, making use of everything we've learned in the sections about references, properties, and methods.

Getting ready

`Ranges.xlsm` needs to be kept open. Now, follow these steps:

1. Insert a new sheet, and then add the following data to **Sheet2**:

	A	B	C
1	#	Name	D.O.B.
2	1	Tim	6/25/1992
3	2	Sue	1/15/1995
4	3	Bill	8/6/1991

Figure 7.8 – Preparation

2. Press *Alt + F11* to activate the VBA Editor, and then insert a new module and change its name to `Range_Select`.

How to do it...

1. In the Editor, create a new Sub procedure:

```
Sub RangeSelect()

End Sub
```

2. Add the following line of code to select cell A5:

```
Sub RangeSelect()
    Range("A5").Select
End Sub
```

3. Next, change the value of cell A5 with the following code:

```
Sub RangeSelect()
    Range("A5").Select
    ActiveCell.Value = 4
End Sub
```

4. Add another line of code to assign a value to cell B5. Instead of the normal referencing, we use the row and column style: *row 5 and column 2*, which is the same as cell B5:

```
Sub RangeSelect()
    Range("A5").Select
    ActiveCell.Value = 4

    Cells(5, 2).Value = "Joe"
End Sub
```

5. The last line of code selects cell C5 and then assigns a date value to the cell. This way of referencing a range is not commonly used, but still nice to know about. Take note that dates must be entered in the US style: month, day, year:

```
Sub RangeSelect()
    Range("A5").Select
    ActiveCell.Value = 4

    Cells(5, 2).Value = "Joe"

    [C5].Value = #11/3/1994#
End Sub
```

6. The slow process would be to press *F8* and watch each step as it is executed. The faster way is to press *F5* to run the macro, and then switch back to Excel (*Alt + F11*). New values have been added to cells A5, B5, and C5:

◢	A	B	C
1	#	10	D.O.B.
2	1	Tim	6/25/1992
3	2	Sue	1/15/1995
4	3	Bill	8/6/1991
5	4	Joe	11/3/1994

Figure 7.9 – Added data

By repeating the process, you can add more data to the same table.

How it works...

1. To add data to a cell, you first reference the cell, and then use the `Select` method to focus on it.

2. With that cell being active, you assign a value to the cell.

3. A shorter way of doing this is to refer to a cell and add a value in one line of code. It saves a line of code to combine selection, activation, and the assigning of values.

4. The last line of code makes use of a relatively rare referencing technique, but as in the previous line of code, everything is done in one line.

This is as close as we will get to a real-world example of using references, properties, and methods all in one task.

Do a little bit of research and see whether you can improve on this. Think about writing a procedure to find the first open cell under the last number in column **A**, and then adding the next number under that, but in sequence.

8
Using Functions

In *Chapter 4*, *Working with Procedures*, we covered the basic principles of functions. In this chapter, we're building on that knowledge by adding more detail. Your ability to use and apply functions is another steppingstone to becoming a proficient VBA coder.

In this chapter, we will cover the following recipes:

- Using built-in VBA functions
- Using worksheet functions
- Creating custom functions

By the end of this chapter, you will be able to use and create functions in the VBA environment.

Technical requirements

This cookbook was written and designed to be used with MS Office 2019 and MS Office 365, installed on either Windows 8, 8.1, or 10.

If your hardware and software meet these requirements, you have everything you need.

Demonstration files can be downloaded from `https://github.com/ PacktPublishing/VBA-Automation-for-Excel-2019-Cookbook`.

Please visit the following link to check out the CiA videos: `https://bit. ly/3jQRvVk`.

Using built-in VBA functions

A good starting point for this recipe is a refresher of the definition of a function.

A **function** performs a calculation and returns a single value. Built-in functions are no different in that respect – the end result will always be a single value.

In this recipe, we will be working with built-in functions exclusively. Given the number of available functions, it is important to understand the principles of built-in functions, rather than trying to understand how each function can be used or applied.

A list of every built-in function would take up too much space, so instead refer to the three links here:

- Functions in alphabetical order: `https://bettersolutions.com/vba/functions/complete-list.htm`

- Functions grouped by type: `https://www.excelfunctions.net/vba-functions.html`

- Functions in the VBA Help system: `https://docs.microsoft.com/en-us/office/client-developer/access/desktop-database-reference/visual-basic-for-applications-functions`

Another important aspect of built-in functions is that they are predefined. In other words, they cannot be defined or changed by users.

Take note that some built-in VBA functions are exactly the same as Excel workbook functions, as follows:

- `Average()`: Calculates the average of a series of values

- `Sqr()`: Calculates the square root of a number

- `Abs()`: Calculates the absolute value of a number

- `Sin()`: Calculates the sine of a number

- `Log()`: Calculates the natural logarithm of a number

There are more, but these should be enough to help you understand the principle.

That's enough on that topic. Let's start working on real examples of built-in functions.

Getting ready

Open Excel and make sure that **Sheet1** is active. Save the file and call it `Functions.xlsm`. Press *Alt* + *F11* to activate the VBA Edtior. Insert a new module.

How to do it...

We're going to use some built-in VBA functions as examples of how you can apply these functions.

One of the VBA functions we've used a number of times in this book so far is the `MsgBox` function. Measured by the definition of a function, it doesn't do any calculations, but it does return a single value.

Let's start coding:

1. Create a new Sub procedure and call it `Function_Samples`. Add the following line of code to the procedure:

```
Sub Function_Samples
    MsgBox Date
End sub
```

2. Press *F5* to run the macro. The following message box will appear:

Figure 8.1 – Message box displaying a date

3. Click **OK** to return to the VBA Editor.

4. Another example of a built-in function and how to use it is the following. We will continue with the same recipe. Create a new Sub procedure and call it `FormatFunction`. Add the three lines of code in the following example:

```
Sub FormatFunction()
    Dim FormatSample
    FormatSample = Format(0.75657, "Percent")
    MsgBox FormatSample
End sub
```

5.   Press *F5* to run the macro. The message box that appears is the following:

Figure 8.2 – Message box displaying the percentage

Here is a final example:

6.   Create yet another Sub procedure:

```
Sub StringFunction()
    Dim StrSearch
    StrSearch = InStr(1, "Find the position of A _
    in the text", "A")
    MsgBox StrSearch
End sub
```

7.   Press *F5* to run the macro. The following message box will appear.

Figure 8.3 – Message box displaying the position of A in the text string

These three functions are by no means representative of all the built-in functions, but at least you've had the opportunity to use your first functions.

How it works...

Let's take a closer look at each of the function examples:

1. The Date function simply returns the system date. However, if you don't know what the code should look like, press *F1* to invoke the VBA help function. After searching for the Date function, the following screen will appear:

Date function

Returns a **Variant** (**Date**) containing the current system date.

Syntax

Date

Remarks

To set the system date, use the **Date** statement.

Date, and if the calendar is Gregorian, **Date$** behavior is unchanged by the **Calendar** property setting. If the calendar is Hijri, **Date$** returns a 10-character string of the form *mm-dd-yyyy*, where *mm* (01–12), *dd* (01–30) and *yyyy* (1400–1523) are the Hijri month, day, and year. The equivalent Gregorian range is Jan 1, 1980, through Dec 31, 2099.

Example

This example uses the **Date** function to return the current system date.

```vba
Dim MyDate
MyDate = Date    ' MyDate contains the current system date.
```

Figure 8.4 – The Date function help page

2. Under **Syntax**, it indicates that there are no extra arguments for this function.

3. Under **Example**, it shows you how to use the function. You can either declare a variable to assign the Date value to, or if you want to display the system date, you can do so via a message box.

4. The Format function has a different syntax, with more than one argument. In our example, you first type the function and then, in parentheses, the value you want to format, and after that, the actual format. In this case, we wanted the decimal number to be displayed as a percentage.

5. The `InStr` function has three arguments. The first argument indicates the starting point, followed by the text string you are investigating, and finally, the character you are looking for:

```
InStr(1, "Find the position of A in the text", "A")
```

The examples are endless, but the principles are always the same:

- Understand the structure of the function. Press *F1* for help.

- Always use built-in functions in a Sub procedure.

- Display the result via a message box. In later examples, we will declare variables to display results.

As you progress as a programmer, you will discover how important built-in functions are. Make *F1* your best friend, because there are too many functions to remember them all.

Using worksheet functions

This recipe explains the use of worksheet functions in VBA. Despite the impressive list of built-in functions, you might sometimes find the need for one of the old favorites, such as sum, average, or even count. In fact, you can use most of Excel's worksheet functions, unless they have an equivalent VBA function.

Getting ready

With `Functions.xlsm` still open, type the following data into **Sheet1**:

	A
1	68
2	65
3	75
4	28
5	70

Figure 8.5 – Data for worksheet functions

Once done, press *Alt + F11* to activate the VBA Editor, and insert a new module.

How to do it...

Let's start with some of the most popular, or at least the most used, worksheet functions:

1. Start a new Sub procedure and call it `WorksheetFunctions`.

2. Declare variables for `SumValues`, `AvgValue`, and `MaxValue` with the following code:

```
Sub WorksheetFunctions()
    Dim SumValues As Integer
    Dim AvgValue As Double
    Dim MaxValue As Integer
End Sub
```

3. After that, set the variables equal to the range A1:A5, using the `Application.WorksheetFunction` qualifier before the first variable. For the last two variables, use only the `WorksheetFunction` qualifier:

```
Sub WorksheetFunctions()
    Dim SumValues As Integer
    Dim AvgValue As Double
    Dim MaxValue As Integer

    SumValues = Application.WorksheetFunction.Sum _
    (Range("A1:A5"))
    AvgValue = WorksheetFunction.Average(Range("A1:A5"))
    MaxValue = WorksheetFunction.Max(Range("A1:A5"))

End Sub
```

4. Once done, activate the **Locals** window (**View | Locals Window**).

5. Press *F8* to step into the procedure. Continue pressing *F8*, but keep your eye on the **Locals** window to see how the values are assigned to each variable:

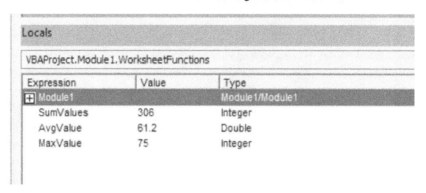

Figure 8.6 – Results in the Locals window

How it works...

Let's take a closer look at what happened here:

1. We declared a variable for each function: `SumValues` for sum, `AvgValue` for average, and `MaxValue` for the maximum function.

2. Because we are dealing with worksheet functions, we couldn't assign values to these variables in the normal way. In each case, we had to use the `WorksheetFunction` qualifier before the function.

3. Using this technique, you can use any of the worksheet functions in VBA, on the condition that VBA doesn't have an equivalent function.

If you have some experience with Excel, worksheet functions will save you a lot of time.

Creating custom functions

Between the built-in functions and the worksheet functions, it is difficult to imagine that you would need anything more. It does, however, sometimes happen that you need something specific. Custom functions are exactly what the name says; they're customized for your specific needs. You develop this function yourself by using VBA.

This recipe will take you through the steps of creating a custom function.

Getting ready

`Functions.xlsm` is still open in **Sheet1**. As always, press *Alt + F11* to activate the VBA Editor, and insert another new module.

How to do it...

The first thing about custom functions is that they must be defined in the workbook where they will be used. This makes sense because you won't find them among the built-in functions or the worksheet functions.

Imagine you have to repeatedly – but at intervals and in different places on a worksheet – calculate the number of days between two dates. Of course, you can do this with a simple Excel calculation, but it would be so much faster and easier if you had a function to do it for you. Let's create this custom function:

1. Let's first define the new function by calling it `DaysCalc`. We also want to set the two arguments, `EndDate` and `Startdate`:

    ```
    Function DaysCalc(EndDate As Date, StartDate As Date) _
    As Integer
        DaysCalc = (EndDate - StartDate)
    End Function
    ```

2. Next, we want to use this custom function in a VBA Sub procedure:

    ```
    Sub TimeLapse()
        Dim StartDate As Date
        Dim EndDate As Date

        StartDate = InputBox("Type the date on which you _
        started")
        EndDate = InputBox("Type the date on which you _
        ended")
        MsgBox DaysCalc(EndDate, StartDate)
    End Sub
    ```

3. Press *F5* to run the macro. When the first input box appears, enter a date from roughly 4 to 6 months ago. Click **OK**:

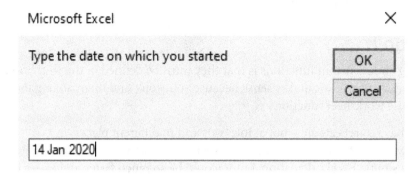

Figure 8.7 – The input box for the start date

4. In the next input box, type today's date. Click **OK**:

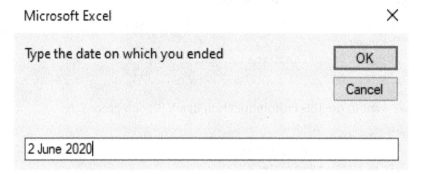

Figure 8.8 – The input box for the end date

5. A message box will appear, displaying the number of days between the first and the last date:

Figure 8.9 – Message box with result

You don't need to make use of input boxes, but in this case, it worked well enough.

How it works...

1. Once the custom function has been defined, it is available for use in the Sub procedure in the workbook. It can also be used from Excel in the same way that other functions are used.

2. To use the custom function in VBA, it must be used in a Sub procedure. Arguments must be declared as variables, and values must be assigned. In this case, we assign values via the input boxes.

3. The result can be assigned to a specific cell, or in this case, to a message box. This is your function, and you can use it any way you find best.

There's more...

As a matter of interest, it is nice to see how this custom function can be used from within Excel:

1. Switch to Excel by pressing *Alt + F11*.

2. In **Sheet1**, click in cell C1 and type a start date.

3. In cell E1, type an end date:

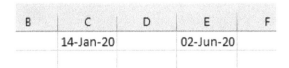

Figure 8.10 – Start and end dates

4. Click in cell G1. This is where we want to see the result – the number of days between the two dates.

5. Enter the = sign and start typing the first few letters of the newly created function. Once you see the function on the list, double-click on it:

Figure 8.11 – The function list in Excel

6. Now, click on the end date first, cell E1. That's the first argument for this function.

7. Enter the comma, and then click on the start date, cell C1.

8. Press *Enter*. The result will be displayed in cell G1:

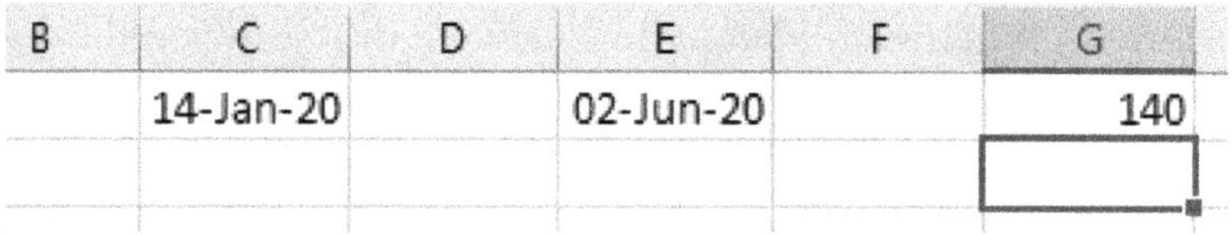

B	C	D	E	F	G
	14-Jan-20		02-Jun-20		140

Figure 8.12 – Result

This was only the beginning, but it's a good start. A small word of warning, though: make sure that there is not a built-in or worksheet function already available before wasting a lot of time writing your own function.

9
Implementing Program Flow

So far, we've mostly worked with either recorded macros, or relatively simple and short procedures. The code was easy to follow, since it started on line one and flowed line by line, until the procedure ended. Your life is about to change, however, because program flow will introduce you to conditions and decisions. It will be up to you to anticipate what users will do or expect, and write code to meet those expectations.

In this chapter, we will cover the following recipes:

- Exploring program flow
- Changing the flow using the `GoTo` statement
- Using `If` and `If-Then` structures to make decisions
- Using the `Select Case` structure
- Using loops

By the end of this chapter, you will be able to implement program flow principles in your VBA Sub procedures.

Technical requirements

This cookbook was written and designed to be used with MS Office 2019 and MS Office 365, installed on either Windows 8, 8.1, or 10.

If your hardware and software meet these requirements, you have everything you need.

Demonstration files can be downloaded from `https://github.com/PacktPublishing/VBA-Automation-for-Excel-2019-Cookbook`.

Please visit the following link to check out the CiA videos: `https://bit.ly/3jQRvVk`.

Exploring program flow

This chapter will open the door for you to a whole new way of thinking about programming. In the previous chapters, we've merely scratched the surface – making sure that you know your way around some basic, and some not so basic, aspects of VBA.

Program flow controls how your code is executed. This is where the real programming starts. Instructing a machine to make decisions has always been a challenge for programmers. A PC, by definition, is an unintelligent piece of hardware. Everything it does is done via software that has been designed by humans. Every command that software executes is based on a set of choices – options between two or more actions.

It's up to you, the programmer, to think of all the possible options your code has to choose between. You need to control the flow of your code by skipping over some statements and executing others, once or several times, until certain conditions are met. Every step of the way, your code must test conditions to determine what the procedure does next.

Changing the flow using the GoTo statement

In this recipe, we will be exploring the GoTo statement. Before I say another word, it is important to mention that whatever we do in this recipe is nothing more than a basic explanation of how to use the GoTo statement. The only time you should ever use it is when you do error handling, which will be discussed in *Chapter 11*, *Handling Errors*. The Sub procedure we create here is, however, a good example of how you can control program flow.

Let's see how the GoTo statement works.

Getting ready

Open Excel and activate a new workbook. Save the file as a macro-enabled file on your desktop and call it `ProgramFlow`. **Sheet1** should be active. Press *Alt + F11* to switch to the VBA Editor. With that open, insert a new module.

How to do it...

1. Create a new Sub procedure and call it `GoToSample`:

```
Sub GotoSample()

End Sub
```

2. Add the following lines of code:

```
Sub GotoSample()
    Password = InputBox("Enter your password:   ")
    If Password <> "aBc" Then GoTo WrongPassword

End Sub
```

3. Create code to display a message box for when the correct password is entered:

```
Sub GotoSample()
    Password = InputBox("Enter your password:   ")
    If Password <> "aBc" Then GoTo WrongPassword
    MsgBox "Welcome to our website"
    'Lines of code
    'More lines of code
    Exit Sub

End Sub
```

4. The last bit of code will take care of incorrect entries or errors:

```
Sub GotoSample()
    Password = InputBox("Enter your password:   ")
    If Password <> "aBc" Then GoTo WrongPassword
    MsgBox "Welcome to our website"
    'Lines of code
    'More lines of code
    Exit Sub
```

```
WrongPassword:
    MsgBox "Sorry, wrong password"

End Sub
```

5. Press *F5* to run the procedure. Type the correct password, aBc, in the message box and click **OK**. Another message box will appear with a welcome message. Click **OK**.

6. Now, run the code again, this time entering an incorrect password. Click **OK**. This message box is less welcoming, informing you that your password was incorrect.

How it works...

Let's see how this most basic decision-making process works:

1. In this procedure, users are asked for a password. Using InputBox works well in this case.

2. Should you enter the correct password, it stands to reason that the bypassing procedure will not be invoked. A message box will welcome you, after which the rest of the code in the procedure will be run.

3. Once the procedure comes to the last line of code, it will exit without activating the WrongPassword code, and end the Sub procedure.

4. When the password is incorrect – not corresponding to the correct password – the rest of the procedure is bypassed. The GoTo command stops further execution of the rest of the code by sending you to the indicated area, in this case, WrongPassword.

5. Once there, a message box will be activated, telling you that your password is incorrect (in *Chapter 11*, *Handling Errors*, we will discuss a more elegant way of returning to the procedure).

Using If and If-Then structures to make decisions

Of all the control structures in VBA, the If-Then and ElseIf structures are probably the most important. You will use these more than any of the other structures.

The word *If* sets a condition. It works like normal English; *If you do not study, you may fail your exam*. In other words, you need to make a decision. If you study, you pass, or else you fail.

In this recipe, we explain this control structure and its conditional statement with two examples, the first being very basic, and the second slightly more complex. Simplistic or not, you will see how you can use code to make your life easier. PCs are much faster than the human brain when it comes to repetitive tasks and decisions.

Getting ready

With `ProgramFlow.xlsm` still open on **Sheet1**, enter the single word `Red` in cell A1.

Press *Alt + F11* to switch to the VBA Editor. With that active, insert a new module.

How to do it...

There are many ways of using the `If` statement. The simplest form is a single line of code, using only `If` and `Then` as keywords:

1. As always, we start with a new Sub procedure. Call it `IfThenSample`, and then enter the following code:

```
Sub IfThenSample()
    If Range("A1") = "Red" Then MsgBox "Danger"
End Sub
```

This is how it will appear on screen:

Figure 9.1 – Message box

2. Press *F5* to run the code. Observe the message box with the **Danger** message. Click **OK** to return to the Editor.

3. Press *Alt + F11* to switch to Excel. Replace the word `Red` in cell A1 with `Green`. Switch back to the Editor, and then press *F5* again. Nothing happens, which is not surprising.

4. To make the code slightly more useful, add another line of code after the first:

```
Sub IfThenSample()
    If Range("A1") = "Red" Then MsgBox "Danger"
    If Range("A1") = "Green" Then MsgBox "Proceed"
End Sub
```

5. Running the procedure this time will display a message box with the
    Proceed message.

    There are obvious limitations, and limited use for this type of decision making.
    Let's investigate something slightly more useful. This time, we will use the `If` and
    `ElseIf` keywords to create a nested `If` statement. We will continue with the
    same recipe.

6. Switch back to Excel and enter the value 4 in cell A1. Return to the Editor. Create
    a second Sub procedure below the first one and call it `ElseIfSingle`. Copy the
    following sample code and paste it into the procedure:

```
Sub ElseIfSingle()
    If Sheet1.Range("A1").Value > 5 Then
        Debug.Print "Value is greater than five."
    ElseIf Sheet1.Range("A1").Value < 5 Then
        Debug.Print "Value is less than five."
    Else
        Debug.Print "Value is equal to five."
    End If
End Sub
```

7. Activate the **Immediate** window (**View | Immediate Window** or *Ctrl + G*).

8. Run the code by pressing *F5*, first with the value 4 in cell *A1*. Observe the message
    in the **Immediate** window. Next, run it after replacing 4 with 5 in cell A1. Finally,
    run it one final time with the value 6 in cell A1. Three messages should be visible in
    the **Immediate** window.

How it works...

The program flow in this example can be explained as follows:

1. The first line of code tests the value in cell A1. Since it is not larger than 5, in other words, it doesn't meet the condition, the line of code directly after that will be skipped. No message will be displayed in the **Immediate** window.

2. The second condition will now be tested and found true. 4 is, after all, less than five. As per the next instruction, the message will now be displayed in the **Immediate** window:

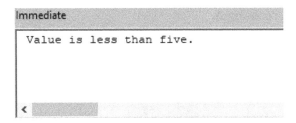

Figure 9.2 – Message in the Immediate window

3. The third condition test will be skipped, since the purpose of the code was to test for one condition only; less than, equal to, or larger than.

There's more...

1. Change the value in cell A1 back to 4. This time, cycle through the lines of code, step by step, by pressing *F8*, the keyboard shortcut for **Step Into**. Check which lines are skipped, and which message is displayed in the **Immediate** window every time.

2. Once done, change the value in cell A1 to 5. Step into the code again. Once finished with 5, change the value to 6. Stepping into the code should show you how the first condition is met, and the rest of code is skipped to end the procedure.

There is a lot more you can do with the If-Then control structure. As you gain experience, you will discover the power of long and complex nested If controls. As long as you understand the basic principles, the rest will come easy.

Using the Select Case structure

This recipe covers yet another control structure, the **Select Case** structure. There are similarities between this and the **If-Then-Else** structure, which will make it easier to understand the working process. This structure works well enough when you have only two options to choose between, but excels when you have to make decisions between three or more options.

Getting ready

Make sure that `ProgramFlow.xlsm` is still active. Clear **Sheet1** of any data and enter the following numbers in column **A**:

◢	A
1	85
2	75
3	65
4	55
5	45
6	

Figure 9.3 – Data for Select Case

Press *Alt + F11* to switch to the VBA Editor. With that open, insert a new module.

How to do it...

1. Create a new Sub procedure. Call it `SelectCaseSample`, and then copy the following code:

```
Sub SelectCaseSample()
    Dim Mark As Integer
    Range("A1").Select
    Mark = ActiveCell.Value
    Select Case Mark
        Case Is < 50
            ActiveCell.Offset(0, 1).Value = "Try again"
        Case Is < 60
            ActiveCell.Offset(0, 1).Value = "D"
        Case Is < 70
            ActiveCell.Offset(0, 1).Value = "C"
        Case Is < 80
            ActiveCell.Offset(0, 1).Value = "B"
        Case Else
```

```
        ActiveCell.Offset(0, 1).Value = "A"
    End Select

End Sub
```

2. Resize Excel and the VBA Editor in such a way that you can see both windows on one screen:

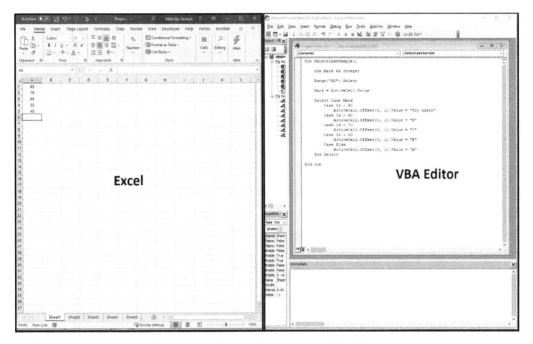

Figure 9.4 – Viewing Excel and the VBA Editor

3. Click in the code window and press *F8* to step into the code. Keep pressing *F8* until the letter **A** appears in cell B1.

4. Reset the procedure and change the first range reference to A2:

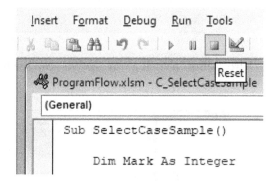

Figure 9.5 – The Reset button

5. Repeat the process until you reach cell A5, each time changing the range reference to the next cell in column **A**. The data on **Sheet1** should now look like this:

	A	B
1	85	A
2	75	B
3	65	C
4	55	D
5	45	Try again
6		

Figure 9.6 – Results

How it works...

This was a rather long-winded and ineffective process. Let's see what happened, and how we can improve on it.

Before starting, close the **Immediate** window in the VBA Editor, and replace it with the **Locals** window (**View** | **Locals Window**):

1. Change the range reference back to cell A1, and press *F8* to step into the code. Your screen should look like this:

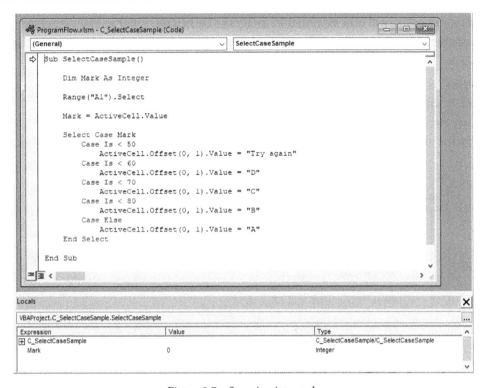

Figure 9.7 – Stepping into code

2. Press *F8* twice more, until the focus is on the Mark variable. Observe how the active cell (cell A1)'s value has been assigned to the variable. To see the assigned value, hover the mouse curser over ActiveCell.Value:

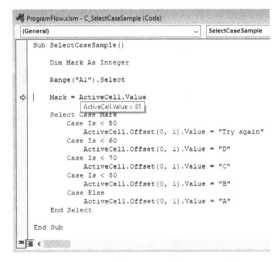

Figure 9.8 – Value assigned to a variable

3. This value, 85, will now be tested in each case against the criteria. The first case is less than 50, meaning it will be skipped. Ditto for each case where 85 is larger than the set standard.

4. Press *F8* until you are on the last case, `Case Else`. This time, when you press *F8*, it will execute the next line because 85 is larger than 80. According to the case structure, any values not smaller than 80 must be assigned the value A. Furthermore, it must be placed in the same row, one column to the right:

```
ProgramFlow.xlsm - C_SelectCaseSample (Code)

(General)                                              SelectCaseSample

    Sub SelectCaseSample ()

        Dim Mark As Integer

        Range ("A1") .Select

        Mark = ActiveCell.Value

        Select Case Mark
            Case Is < 50
                ActiveCell.Offset(0, 1).Value = "Try again"
            Case Is < 60
                ActiveCell.Offset(0, 1).Value = "D"
            Case Is < 70
                ActiveCell.Offset(0, 1).Value = "C"
            Case Is < 80
                ActiveCell.Offset(0, 1).Value = "B"
            Case Else
                ActiveCell.Offset(0, 1).Value = "A"
        End Select

    End Sub
```

Figure 9.9 – Meeting the criteria

5. Pressing *F8* now will end `Case Select`, while the next *F8* will end the procedure.

6. To add the correct symbol next to the value in cell A2, you will have to change the first range reference to A2 and step into the procedure again. Observe how every case is skipped, until it meets the *less than 80* criterion. The line after that is executed, and because the value has been found, the case will be ended, after which the procedure will be ended.

7. Repeat this process, each time changing the first range reference to the next cell in column **A**, until all the values have symbols in column **B**.

8. It is quite obvious that this is a highly inefficient process. The problem is that neither the If-Then nor the Select Case structure can go through the code repetitively, at least not without manual intervention. In the following section, we will introduce you to loops, and when we finally combine If-Then or Case structures with a loop structure, you will never look back.

Using loops

In this final recipe of this chapter, we will show you how to use loops.

Loops are used to automatically repeat a set of statements until a condition is met. There are different types of loops that can be used in VBA:

- The Do loop
- The Do-Until loop
- The For Next loop

  For and For Each loops can both be used to iterate through collections and arrays. Only the For loop can be used to iterate through a range of specified values, for example, 1 to 10. Only the For loop can be used to replace items of an iterated collection or array.

- Looping through a collection of objects

Getting ready

With ProgramFlow.xlsm still open on **Sheet1**, press *Alt + F11* to switch to the VBA Editor With that open, insert a new module.

How to do it...

The first loop under discussion is the Do loop:

1. Type the following code into the LoopSample Sub procedure:

```
Sub LoopSample()
    Range("A1").Select
    Do
        ActiveCell.Offset(1, 0).Select
    Loop Until ActiveCell.Value = ""
End Sub
```

2. Resize the two windows again before stepping into the procedure.

3. Press *F8*, and observe how cell A1 is selected in Excel.

4. Press *F8* again until you enter the Do loop. Press it again and observe how cell A2 is selected.

5. Keep stepping through the code with *F8* until you reach the final entry in cell A5. Pressing *F8* one last time will exit the loop and end the procedure.

In the next Do Until loop, I've inserted the If Else structure in order to automate the process:

1. Clear the data in cells B1:B5, and then insert a new module. Create the following Sub procedure in the code window:

```
Sub ElseIfDoLoop()
    Dim Mark As Integer
    Dim Symbol As String
    Range("A1").Select
    Do Until ActiveCell.Value = ""
        Mark = ActiveCell.Value
        If Mark < 50 Then
            Symbol = "Try again"
        ElseIf Mark < 60 Then
            Symbol = "D"
        ElseIf Mark < 70 Then
            Symbol = "C"
        ElseIf Mark < 80 Then
            Symbol = "B"
        ElseIf Mark <= 100 Then
            Symbol = "A"
        Else
        End If
```

```
        ActiveCell.Offset(0, 1).Value = Symbol
        ActiveCell.Offset(1, 0).Select
    Loop
End Sub
```

2. To speed things up a bit, simply press *F5* to execute the Sub procedure. Observe the newly inserted values in cells B1 to B5. The inserted `If` structure in the loop automated the process of assigning symbols to the values, saving us a lot of time.

The `For Next` loop is next:

1. Create yet another module, and then insert the following text in the code window:

```
Sub ForNextSample()
    Dim Count As Integer
    Range("D1").Select
    For Count = 1 To 20
        ActiveCell.Value = Count
        ActiveCell.Offset(1, 0).Select
    Next Count
End Sub
```

2. Once again, press *F5* to execute the code. Column **D** will now display a series of values, in sequence, starting in cell D1 and ending in cell D20.

Finally, we have to loop through a collection of objects. A collection is a series of objects of the same type: workbooks, worksheets, ranges, and even cells fall into that category. There are various ways in which the concept can be demonstrated. In this recipe, we will be investigating two possible ways.

1. The first example will loop through all the worksheets in the active workbook. In preparation for this Sub procedure, insert four extra worksheets into the workbook, and open the **Immediate** window in the Editor. Then, enter the following code in the code window:

```
Sub ListWorkSheetNames()
    Dim SingleSheet As Worksheet
    For Each SingleSheet In Worksheets
        Debug.Print SingleSheet.Name
    Next SingleSheet
End Sub
```

2. When you press *F5*, the names of the five sheets will be displayed in the **Immediate** window.

In the final example, we will be looping through a range of cells. To make the most of this, we will have to combine a number of loops in a single Sub procedure.

In preparation, we need to clear **Sheet1** and then add some data to the blank sheet:

1. Enter a series of values in cells D1:D10. Start at 85 and use the **Autofill** feature to create a decreasing series with a step value of 4:

D
85
81
77
73
69
65
61
57
53
49

Figure 9.10 – Values in cells D1:D10

2. Before running the `ElseIfDoLoop` procedure, change the starting reference to D1. Now run the `ElseIfDoLoop` procedure from cell D1. The result should look like this:

D	E
85	A
81	A
77	B
73	B
69	C
65	C
61	C
57	D
53	D
49	Try again

Figure 9.11 – Values with symbols

3. Create a final new module and copy the following text into the code window.

The first part of the code declares all the variables:

```
Sub CountSymbols()
    Dim SingleCell As Range
    Dim ListOfCells As Range
    Dim CountSymbol_A
    Dim CountSymbol_B
    Dim CountSymbol_C
    Dim CountSymbol_D
    Dim CountSymbol_TryAgain
```

Now we set the object range, and then the nested If statements:

```
Set ListOfCells = Range("D1", _
Range("E1").End(xlDown))

    For Each SingleCell In ListOfCells

        If SingleCell.Value = "A" Then
          CountSymbol_A = CountSymbol_A + 1
        ElseIf SingleCell.Value = "B" Then
          CountSymbol_B = CountSymbol_B + 1
        ElseIf SingleCell.Value = "C" Then
          CountSymbol_C = CountSymbol_C + 1
        ElseIf SingleCell.Value = "D" Then
            CountSymbol_D = CountSymbol_D + 1
        ElseIf SingleCell.Value = "Try again" Then
          CountSymbol_TryAgain = CountSymbol_TryAgain + 1
        End If

    Next SingleCell
```

Here we assign values to the range F1 to F5:

```
    Range("F1") = "Total A"
    Range("F2") = "Total B"
    Range("F3") = "Total C"
    Range("F4") = "Total C"
    Range("F5") = "Total Try"
```

And finally, we place the variable output in the range G1 to G5:

```
    Range("G1") = CountSymbol_A
    Range("G2") = CountSymbol_B
    Range("G3") = CountSymbol_C
    Range("G4") = CountSymbol_D
```

```
        Range ("G5") = CountSymbol_TryAgain

    End Sub
```

4. Press *F5* and observe the newly inserted information in columns *F* and *G*:

D	E	F	G
85	A	Total A	2
81	A	Total B	2
77	B	Total C	3
73	B	Total C	2
69	C	Total Try	1
65	C		
61	C		
57	D		
53	D		
49	Try again		

Figure 9.12 – Displaying total values

Now this is starting to look like something you could use in the future. Let's investigate the construction of these procedures.

How it works...

Here's how loops work:

1. The first procedure, LoopSample, is the simplest example of what a loop can do. It can start anywhere, but in this case we start in cell A1.

2. Between the Do and Loop keywords, the single line of code tells VBA to move one row down, in the same column, from the active cell.

3. By adding the Until keyword after Loop, we limit the downward movement to the first open cell. In other words, when the active cell is found to be empty, the loop ends.

The next procedure, ElseIfDoLoop, has a nested If inside the loop. Doing a **Step Into** will help a lot to clarify each step of the procedure:

1. After declaring two variables, Mark and Symbol, cell A1 is selected.

2. The same limitation as in the LoopSample procedure is inserted in order to end the loop when reaching the last entry in column **A**.

3. Now, the active cell's value is assigned to the Mark variable. With that value stored in memory, each If statement is checked. The last one meets the criterion because 85 is larger than any of the others. The string A is now assigned to the Symbol variable.

4. The If statement ends, and the next line is executed, meaning that the value A is entered in the cell to the right of the active cell, cell A1.

5. Offset now moves the focus one row down, in the same column.

6. The loop is repeated, adding symbols to the right of each value, until cell A6 becomes the active cell. Being empty, the loop is forced to end, after which the procedure also ends.

The ForNextSample procedure works as follow:

1. A variable called Count is declared.

2. Cell D1 is selected.

3. The count start and end values are set.

4. The first Count value is assigned to the active cell.

5. Focus moves one row down, in the same column.

6. The count loop now starts again, because the end value, 20, has not been reached.

7. The loop continues until the value 20 is entered in the last cell, after which the loop ends and the procedure also ends.

Finally, the collection loop must be explained. In the first example, ListWorkSheetNames, we print the names of each worksheet in the immediate window. Here's how it works:

1. A variable called SingleSheet is declared as a worksheet object.

2. The For loop is given its parameters, which is to find all worksheet objects and print their names in the **Immediate** window.

3. By stepping into the code (pressing *F8*), you will see how each sheet name is found and printed, until the loop ends after printing the last name.

The second example of a loop structure is essentially a loop through a range of cells. By adding some extra coding, it has the potential to become something useful.

The aim of this procedure is to count the number of symbols in each category, add them, and then print the totals in a new position. Here's how the code works:

1. Declare range variables for the range that we will loop through, as well as the individual cells in the range.

2. Next, declare variables for each symbol to be counted.

3. Now, set the range for the `ListOfCells` variable. Observe that this range covers the entire column.

4. Start the `For` loop, telling it to investigate each cell in the range.

5. Insert a nested `If` structure inside the `For` loop. Observe how each symbol is detected and then added to the category variable. It will help a lot if you use the **Step Into** shortcut, *F8*, to cycle through each step here.

6. Once the end of the range has been reached, the `For` loop ends. The procedure, however, has more commands waiting.

7. The title for each symbol count is assigned to cells F1:F5.

8. Finally, in the range G1:G5, the total values for each symbol category are assigned.

9. The procedure ends.

Like everything else in life, it will take time for you to assimilate this information. Work through these examples repeatedly, and then try some of your own.

10
Implementing Automation

Automation comes in different flavors. Simple recorded macros, for instance, can be used to eliminate the drudgery of repetitive tasks. Even keyboard shortcuts are a form of automation. However, when messages start popping up while you open or close a file or because you forget to make backups, the word automation takes on a new meaning. This chapter is all about those event-driven procedures, which is a major step toward automation in VBA. Therefore, the benefits of event procedures are increased production and better interaction with users.

In standard English, an event is something that happens – a wedding or a conference, for example. In VBA, an event is also something that happens, such as when you click on a button, or when you save, open, or close a file. You can also say that an event procedure is a sub-routine that runs automatically in response to an event in the workbook.

In this chapter, we will cover the following recipes:

- Writing event handler procedures
- Discovering events
- Creating workbook-related events
- Creating worksheet-related events
- Creating non-object events

By the end of this chapter, you will be able to write event handler procedures.

Technical requirements

This cookbook was written and designed to be used with MS Office 2019 and MS Office 365, installed on either Windows 8, 8.1, or 10.

If your hardware and software meet these requirements, you have everything you need.

Demonstration files can be downloaded from `https://github.com/ PacktPublishing/VBA-Automation-for-Excel-2019-Cookbook`.

Please visit the following link to check out the CiA videos: `https://bit. ly/3jQRvVk`.

Writing event handler procedures

In this recipe, we will be working with a new type of procedure, known as **event handler procedures**. This is a special type of procedure, designed and placed in such a way that it will do nothing else but handle events.

> **Important note**
> For a list of every possible event available in VBA, follow this link:
> `https://docs.microsoft.com/en-us/dotnet/api/ microsoft.office.tools.excel.workbook?redirectedfr om=MSDN&view=vsto-2017#events`.

Getting ready

Open Excel and activate a new workbook. Save the file as a macro-enabled file on your desktop and call it `Events`. **Sheet1** should be active. Press *Alt + F11* to switch to the VBA Editor.

How to do it...

Let's create our first event handler procedure:

1. Instead of inserting a new module, double-click on the workbook object in **Project Explorer**:

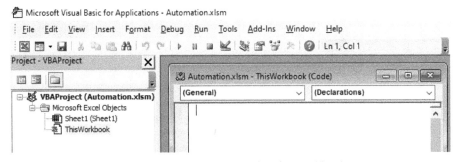

Figure 10.1 – Code window for ThisWorkbook

2. In the code window, click on the drop-down arrow on the left and choose the object that you're coding for; `Workbook`:

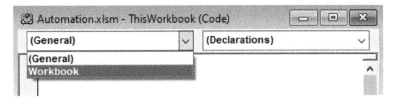

Figure 10.2 – Workbook object

3. This will automatically generate the default event for this object, which is the open event:

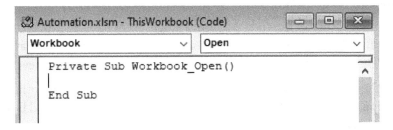

Figure 10.3 – Generated code

4. Insert the following code into the existing procedure:

```
Private Sub Workbook_Open()
    MsgBox "Welcome to Automation"
End Sub
```

5.   Save the file and close Excel. When you open the saved file, click the **Enable Macros**
      notification. A message box will appear:

Figure 10.4 – Message box

6.   Click **OK** to close the message box.

How it works...

Creating an event procedure works as follows:

1.   Unlike normal Sub procedures, event procedures are not created in a standard VBA
      module. Event handler procedures go into the code window of an Object module.
      Should they be placed in the wrong module, they will simply not work.

2.   By double-clicking on the **ThisWorkbook** object, the associated code window will
      be activated.

3.   In the top-left corner of the code window, a single event handler procedure is
      available. By selecting that, the Sub and End sub statements will appear in the
      window. This code is the default event handler procedure for an open event.

4.   To the right of that, a procedure drop-down list allows you to choose other events.
      By selecting, for instance, the BeforeClose event, the new event will be created
      and inserted above the current event.

5.   For the Workbook_Open event to work, we need to add some actionable code to
      execute when the workbook opens up. In this case, we want a simple message box to
      appear. Enter the code, together with the text you want to read on the message box.

6.   Unlike other Sub procedures, you can't press *F5* to run the code because it is
      an event that will only run when the workbook opens. So, save the file and then
      close it.

7. Open the saved file, and observe the security warning below the ribbon:

Figure 10.5 – Enabling macros

8. Click on **Enable Content** to enable the macro. The desired message box will appear. Click **OK** to close the message box to enter data on the spreadsheet.

9. The message box will appear every time you open this specific file.

There's more...

Make sure that the security settings on your PC are correct. Check the following settings:

1. Activate the **Developer** ribbon. In the **Code** group, click on **Macro Security** to open the **Trust Center** dialog box:

Figure 10.6 – Macro Security

2. With the **Trust Center** dialog box open, and the **Macro Settings** category selected in the left panel, select **Disable all macros with notification**:

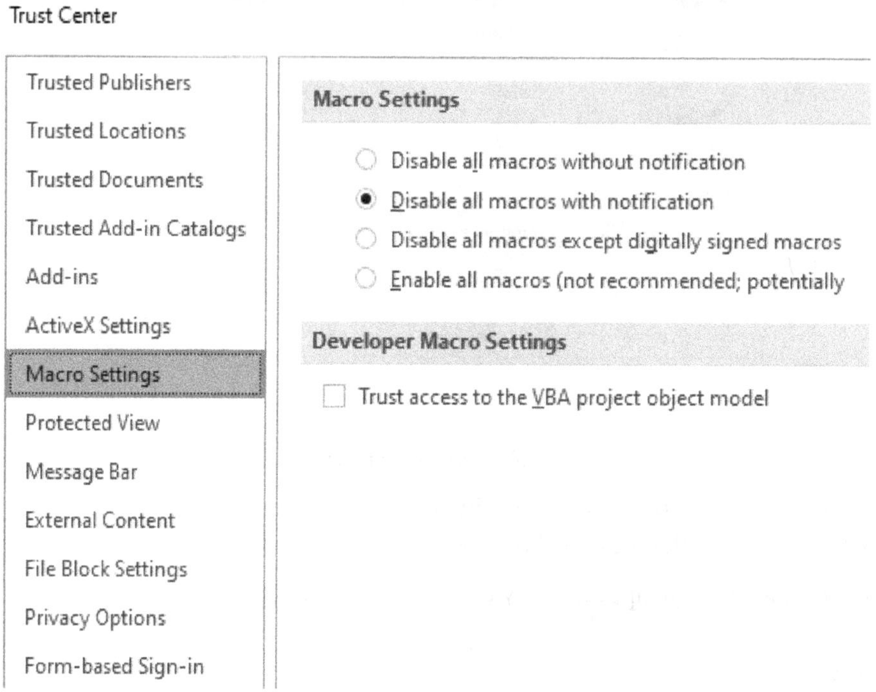

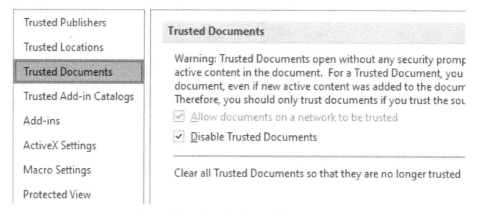

Figure 10.7 – Macro Settings

3. Next, select **Trusted Documents** in the category panel and then tick the **Disable Trusted Documents** checkbox:

Figure 10.8 – Disable Trusted Documents

4. This final setting will ensure that the security warning appears every time you open this file. Without it, the warning will appear only the first time you open the file.

It is seemingly insignificant settings like these that make life so much easier when working with VBA. You can thank me later!

Discovering events

In the following section, we will be creating three different types of events. The principle behind any event will always be the same; in other words, something must happen in Excel to trigger the event procedure.

What has not been mentioned explicitly is that different objects in the Excel VBA environment will respond to different events. It makes sense that you can enter data in the cell of a worksheet, but not in a workbook. Similarly, you cannot save a cell, while a workbook can and must be saved.

The three event types to be discussed will explain this principle in detail, in the remaining recipes of this chapter.

Creating workbook-related events

The `Open` event is one of many workbook-related events. In this recipe, we will be creating more workbook-related events.

Getting ready

Make sure that `Events.xlsm` is still open. **Sheet1** should be active. Press *Alt + F11* to switch to the VBA Editor, and then double-click the `ThisWorkbook` object to activate the code window.

How to do it...

Let's create three workbook-related events:

1. If we can welcome users when they open a file, we can greet them when they leave. In the top-right corner of the code window, select the `BeforeClose` event from the drop-down list:

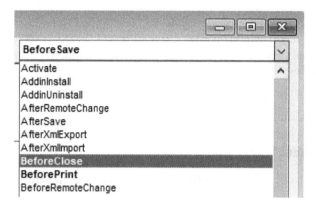

Figure 10.9 – List of events

A new procedure will be created in the code window:

```
Private Sub Workbook_BeforeClose(Cancel As Boolean)

End Sub
```

2. Insert the next line of code in the procedure:

```
Private Sub Workbook_BeforeClose(Cancel As Boolean)
    MsgBox "Goodbye - have a nice day"
End Sub
```

3. After saving the file, close it. A message box will appear, in which you will have to click **OK** before Excel can close down.

4. Open `Events.xlsm` again, enable macros, and click **OK** in the message box. Switch to the VBA Editor.

5. In the `BeforeClose` procedure, set the `BeforeClose` event's parameter to `Cancel` by adding the following line:

```
Private Sub Workbook_BeforeClose(Cancel As Boolean)
    MsgBox "This file cannot be closed"
    Cancel = True
End Sub
```

6. If you now try to close the file, it will not allow you to do so. You can, however, close the file on a conditional basis. Add the following code to the procedure:

```
Private Sub Workbook_BeforeClose(Cancel As Boolean)
    If Hour(Now) < 17 Then
        MsgBox "You have to work until 5pm"
        Cancel = True
    End If
End Sub
```

Change the hour until it is earlier than your current time in order to meet the condition.

7. The second workbook-related event is the `BeforeSave` event. In the top-right corner of the code window, select the `BeforeSave` event from the drop-down list. A new procedure will be created in the code window:

```
Private Sub Workbook_BeforeSave(ByVal SaveAsUI As _
Boolean, Cancel As Boolean)

End Sub
```

8. Insert the next line of code in the new procedure:

```
Private Sub Workbook_BeforeSave(ByVal SaveAsUI As _
Boolean, Cancel As Boolean)
    MsgBox "You do not have permission to save this file"
    Cancel = True
End Sub
```

9. Whether you click on **Save** in Explorer, or switch to Excel and try to save the file there, a message box will inform you that you cannot save the file.

10. Next, we want to prevent users from printing a file. Insert the `BeforePrint` event, and insert the following code into the procedure:

```
Private Sub Workbook_BeforePrint(Cancel As Boolean)
    MsgBox "You cannot print this file"
    Cancel = True
End Sub
```

11. Switch to Excel and type your name in cell A1. Press *Ctrl + P* to activate the print window. Click on the **Print** button. A message box will tell you that you cannot print the file.

12. To save the file, and also to exit Excel, you will have to comment out any line of code preventing you from doing so.

How it works...

Let's start with the BeforeClose event.:

1. With this event active, you can set reminders, or even warnings, before users can close Excel. In the first case, we're simply wishing them a nice day.

2. By setting the Cancel parameter to True, the file cannot be closed at all, which doesn't make sense. If you add a condition, as in the third example, you can force users to obey certain rules.

3. The BeforeSave event will have the same effect, but only when users try to save a file. Without any conditions, it will prevent saving. With conditions, such as providing a password or code, the event would be more useful.

4. The last event, BeforePrint, will activate when users try to print the file. There may be good reason for you to prevent printing, but adding a condition will make it more flexible and user-friendly.

Creating worksheet-related events

The next logical step will be to create events that influence only worksheets. This recipe will discuss the principles behind these events.

Getting ready

Open Excel and activate a new workbook. Save the file as a macro-enabled file on your desktop and call it Worksheets. Enter the following data in **Sheet1**:

	A	B	C	D	E	F	G
1	Monday	Tuesday	Wednesday	Thursday	Friday	Saturday	Sunday
2	100	100	100	100	100	100	100
3	100	100	100	100	100	100	100
4	100	100	100	100	100	100	100
5	100	100	100	100	100	100	100

Figure 10.10 – Working data

Finally, press *Alt + F11* to switch to the VBA Editor.

How to do it...

The first worksheet event we will create is the `SelectionChange` event. The steps are virtually the same as with the workbook event handler procedure:

1. Double-click the **worksheet** object in **Project Explorer, Sheet1**.

2. In the code window that appears, click on the drop-down arrow on the left, and choose the object that you're coding for; **Worksheet**.

3. This will automatically generate the default event for this object, which is the `SelectionChange` event.

4. Insert two lines of code into the procedure:

```
Private Sub Worksheet_SelectionChange(ByVal Target _
As Range)
    Target.Font.Color = vbBlue
    Target.Font.Bold = True
End Sub
```

5. Press *Alt + F11* to switch to Excel. Click on any of the filled cells and observe how the text changes to blue and bold. The event is working as intended, but is not really useful.

6. Switch back to the VBA Editor. Add the following condition:

```
Private Sub Worksheet_SelectionChange(ByVal Target _
As Range)
    If Target.Row = 1 Then
        Target.Font.Color = vbBlue
        Target.Font.Bold = True
    End If
End Sub
```

7. Switch back to Excel one last time. Use *Ctrl + A* to select the entire sheet, and then click **Home | Editing | Clear | Clear Formatting** to clear all formatting.

8. Click on any cell in the sheet, and observe how only the top row will turn blue and bold, while clicking on any other cell has no effect.

Another example of a worksheet event is the Change event:

1. In the VBA Editor, create the Change event. Click on the drop-down arrow on the left, and choose the object that you're coding for; **Worksheet**.

2. From the drop-down box on the right, select the Change event.

3. Create the code for a simple message box:

```
Private Sub Worksheet_Change(ByVal Target As Range)
    MsgBox "Change!"
End Sub
```

4. Switch to Excel and delete or edit the content of any cell in the table. A message box will appear:

Figure 10.11 – Message box for a change event

5. Switch back to the Editor. Add the following code to the procedure:

```
Private Sub Worksheet_Change(ByVal Target As Range)
    If Target.Address = Range("A6").Address Then
        MsgBox "Change!"
    End If
End Sub
```

6. Switch back to Excel and once again delete or edit the content of any cell in the table. A message box will appear only when you change something in cell A6.

7. Switch back to the Editor one last time. Add the following code to the procedure:

```
Private Sub Worksheet_Change(ByVal Target As Range)
    If Not Intersect(Target, Range("A6:G6")) Is Nothing _
    Then
        MsgBox "Change!"
    End If
End Sub
```

8. This time, the message box will appear only when you change something in the range A6 to G6.

How it works...

The events work as follows:

1. The `SelectionChange` event will activate every time you select a cell in the worksheet. By adding methods, such as making the font blue and bold, you can change every cell you select. Nice, but with little value.

2. Using the `If` condition to limit the event to row one of the worksheet, you can now use the event to format headings on **Sheet1**.

3. The `Change` event will trigger when something in a cell changes, such as adding or deleting values. The message box displays every time a change is made anywhere in the sheet.

4. To focus the event on a single cell, set the `Target` address equal to that cell. The `Change` event will only fire when that specific cell is changed.

5. To cover a range of cells for a `Change` event, use the `Intersect` function to specify the **Target** range.

Creating non-object events

This recipe deals with objects other than workbooks and worksheets. The principle is, however, exactly the same as with the previous events; an action of sorts triggers the event. Let's get working!

Getting ready

Open Excel and activate a new workbook. Save the file as a macro-enabled file on your desktop and call it `NonObjectEvents`. **Sheet1** should be active. Press *Alt + F11* to switch to the VBA Editor.

How to do it...

When dealing with workbook and worksheet events, we created code for the event in the object's code window. Non-object events are exactly what the name says; events that are not associated with objects. These events are programmed in a normal VBA module.

1. Insert a new module in the VBA Editor; **Insert | Module**.

2. Enter the following code in the code window:

```vba
Sub WakeUpCall()
    Application.OnTime 0.5, "Alarm"
End Sub
```

3. Create a second Sub procedure – the one that is referred to in the first Sub procedure:

```vba
Sub Alarm()
    MsgBox "Time for a break!"
End Sub
```

4. You will have to wait until noon, in other words 12:00 P.M., for this event to be triggered, but it will work.

5. Let's do another, somewhat more useful non-object event. Insert a new module, and then create the following Sub procedures:

```vba
Sub KeyAssign()
    Application.OnKey "+^{RIGHT}", "SpecialSign"
    Application.OnKey "^{z}", "OwnUndo"
    Dim SpecialSign As String, OwnUndo As String
    SpecialSign = "+^{RIGHT}"
    OwnUndo = "^{z}"
End Sub

Sub SpecialSign()
    MsgBox "You pressed Shift+Ctrl+Right Arrow"
End Sub

Sub OwnUndo()
```

```
        MsgBox "You pressed Undo"
    End Sub
```

6. Set up the `OnKey` event by running the `KeyAssign` procedure. Switch to Excel.

7. Press either of the two keyboard shortcuts: *Shift + Ctrl + right arrow*, or *Ctrl + Z*. A message box will appear in each case, confirming the keystrokes.

How it works...

These non-object events work as follows:

1. In the `WakeUpCall` procedure, the `OnTime` method of the `Application` object does the work. It has two arguments: the time and the name of the Sub procedure that must be executed.

2. For this procedure to do what it's supposed to do, it must be executed. Remember, this is not an `Open` or `Close` event associated with a workbook.

3. Apart from executing the procedure, you must also have this specific workbook open for the `OnTime` event to be activated. When your PC's system clock reaches 12:00 P.M., a message box will appear, telling you to take a break.

4. The `KeyAssign` procedure also takes two arguments: first, the code for the kkeystrokes (`"+^{RIGHT}"`) and then the Sub procedure.

5. Next, we declare two variables, one for each keystroke:

```
    Dim SpecialSign As String, OwnUndo As String
```

6. After this, we assign the keyboard strokes to the variables:

```
    SpecialSign = "+^{RIGHT}"
    OwnUndo = "^{z}"
```

7. The final step involves writing messages to be displayed when each procedure is triggered.

This brings us to the end of this section. It must be mentioned that not all events have been covered here. Do yourself a favor and do some research on the Microsoft site for `Application` events, `Chart` events, and `UserForm` events.

Whatever we have done here will give you a solid foundation, enough anyway to easily apply other events with equal success.

11
Handling Errors

Try as you may, mistakes will be made. After all, we're only human. There are three types of errors in the VBA world of coding; syntax errors, compile errors, and runtime errors. Even experienced programmers encounter these problems to some extent. In the world of programming, errors are part of the territory, so consider yourself in good company.

The sooner you learn how to deal with all types of errors, the easier your life as a programmer will be.

In this chapter, we will cover the following recipes:

- Handling different types of errors
- Correcting a runtime error
- Testing to find errors
- Using the On Error statement
- Resuming after an error

By the end of this chapter, you will be able to do error handling in VBA.

Technical requirements

This cookbook was written and designed to be used with MS Office 2019 and MS Office 365, installed on either Windows 8, 8.1, or 10.

If your hardware and software meet these requirements, you are good to go.

Demonstration files can be downloaded from `https://github.com/PacktPublishing/VBA-Automation-for-Excel-2019-Cookbook`.

Please visit the following link to check out the CiA videos: `https://bit.ly/3jQRvVk`.

Handling different types of errors

All errors are not equal.

OK, let me clarify that statement. All errors will prevent a procedure from executing flawlessly, but there are several different types of errors, each with specific characteristics and consequences. Not all sources agree on the number of error types. However, in this manual, I have identified and described the following three errors:

- **Syntax error**: A very common error, especially when you're new to the VBA environment, is syntax-related, or grammar-related errors. It could be that you spell a word incorrectly, or accidentally drop a number somewhere. It could even be something as small as a missing comma, full stop, or bracket (parenthesis). Whichever *spelling mistake* it is, VBA is unforgiving in that department. It has to be done the right way, 100% correct, or nothing.

- **Compile error**: Compiling is done automatically for you when you run a Sub procedure, checking whether your code makes sense. Where syntax errors check individual words, compile errors are only revealed when an entire Sub procedure is incorrect or does not make sense.

- **Runtime error**: This type of error is very common, even among more experienced coders, and can occur for a great number of reasons. It should be observed that, unlike syntax and compile errors, runtime errors will only be revealed once you run your Sub procedure. A typical runtime error could be referring to a cell that doesn't actually exist. In such a case, your code will compile without problems, but a runtime error will occur because the cell reference does not exist.

In this recipe, we will be working on resolving these errors.

Getting ready

Open Excel and activate a new workbook. Save the file as a macro-enabled file on your desktop and call it `ErrorHandling.xlsm`. **Sheet1** should be active. Press *Alt + F11* to switch to the VBA Editor, and then insert a new module.

How to do it...

First-hand experience is always the best way to learn. Let's see how syntax errors present themselves:

1. Copy the following code into the code window:

```
Sub ErrorSamples()
    Range("A1").Value = "Name"
    Range("B1").Value = "Dept"
    Range("C1").Value = "Date"

    Range("A2").Value = InputBox("Type your name")
    Range("B2").Value = InputBox("Type your Department")
    Range("C2").Value = InputBox("Enter today's date")

    Range("A1:C1").Select
    With Selection.Font
        .Name = "Verdana"
        .Size = 10
        .Bold = True
    End With
End Sub
```

2. Once done, remove the parentheses after cell reference A2 so as to simulate an error. Click in the next line, and observe the immediate warning:

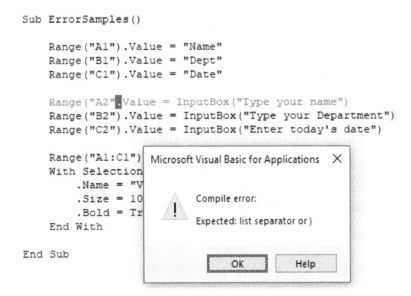

Figure 11.1 – Syntax error showing in red

A message box pops up, informing you that a **list separator or)** is expected. It also highlights the position where it thinks the parentheses should appear. This is not a true compile error, so ignore the heading on the message box for the moment. There is a solution for this at *Step 7* in this recipe.

3. Click **OK** to close the dialog box, and then replace the parentheses you've just removed. The font turns back to black, which is confirmation that you've removed the error.

4. Next, let's remove the quotation mark directly following cell reference A2. Click in the next line to activate the error:

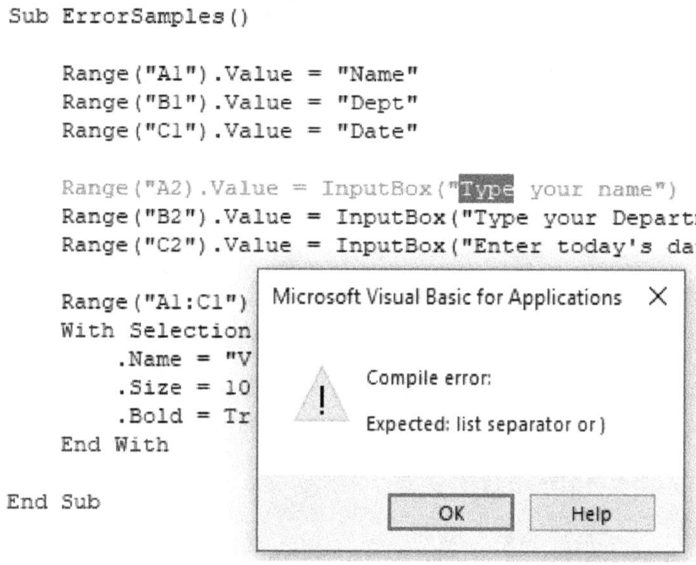

```
Sub ErrorSamples()

    Range("A1").Value = "Name"
    Range("B1").Value = "Dept"
    Range("C1").Value = "Date"

    Range("A2").Value = InputBox("Type your name")
    Range("B2").Value = InputBox("Type your Department")
    Range("C2").Value = InputBox("Enter today's date")

    Range("A1:C1")
    With Selection
        .Name = "V
        .Size = 10
        .Bold = Tr
    End With

End Sub
```

Microsoft Visual Basic for Applications   ✕

!   Compile error:

Expected: list separator or)

OK   Help

Figure 11.2 – Syntax error marking the wrong area

5. The line turns red again, but this time the highlighted area is in completely the wrong place. Even the message box is wrong; we're missing a quotation mark, not a parenthesis. As with the previous confusing message box, there is a solution at *Step 7*

6. Click **OK** to close the message box, and replace the missing quotation mark.

7. Now, let's prevent the confusing dialog boxes from appearing. In the VBA Editor, on the menu bar, click on **Tools | Options**. The **Options** dialog box appears:

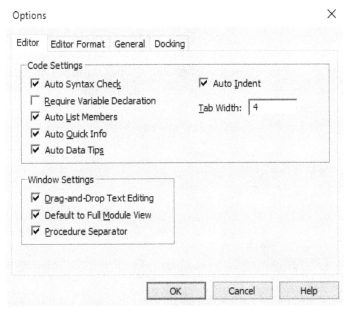

Figure 11.3 – The Options dialog box

8. In the **Code Settings** group, remove the tick mark in front of **Auto Syntax Check**. Click **OK** to close the dialog box. Whenever you make a syntax error again, no dialog box will appear, while the erroneous code will still be marked in red.

9. Remove the quotation mark after cell reference A2 again, and click in the next line:

```
Sub ErrorSamples()

    Range("A1").Value = "Name"
    Range("B1").Value = "Dept"
    Range("C1").Value = "Date"

    Range("A2).Value = InputBox("Type your name")
    Range("B2").Value = InputBox("Type your Department")
    Range("C2").Value = InputBox("Enter today's date")

    Range("A1:C1").Select
    With Selection.Font
        .Name = "Verdana"
        .Size = 10
        .Bold = True
    End With

End Sub
```

Figure 11.4 – Syntax error without dialog box

10. This time, the dialog box with its confusing messages does not appear. The line is still marked in red, though, which is all you want – an indication where the syntax error is.

11. To cause a compile error, delete the letter e in the first instance of the word `Range`. Click in the next line. Observe that the text of the first line does not turn red:

```
Sub ErrorSamples()

    Rang("A1").Value = "Name"
    Range("B1").Value = "Dept"
    Range("C1").Value = "Date"

    Range("A2").Value = InputBox("Type your name")
    Range("B2").Value = InputBox("Type your Department")
    Range("C2").Value = InputBox("Enter today's date")
```

Figure 11.5 – Error in code

12. Try to run the procedure by pressing *F5*. The following dialog box appears:

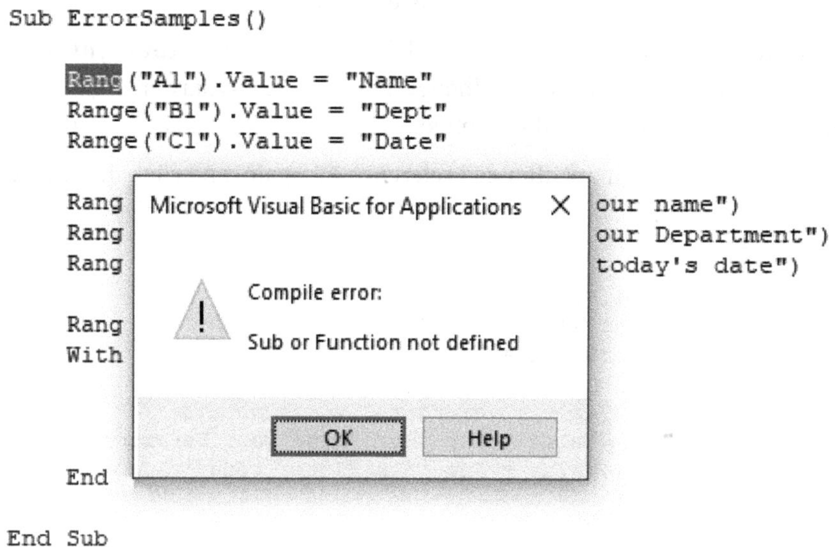

```
Sub ErrorSamples()

    Rang("A1").Value = "Name"
    Range("B1").Value = "Dept"
    Range("C1").Value = "Date"

    Rang                                           our name")
    Rang                                           our Department")
    Rang                                           today's date")

    Rang     Compile error:
    With
              Sub or Function not defined


                    OK         Help

    End
```

Microsoft Visual Basic for Applications   X

End Sub

Figure 11.6 – Compile error warning and highlight

13. More than an accurate assessment of what the problem is, the correct area where the mistake was made is highlighted in the code. Click **OK** to close the dialog box and correct the mistake by rectifying the spelling for the word `Range`.

14. Run the procedure again to confirm that all errors have been removed.

How it works...

Here is an explanation of what we just did in this recipe:

1. Syntax errors are essentially errors in the structure or the grammar of the code. Examples of this type of error would be double quotes left out, parentheses omitted, double spaces, incorrect line breaks, declared variables spelt incorrectly in references, and so on. Syntax errors will mark the line in red, plus a dialog box will appear, sometimes with confusing information.

2. By removing the **Auto Syntax Check** option from the **Options** dialog box, a dialog box will not appear when syntax errors are made, while the line of code will still be marked in red.

3. Compile errors only reveal themselves immediately before a Sub procedure is executed. By spelling a **keyword** incorrectly, for instance, a message box informs you of your error.

4. The dialog box information for compile errors is much more accurate than that of syntax errors. At the same time, compile errors are highlighted with much greater accuracy.

Syntax errors and compile errors both have the same effect: they prevent the code from running. Don't make too much of an issue of this, though. There are only two rules to remember:

- Correct the spelling mistakes (marked in red, and known as syntax errors) when the code turns red.

- Correct compile errors when you try to run the code, and a message box tells you to correct the compile error.

Correcting a runtime error

Runtime errors are by far the most common type of error you'll come across when working in VBA. As the name suggests, these errors only occur once you run the code. Unlike with syntax and compile errors, there is no way for VBA to check your code for actions that will happen after the procedure starts running.

To come up with a list of possible runtime errors is virtually impossible because situations and procedures are never the same.

One typical runtime error that occurs from time to time is when you create a link to an external file, and then accidentally delete that file. Only when you run the code will an error message be displayed. Another example is when you refer to a range that does not exist.

In this recipe, we will be correcting a runtime error.

Getting ready

Make sure that `ErrorHandling.xlsm` from the preceding recipe is still open. **Sheet1** should be active. Press *Alt + F11* to switch to the VBA Editor. If it is not open, double-click on **Module 1** to activate the code window.

How to do it...

Let's manipulate our code to create an error:

1. In the code window of **Module 1**, edit the code as follows. In other words, change the reference A1 to XFE1:

```
Sub ErrorSamples()

    Rang("XFE1").Value = "Name"
    Range("B1").Value = "Dept"
    Range("C1").Value = "Date"
```

Figure 11.7 – Deliberate runtime error

2. Observe that no errors are displayed when clicking in the next line.

3. Press *F5* to run the code. The following dialog box appears:

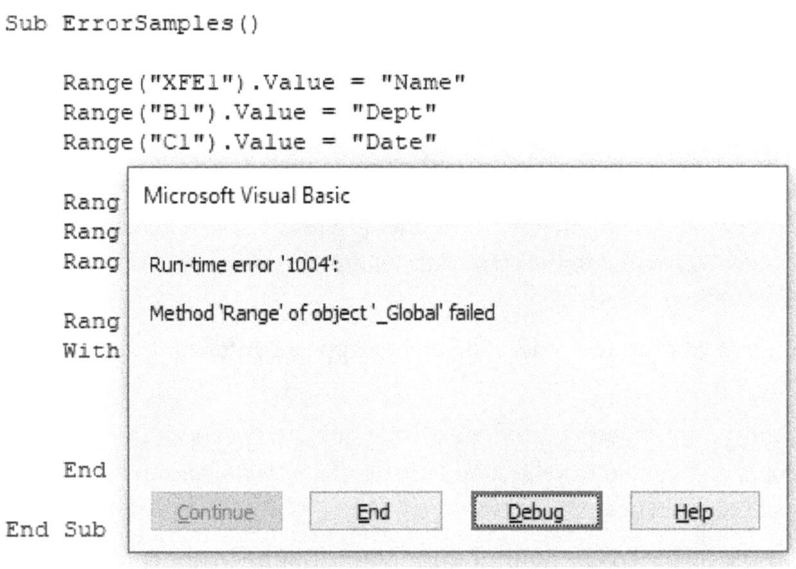
Sub ErrorSamples()
Range("XFE1").Value = "Name"
Range("B1").Value = "Dept"
Range("C1").Value = "Date"
Rang
Rang
Rang
Rang
With
End
End Sub
Microsoft Visual Basic
Run-time error '1004':
Method 'Range' of object '_Global' failed
Continue
End
Debug
Help

Figure 11.8 – Runtime error indicated by the dialog box

4. Click on **Debug** to close the dialog box. Observe that the line containing the error is now highlighted in yellow:

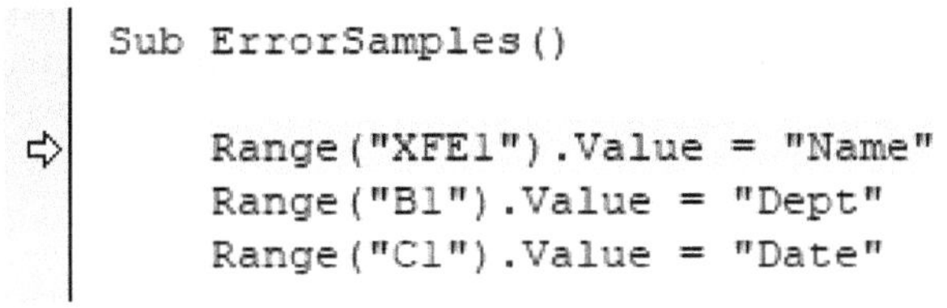
Sub ErrorSamples()
Range("XFE1").Value = "Name"
Range("B1").Value = "Dept"
Range("C1").Value = "Date"

Figure 11.9 – Highlighted line with error

5. Correct the error by deleting the incorrect cell reference, replacing it with the original reference to cell A1. Click on the next line. The line is still highlighted:

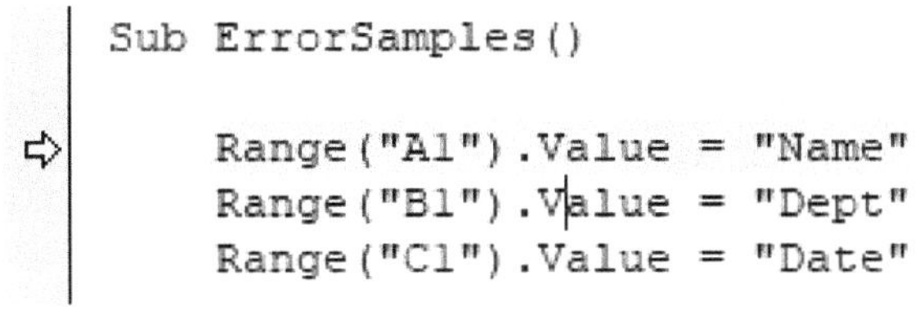
Sub ErrorSamples()
Range("A1").Value = "Name"
Range("B1").Value = "Dept"
Range("C1").Value = "Date"

Figure 11.10 – Highlighted line with correction

6. Since the error has been corrected, you can simply press *F5* to run the rest of the procedure.

How it works

Let's look at the details of what's just happened.

1. The last column in Excel is column *XFD*. Referring to column XFE is guaranteed to cause a runtime error because there is no such a reference in Excel.

2. Since this incorrect cell reference is neither a syntax error nor a compile error, you can click anywhere else in the code without error messages popping up, or lines being highlighted in red.

3. The moment you run the code, a dialog box appears, informing you of a runtime error.

4. By clicking on the **Debug** button, the dialog box disappears and the line containing the error is highlighted in yellow. You are now in *break mode*, and can rectify the incorrect cell reference.

5. Once you've corrected the runtime error, the yellow highlight on the line does not disappear. It simply means that you are still in break mode, and can either exit break mode, or press *F5* to finish the procedure.

6. If there are no other runtime errors, your procedure will execute successfully.

Correcting runtime errors requires vigilance and a thorough understanding of the application, as well as knowledge of general principles within the PC environment.

Testing to find errors

Errors that occur while Excel executes your code – the typical runtime errors – do not always reveal themselves immediately. It is quite possible to work with a specific Sub procedure for a while before a dialog box will pop up and spoil your fun. "How's that possible?", you may ask.

The simple answer is that users often use a procedure without making any so-called mistakes. However, being human, we sometimes use text instead of numerical values. That's just one example. The point is, these *errors* are not always predictable, and it happens all the time, especially if you are new to programming. Programming is not only about knowing syntax, but also about being able to think logically.

A good understanding of math will also come in handy. For instance, dividing by zero, or trying to calculate the square root of a negative number, is guaranteed to invoke a runtime error.

Add to this other *mistakes*, such as typing text into a field that expects a value, and you'll understand that programmers have to think about much more than simple lines of code.

In this recipe, we will be testing a Sub procedure repeatedly. Testing, followed by more testing, trying to imagine every possible action a user might take when using your code, is the only way to eliminate runtime errors.

Getting ready

Make sure that `ErrorHandling.xlsm` is still open. **Sheet1** should be active. Press *Alt + F11* to switch to the VBA Editor. Insert a new module.

How to do it...

Let's start with a very simple example:

1. Copy the following code into the code window:

```vba
Sub Test()
    Dim Num As Double
    Num = InputBox("Enter a value to divide by")

    ActiveCell.Value = ActiveCell.Offset(0, -1). _
    Value / Num
End Sub
```

2. Resize both the VBA Editor and Excel in such a way that both windows are visible next to each other:

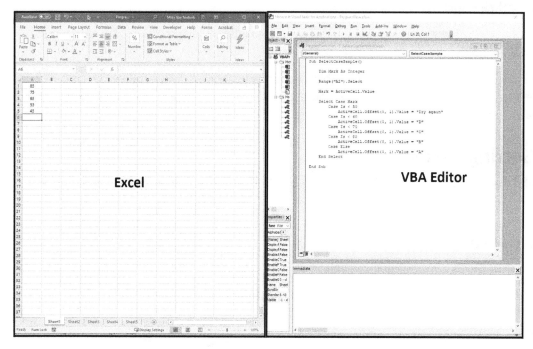

Figure 11.11 – Viewing Excel and the VBA Editor

3. In Excel, type the value 12 in cell A1, and then select cell B1.

4. Click in the code window of **Module 2** and press *F5* to run the code. Enter the value 2 in the input box and click on **OK**. The value **6** will appear in cell B1.

5. Test the procedure several times, each time using a positive value.

6. Next, test the procedure two or three times by entering a negative value.

7. Finally, run the procedure, but this time enter the value 0 in the input box. A dialog box appears, announcing a runtime error:

```
Sub Test()

    Dim Num As Double
    Num = InputBox("Enter a value to divide by")

    ActiveCell.Value = ActiveCell.Offset(0, -1).Value / Num

End Sub
```

Microsoft Visual Basic

Run-time error '11':

Division by zero

| Continue | End | Debug | Help |

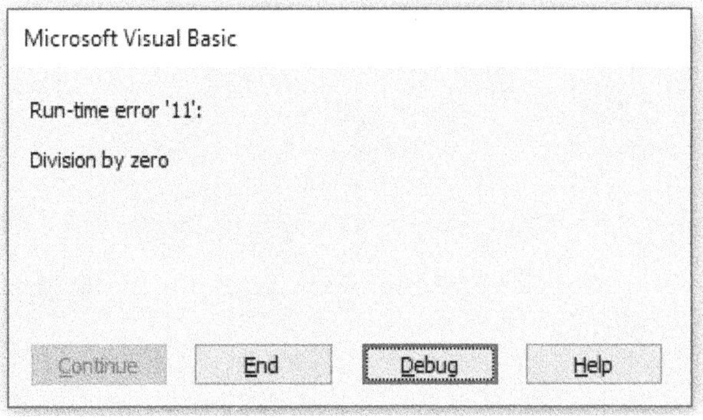

Figure 11.12 – Runtime error

8. Click **End** to stop the procedure. Click in the code window, and then edit the code as follows:

```
Sub Test()
    Dim Num As Double
    Num = InputBox("Enter a value to divide by")

    If Num = 0 Then
        MsgBox "You cannot divide by zero"
        Exit Sub
    End If

    ActiveCell.Value = ActiveCell.Offset(0, -1). _
    Value / Num
End Sub
```

9. Run the procedure, once again using 0 as the divider. Instead of a runtime error, the following message box appears:

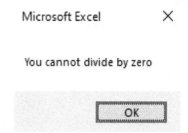

Figure 11.13 – Message box explaining the error

10. Let's do another test. Run the procedure and type your name in the input box. The following runtime error occurs:

```
Sub Test()

    Dim Num As Double
    Num = InputBox("Enter a value to divide by")

    If Num = 0 Then
        MsgBox "You cannot divide by zero"
        Exit Sub
    End If

    ActiveCell.Value = ActiveCell.Offset(0, -1).Value / Num

End Sub
```

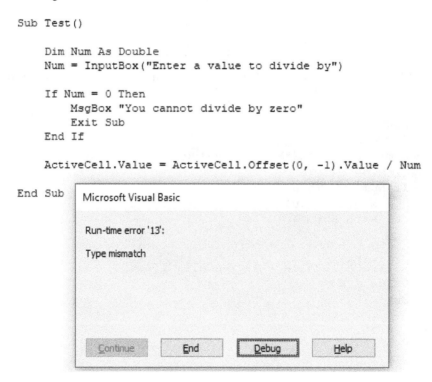

Figure 11.14 – Value runtime error

11. Click **End**, and then edit the code as follows. We will be working with debugging in the next chapter. Take care to change the data type for the Num variable to Variant:

```
Sub Test()
    Dim Num As Variant
    Num = InputBox("Enter a value to divide by")

    If Num = 0 Then
        MsgBox "You cannot divide by zero"
        Exit Sub
    End If

    If Not IsNumeric(Num) Then
        MsgBox "You must enter a number"
        Exit Sub
    End If

    ActiveCell.Value = ActiveCell.Offset(0, -1). _
    Value / Num
End Sub
```

12. Run the procedure, again typing your name in the input box. Instead of a runtime error, the following message box appears:

Figure 11.15 – Text runtime error

By anticipating typical mistakes that users make, it is possible to prevent most runtime errors. In the next recipe, we will reveal the last secret regarding runtime errors. For now, let's see how our recipe works!

How it works...

Let's look at what we've just done, but in more detail:

1. The `Test` procedure is a very simple piece of coding that I often use for training purposes. The objective, in this example, is to give users the opportunity to divide the value in cell A1 by any chosen value.

2. In its simplest form, using any value other than zero, the procedure works without any problems. Then, a user decides to divide by zero, and the first runtime error upsets your stable procedure.

3. By inserting an `If` statement to handle this specific *error* made by users, we've added typical error-handling code. In simple English, this means that we can enter zero as the divider, without ugly dialog boxes bringing our procedure to a standstill.

4. The same thing happens when we add text (your name), instead of a numerical value, to the input box. Your error-handling code will smooth away the dialog box.

There are more errors than these two, such as when users cancel the input box, when the correct sheet is not activated, or when the sheet is protected. As mentioned previously, the only way to find these errors is to test for every possible error you can think of. The next recipe will discuss the technique of handling all errors in a procedure.

Using the On Error statement

In this recipe, we will be using the `On  Error` statement in a procedure.

Instead of trying to anticipate every possible error that can be made or invoked, the `On Error` statement handles every and all possible errors.

This statement lets you bypass Excel's error handling – the dialog boxes – and allows you to use your own error-handling code.

Let's see how it's done.

Getting ready

`ErrorHandling.xlsm` is still open, with **Sheet1** active. Both Excel and the VBA Editor windows are visible next to each other.

How to do it...

Insert a new module and follow these steps:

1. Enter the following code:

```
Sub Test()
    Dim Num As Variant
    Dim Msg As String

    On Error GoTo WrongEntry   'Set up error handling

    Num = InputBox("Enter a value to divide by")

    If Num = "" Then Exit Sub  'Exit the procedure if _
    nothing is entered

    ActiveCell.Value = ActiveCell.Offset(0, -1). _
    Value / Num
    Exit Sub

WrongEntry:
Msg = "An error occurred. Please check your entry."
MsgBox Msg, vbCritical
End Sub
```

2. Run the procedure as many times as you like, testing different entries each time; entering zero as the divider, typing text in the input box, and canceling the input box. In each case, the following dialog box will appear:

Figure 11.16 – Custom dialog box

Error handling is a very important element in an VBA Sub procedure. Use and apply the On Error statement whenever you have to manage a series of possible errors.

How it works...

1. Instead of trying to handle each error individually, we inserted the `On Error` statement directly after declaring the variables. The purpose of this statement is to take care of all errors.

2. Any errors occurring while the procedure is running will be taken care of this way.

3. The only exception is when the input box is canceled, hence the line dedicated to that, which reads as follows:

    ```
    If Num = "" Then Exit Sub  'Exit the procedure if _
    nothing is entered
    ```

4. When an error occurs, the `GoTo` error-handling statement skips the rest of the procedure and goes directly to `WrongEntry`, where an appropriate and personalized dialog box is created.

5. It might be a good idea to be a bit more specific about the possible errors that caused the procedure to end. I'll leave that to you.

Error handling can be a nightmare if you don't know how to trap errors. Dealing with errors by using the `On Error GoTo` statement makes life much easier for programmers as well as users.

Resuming after an error

One way of handling errors is to display a dialog box with some explanation as to why the procedure stopped. It's rather abrupt, though, sometimes leaving us with a lack of full understanding as to what really happened. Furthermore, we are often unsure as to what we should do after closing the dialog box.

In cases where we want to recover from errors, the `Resume` statement will achieve this.

In this recipe, we will be resuming after errors occurred in three different ways.

Getting ready

With `ErrorHandling.xlsm` still open, and **Sheet1** active, arrange the Excel and VBA Editor windows in such a way that both are visible next to each other.

How to do it...

Insert a new module and follow these steps:

1. Enter the following code:

```
Sub Test()
    Dim Num As Variant
    Dim Msg As String
    Dim Answer As Integer

TryAgain:
    On Error GoTo WrongEntry    'Set up error handling

    Num = InputBox("Enter a value to divide by")
    If Num = "" Then Exit Sub    'Exit the sub if cancelled

    ActiveCell.Value = ActiveCell.Offset(0, -1). _
    Value / Num
    Exit Sub

WrongEntry:
    Msg = Msg & "An error occured. Please check your _
    entry."
    Msg = Msg & vbNewLine & vbNewLine & "Try again?"
    Answer = MsgBox(Msg, vbYesNo + vbCritical)

    If Answer = vbYes Then Resume TryAgain
End Sub
```

2. Run the procedure two or three times, testing different entries again; entering zero as the divider, typing text in the input box, and canceling the input box. In each case, the following dialog box will appear:

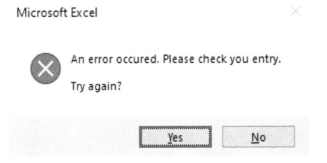

Figure 11.17 – Resulting dialog box

3. Click on **Yes** to resume the procedure.

4. Fix whatever *error* you made in order to successfully perform the calculation.

How it works...

1. We added another label to the code, directly after declaring the variables: TryAgain.

2. When an error occurs, the GoTo error-handling statement skips the rest of the procedure and goes directly to WrongEntry.

3. This time, when the user clicks **Yes**, the Resume statement makes the code return to the TryAgain label.

Giving users the opportunity to correct their mistakes will cause less confusion and uncertainty.

12
Debugging

In the real world of programming, all applications have bugs. In simple English, this means that programs do not always perform the way we expect them to. Even Excel, Word, and PowerPoint have bugs. Before you get too worried, let me assure you that the majority of these bugs will only appear in highly exceptional cases or circumstances.

One example will be when you run an older version of an application on the latest version of the Windows operating system. At the time of release, developers of the old applications could not foresee what Windows 10 would look like or require from installations. When things go wrong in such a case, no one is to blame, even though runtime errors will more than likely cause those applications to malfunction.

In a situation where individuals work on some simple procedures in Excel, runtime errors are less likely to cause such dramatic problems. It would be relatively easy to detect and eliminate them, but you still need to understand what debugging is. Bugs of this nature include error types such as undefined object errors, division by zero errors, logic errors, and data type errors.

The process of detecting and removing existing and potential errors (also called bugs) is known as **debugging**. Errors in software code that can cause it to behave unexpectedly or crash are called **bugs**.

There are various **debugging techniques** that can be employed in the VBA Editor to eliminate these errors.

In this chapter, we will cover the following recipes:

- Exploring various bugs
- Debugging techniques
- Using the debugger in Excel

By the end of this chapter, you will be able to identify different bugs. You will also be able to use various debugging techniques to eliminate bugs.

Technical requirements

This cookbook was written and designed to be used with MS Office 2019 and MS Office 365, installed on either Windows 8, 8.1, or 10.

If your hardware and software meet these requirements, you're good to go.

Demonstration files can be downloaded from `https://github.com/ PacktPublishing/VBA-Automation-for-Excel-2019-Cookbook`.

Please visit the following link to check out the CiA videos: `https://bit. ly/3jQRvVk`.

Exploring various bugs

Before getting too excited about eliminating bugs, we need to understand what we're dealing with. Some errors are obvious, and therefore, easy to find and eliminate. The syntax and compile errors discussed in *Chapter 11, Handling Errors*, fall into this category, because we eliminate them before running the procedure.

What we're dealing with here is the typical **runtime error**, which will only rear its ugly head once we run the procedure.

This is a theoretical recipe, in the sense that we are going to identify and list various bugs. Other than making notes, either in Word or Excel, nothing else is needed.

Here is a list of the different categories of bugs:

- **Logic error bugs**: The name says it all, meaning that whatever you're trying to do with your code doesn't make logical sense. A simple example would be when you assign the wrong value to a variable. All calculations related to that variable will result in incorrect results.

- **Incorrect reference bugs**: These bugs will present themselves when you refer to a range that doesn't exist, or when you refer to a file that has been moved or deleted.

- **Extreme-case bugs**: This is a less common bug, but still an annoyance. It happens when a database presents you with numbers you did not expect or plan for. These numbers would be either extremely large or extremely small, hence the reason we refer to them as extreme-case bugs.

- **Data error bugs**: Once again, the bug's name tells us what it does. This occurs, for example, when users enter text in fields where numbers are expected, or when you try to perform mathematical calculations with text strings.

- **Version bugs**: This type of bug is associated with incompatibilities between older and newer versions of Microsoft applications. Whether it's the operating system that's old, or that you developed a program in the latest version of Excel, and your users are working on an ancient version from 1995, the result will be a program crash.

- **Exceptional bugs**: These bugs are normally beyond your control in the sense that Microsoft sometimes makes updates that cause previously working procedures to end unexpectedly. Another example of an exceptional bug will be security updates, over which you obviously have no control.

Debugging techniques

We often use the word **technique** without thinking of its exact meaning. According to various dictionaries, the word refers to *a way of carrying out a particular task or a scientific procedure*, or *a skillful or efficient way of doing or achieving something*.

That is exactly what a debugging technique is; *a proven method or procedure of finding and eliminating errors in our code*.

In this recipe, we will be investigating four specific debugging techniques:

- Hover
- Message box
- `Debug.Print`
- The **Locals** window

Each of these will enable us to see what values the variables have taken on. Any errors can, therefore, be corrected before finalizing the procedure.

Getting ready

Open Excel and activate a new workbook. Save the file as a macro-enabled file on your desktop and call it Debugging.xlsm. **Sheet1** should be active. Press *Alt + F11* to switch to the VBA Editor, and then insert a new module. Switch back to Excel to enter data in **Sheet1**.

How to do it...

Let's first create some data to work with and start with the *hover* technique:

1. Enter the following data in **Sheet1**:

◢	A	B	C
1	**Name**	**Age**	**Weight(kg)**
2	Joe	35	95
3			
4			

Figure 12.1 – Data

2. Switch to the VBA Editor. In the code window, type the following code:

```
Sub DebugSample()
    Dim Name As String
    Dim Age As Integer
    Dim Weight As Double

    Name = Range("A2").Value
    Age = Range("B2").Value
    Weight = Range("C2").Value
End Sub
```

3. Press *F8* to step into the code, and then hover the mouse cursor over the Name variable:

```
⇨  Sub DebugSample()

        Dim Name As String
        D  Name = ""   Integer
        Dim Weight As Double

        Name = Range("A2").Value
        Age = Range("B2").Value
        Weight = Range("C2").Value

    End Sub
```

Figure 12.2 – Hovering over a variable

4. Press *F8* until the `Age` variable line is highlighted. Then, hover over the `Name` variable:

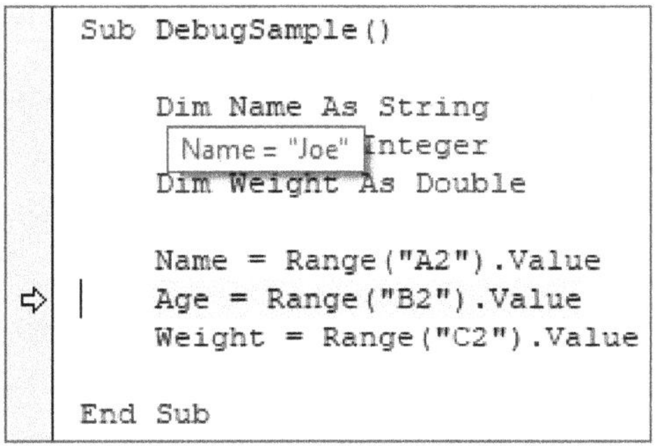

```
Sub DebugSample()

    Dim Name As String
    Name = "Joe" Integer
    Dim Weight As Double

    Name = Range("A2").Value
⇨ |  Age = Range("B2").Value
    Weight = Range("C2").Value

End Sub
```

Figure 12.3 – Name variable value

5. Press *F8* again, and then hover over the `Age` variable:

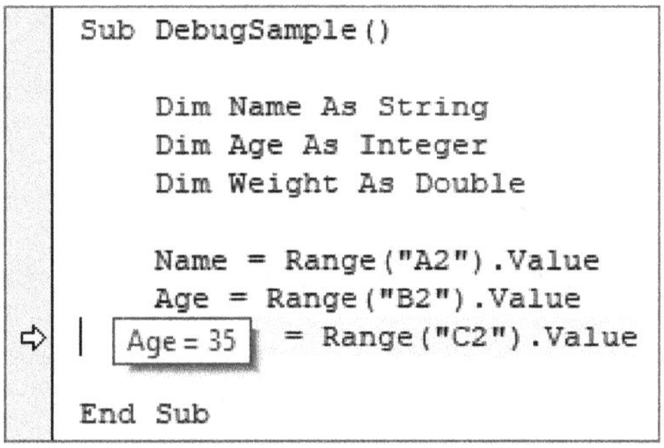

```
Sub DebugSample()

    Dim Name As String
    Dim Age As Integer
    Dim Weight As Double

    Name = Range("A2").Value
    Age = Range("B2").Value
⇨ |  Age = 35   = Range("C2").Value

End Sub
```

Figure 12.4 – Age variable value

6. Now, press *F8* for the last time and then hover over the `Weight` variable to view the value of the variable.

Now, let's move on to the second technique, which is message box:

1. Add the following line of code:

```
MsgBox Name & vbNewLine & Age & vbNewLine & Weight
```

The complete procedure should look like this:

```
Sub DebugSample()
    Dim Name As String
    Dim Age As Integer
    Dim Weight As Double
```

```
    Name = Range("A2").Value
    Age = Range("B2").Value
    Weight = Range("C2").Value

    MsgBox Name & vbNewLine & Age & vbNewLine & Weight
End Sub
```

2. Press *F5* to run the procedure:

Figure 12.5 – Message box displaying values

3. Click **OK** to close the message box.

The third technique that we will implement now is the Debug.Print technique:

1. First, either delete the line with the MsgBox instruction or simply turn it into a comment by placing an apostrophe in front.

2. Start by activating the **Immediate** window – click **View | Immediate Window**.

3. Add the following line to the procedure:

```
Debug.Print Name, Age, Weight
```

The complete procedure should look like this:

```
Sub DebugSample()
    Dim Name As String
    Dim Age As Integer
    Dim Weight As Double

    Name = Range("A2").Value
    Age = Range("B2").Value
    Weight = Range("C2").Value

    Debug.Print Name, Age, Weight
End Sub
```

4. Step into the code with *F8*, or press *F5* to run the procedure. The variable values appear in the **Immediate** window:

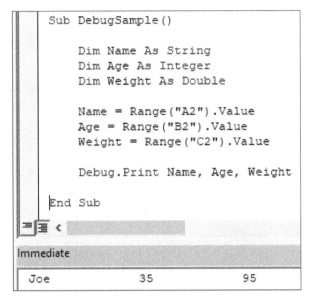

```vba
Sub DebugSample()

    Dim Name As String
    Dim Age As Integer
    Dim Weight As Double

    Name = Range("A2").Value
    Age = Range("B2").Value
    Weight = Range("C2").Value

    Debug.Print Name, Age, Weight

End Sub
```

Immediate

| Joe | 35 | 95 |

Figure 12.6 – Variable values in the Immediate window

The final technique involves the **Locals** window, which will be implemented using the following steps:

1. Activate the **Locals** window by clicking **View | Locals Window** after closing the **Immediate** window.

2. With the **Locals** window open at the bottom of the VBA Editor, press *F8*.

3.　All the variables will appear in this window, without displaying values. Keep pressing *F8* until each variable's value is displayed:

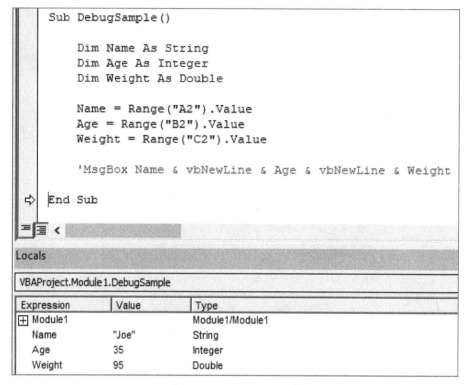

Figure 12.7 – Variable values in the Locals window

These techniques can be used as needed, and not in any specific order of importance.

How it works...

Let's look at the details of the samples we've just worked with:

- **First technique**: Hovering over any of the variable names will display a screen tip. Initially, not one of the variables will have a value assigned to it.

  By pressing *F8*, values will be assigned, one by one, to each variable. Hovering over the variable names will confirm what value has been assigned to which variable.

- **Second technique**: When running the procedure while the message box function is active, variable values will be displayed there. This is another way of confirming variable values.

- **Third technique**: `Debug.Print` can be used if you do not want message boxes to assist you with variable values. Depending on the number of variables in your code, this technique can be used to verify values in one window, all at the same time.

- **Fourth technique**: The **Locals** window is similar to `Debug.Print`, with the added advantage that you do not need any extra line of code to display the values. Furthermore, it also tells you what data type your variable is.

You can use any of these debugging techniques to determine whether variables have taken on the correct values.

Using the debugger in Excel

Using the debugger is yet another debugging technique, but it has greater power and flexibility. It is not necessarily better or easier to use, it is just a slightly more advanced way of checking your code for errors.

The debugger is, in fact, a set of tools in the VBA environment, specifically incorporated in the VBA Editor to ease the process of debugging.

We will be using two tools in this section:

- Setting breakpoints
- Using the **Watch** window

Setting breakpoints

The first tool under discussion allows you to inspect your code by stopping it at specific, pre-set points. It is, in a way, similar to the `MsgBox` function, because it also halts the running of your procedure in the middle of execution. The difference, however, is that you don't have to click on buttons to close dialog boxes, because you'll only work in the VBA Editor.

In this recipe, we will be going through the details of setting breakpoints.

Getting ready

Make sure that `Debugging.xlsm` is still open. Insert a new sheet, and ensure that **Sheet2** is active. Press *Alt + F11* to switch to the VBA Editor. Insert a new module.

If the **Debug** toolbar is not yet active in your VBA Editor, do that now by right-clicking anywhere in the toolbar area. In the pop-up menu that appears, select the top option, **Debug**. A new toolbar will appear to the right of the standard toolbar. If necessary, you can drag and drop this new toolbar to a position below the standard toolbar:

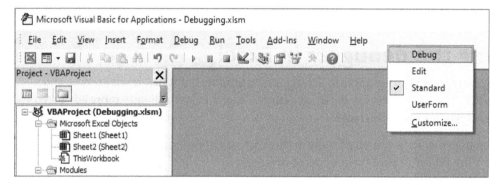

Figure 12.8 – Activating the Debug toolbar

The VBA Editor should now look like this:

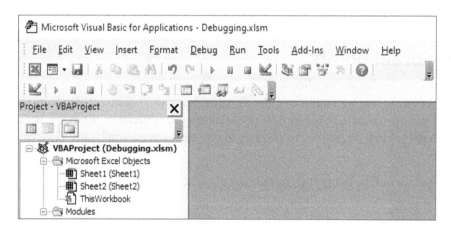

Figure 12.9 – The Debug toolbar in position

Finally, resize both the VBA Editor and Excel in such a way that both windows are visible next to each other:

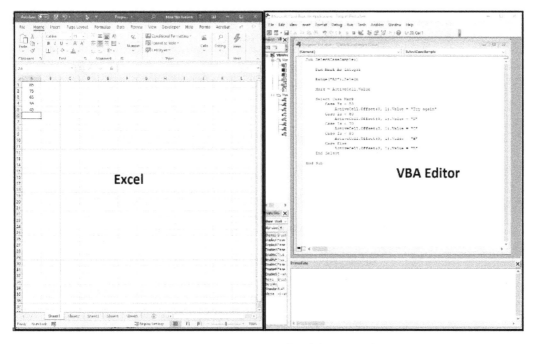

Figure 12.10 – Viewing Excel and the VBA Editor

How to do it...

First, we'll need some data to work with to start with this recipe, so proceed with the following steps:

1. Enter the following data in **Sheet2**:

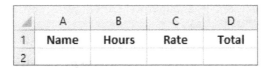

Figure 12.11 – Data

2. Switch to the VBA Editor, and then enter the following code in **Module2**:

```
Sub TotalPay()
    Dim AddName As String
    Dim HoursWorked As Double
    Dim WageRate As Double

    AddName = InputBox("Enter your name")
    Range("A2").Value = AddName
```

```
        HoursWorked = InputBox("Enter your hours worked")
        Range("B2").Value = HoursWorked
        WageRate = InputBox("Enter your hourly rate")
        Range("C2").Value = WageRate
        Range("D2").Value = HoursWorked * WageRate
    End Sub
```

3.   Click in the last line of the code, just before End Sub, where the calculated value will be assigned to cell D2.

4.   Enter a breakpoint in one of the following three ways:

Press *F9*.

Or click on the Toggle Breakpoint icon on the **Debug** toolbar:

Figure 12.12 – Toggle Breakpoint icon

Or click in the gray margin to the left of the line:

```
Sub TotalPay()

    Dim AddName As String
    Dim HoursWorked As Double
    Dim WageRate As Double

    AddName = InputBox("Enter your name")
    Range("A2").Value = AddName
    HoursWorked = InputBox("Enter your hours worked")
    Range("B2").Value = HoursWorked
    WageRate = InputBox("Enter your hourly rate")
    Range("C2").Value = WageRate
    Range("D2").Value = HoursWorked * WageRate

End Sub
```

Figure 12.13 – Inserted breakpoint

5.   Press *F5* to run the procedure.

6.   Enter values in the dialog boxes as they appear, clicking **OK** each time.

7.   With the execution halted, hover over any of the three variables:

```
Sub TotalPay()

    Dim AddName As String
    Dim HoursWorked As Double
    Dim WageRate As Double

    AddName = InputBox("Enter your name")
    Range("A2").Value = AddName
    HoursWorked = InputBox("Enter your hours worked")
    Range("B2").Value = HoursWorked
    WageRa Range("B2").Value = 30  ter your hourly rate")
    Range("C2").Value = WageRate
    Range("D2").Value = HoursWorked * WageRate

End Sub
```

Figure 12.14 – Code stopped at the breakpoint

8. Press *F5* to execute the final line of code.

9. Use any of the three methods again under *step 4* to remove the breakpoint.

How it works...

Let's see how these steps work:

1. We normally set a breakpoint in the code to check for bugs, or to check whether the calculated values of variables are correct.

2. By setting a breakpoint in the final line of code, we allow values to be assigned to all the variables.

3. This debugging technique is less disruptive than others, for the simple reason that we do not leave the VBA Editor environment at any point.

4. It also allows us to edit our code by correcting errors, if there were any.

5. By removing the breakpoint, we can insert it at any other point in the code.

6. If necessary, we can insert more than one breakpoint.

7. To proceed after the execution of the procedure has been stopped, we can either press *F5*, or step into each line of the remaining code by pressing *F8*.

8. To remove the breakpoint, press *F9* again, or click on the red dot in the margin, or use the icon on the toolbar.

Setting a breakpoint is one of a series of tools that assists us in debugging our code.

Using the Watch window

In this recipe, we will be using the **Watch** window, one last debugging tool in the VBA Editor. Every tool discussed in this chapter has its own time and place, meaning that none is better or worse than the other.

Where the **Locals** window displays all the variables simultaneously, the **Watch** window enables us to choose which ones to observe. You can watch a single variable or all the variables in a procedure. You can even place a watch on variables from other modules, should you wish.

Getting ready

Make sure that Debugging.xlsm is still open. **Sheet2** should be active, and Excel and the VBA Editor should be tiled vertically, next to each other. We will be working on the code in **Module2**.

How to do it...

To go about this recipe, we'll need to go through the following steps:

1. First, we need to display the **Watch** window, so close the **Locals** or **Immediate** windows if either one is still open.

2. On the **Debug** toolbar, click the Watch Window icon:

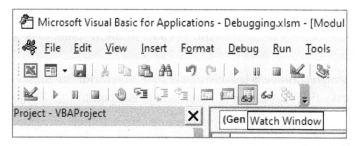

Figure 12.15 – Activating the Watch window

3. The alternative would be to click on **View | Watch Window**.

4. The **Watch** window will appear at the bottom of the VBA Editor:

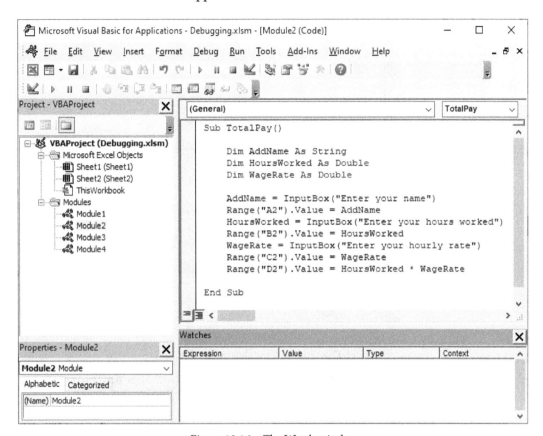

Figure 12.16 – The Watch window

5. Let's watch one specific variable in the procedure. Right-click on the `WageRate` variable. From the pop-up menu, choose **Add Watch…** to display the **Watch** window:

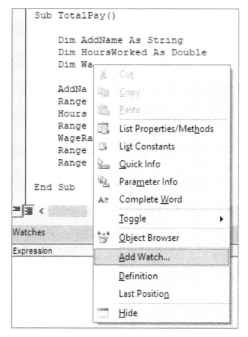

Figure 12.17 – Adding a watch to a variable

6. The following dialog box will appear. Since we don't need to change anything, click **OK**:

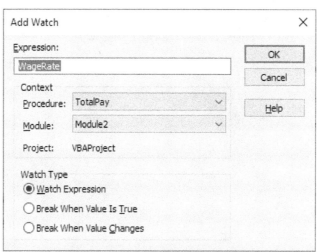

Figure 12.18 – The Add Watch dialog box

7. Another way of adding a watch is to right-click in the **Watch** window itself. Select the **Add Watch…** option:

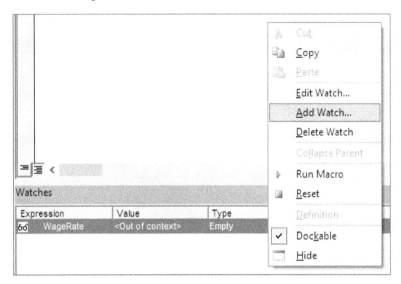

Figure 12.19 – Add Watch… from the Watch window

8. This time, we need to type in the name of the variable we want to watch:

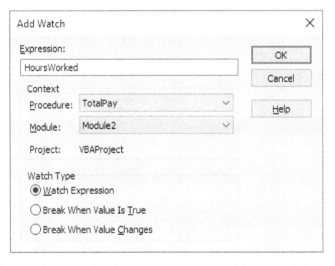

Figure 12.20 – Entering the variable name in the Add Watch dialog box

9. The second variable will now also be displayed in the **Watch** window:

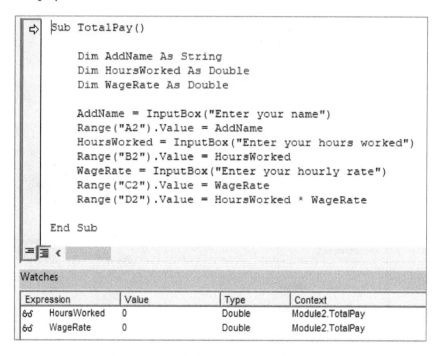

Figure 12.21 – Second watch added

10. Press *F8* to start stepping through the procedure. Only the marked variables' values are displayed:

```
Sub TotalPay()

    Dim AddName As String
    Dim HoursWorked As Double
    Dim WageRate As Double

    AddName = InputBox("Enter your name")
    Range("A2").Value = AddName
    HoursWorked = InputBox("Enter your hours worked")
    Range("B2").Value = HoursWorked
    WageRate = InputBox("Enter your hourly rate")
    Range("C2").Value = WageRate
    Range("D2").Value = HoursWorked * WageRate

End Sub
```

Watches			
Expression	Value	Type	Context
𝖗𝖗 HoursWorked	0	Double	Module2.TotalPay
𝖗𝖗 WageRate	0	Double	Module2.TotalPay

Figure 12.22 – Variables in the Watch window

11. Press *F8* until values have been assigned to both variables. Make changes in the code window, should it be necessary.

The **Watch** window can inspect a single variable at a time or as many as you choose. Once again, it's a debugging tool for specific situations. The choice is yours.

How it works...

1. The **Watch** window will not display any variables unless we nominate the ones we want to check.

2. Once we've selected the variables we want to verify the values of, they will be displayed in the **Watch** window.

3. Whenever the values of the variables change, they will be displayed in the **Watch** window.

4. Any changes we need to make can be done in the code window, without interruption.

5. If we need to recheck the values, then reset the procedure by clicking on the icon in the **Debug** toolbar. Run the procedure, or step through it again.

Debugging tools have been designed to assist us with debugging our code.

13
Creating and Modifying Dialog Boxes

Dialog boxes are an integral part of every application in the Windows environment. The Office Suite is no exception. When it comes to Excel, a dialog box will pop up almost every time we interact with the application.

A dialog box should not be confused with a window. Windows can be resized, maximized, and minimized, while dialog boxes cannot be manipulated in that way. They appear in a standard size when information needs to be gathered or shared, after which they're closed.

This broad description of dialog boxes includes all forms and shapes of the item. For the purposes of this chapter, we will only work with message boxes, input boxes, and the open and close dialog boxes. On the other hand, UserForms, which are a more elaborate type of dialog boxes, will be discussed in the next chapter.

We've used message boxes as well as input boxes in the previous chapters, but we're going to take things to a new level here—we'll add icons and titles this time. Even the humble message box can do more than just display a message.

In this chapter, we will cover the following recipes:

- Using the `MsgBox` function
- Using the `InputBox` function
- Using the `Application.InputBox` method

By the end of this chapter, you will be able to write code to effectively activate message boxes and input boxes.

Technical requirements

This cookbook was written and designed to be used with MS Office 2019 and MS Office 365, installed on either Windows 8, 8.1, or 10. If your hardware and software meet these requirements, you are good to go.

Demonstration files can be downloaded from `https://github.com/PacktPublishing/VBA-Automation-for-Excel-2019-Cookbook`.

Please visit the following link to check out the CiA videos: `https://bit.ly/3jQRvVk`.

Using the MsgBox function

A message box is the easiest, and also the most common, way of sharing information with users. As well as the built-in message boxes that appear in Excel whenever the application needs to inform you of something, we can create and customize our own message boxes in VBA.

In this recipe, we will be using the `MsgBox` function to create and manipulate message boxes to suit our needs.

Getting ready

Open Excel, and activate a new workbook. Save the file as a macro-enabled file on your desktop and call it `DialogBoxes.xlsm`. `Sheet1` should be active. Press *Alt + F11* to switch to the VBA Editor, then insert a new module.

How to do it...

Let's build and expand the code for message boxes:

1. Enter the following code in the code window of **Module1**:

```
Sub SimpleMessage()
    MsgBox "Basic message box."
End Sub
```

2. Press *F5* to run the procedure. This is the message box you should see. Click **OK** to close it:

Figure 13.1 – A simple message box

3. To customize the title of the message box, click at the end of the line of code and type a comma to make the parameter list appear:

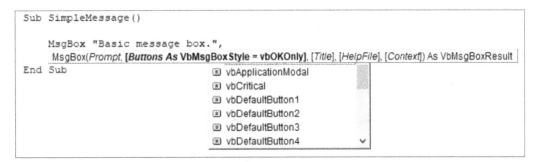

Figure 13.2 – The parameter list

4. With the `Buttons` parameter now highlighted, scroll down the list of available symbols. Select and click on `vbInformation`:

```
Sub SimpleMessage()

    MsgBox "Basic message box.",vb
    MsgBox(Prompt, [Buttons As VbMs  ▣ vbDefaultButton3        ∧ e], [Context]) As VbMsgBoxResult
End Sub                               ▣ vbDefaultButton4
                                      ▣ vbExclamation
                                      ▣ vbInformation
                                      ▣ vbMsgBoxHelpButton
                                      ▣ vbMsgBoxRight
                                      ▣ vbMsgBoxRtlReading  ∨
```

Figure 13.3 – The parameter list

5. Enter another comma after `vbInformation` to enter a title for the dialog box:

```
Sub SimpleMessage()
    MsgBox "Basic message box.", vbInformation, _
    "Announcement"
End Sub
```

6. Press *F5* to run the code. The customized message box should look like this:

Figure 13.4 – Customized message box

7. Close the message box. Let's concatenate, or join, if you will, a message with a VBA function. Create a new Sub procedure under the existing one, still in **Module1**, by adding the following code:

```
Sub ConcatenateLines()
    MsgBox "The date is " & Date
End Sub
```

8. Run the code. The following message box will appear:

Figure 13.5 – Concatenated strings

9. Click **OK** to close, then add more information with another ampersand. Enter the following code:

```
Sub ConcatenateLines()
    MsgBox "The date is " & Date & ", week 32 of the _
    year."
End Sub
```

10. Run the procedure, and see how the message has changed:

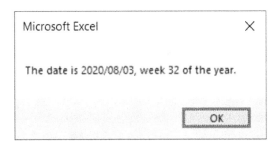

Figure 13.6 – Added information

11. Close the message box. If the information is too much for one line, we can create a new line with the vbNewLine command:

```
Sub ConcatenateLines()
    MsgBox "The date is " & Date & "," & vbNewLine _
    & "week 32 of the year."
End Sub
```

12. When you run the procedure this time, the message box will look like this:

Figure 13.7 – Message over two lines

13. Message boxes can also be used to display values from cells. Press *F11* to switch to Excel, then enter the following data in `Sheet1`:

	A	B	C
1	**Name**	**Dept**	**Age**
2	Joe	HR	25
3	Sue	Sales	32
4	Fred	Tech	30
5	Anne	Training	27

Figure 13.8 – Data

14. Switch back to the VBA Editor. In the code window, create another new Sub procedure by adding the following code:

```
Sub DepartmentInfo()
    Range("A2").Select
    MsgBox ActiveCell.Value & " works in " _
    & ActiveCell.Offset(0, 1).Value
End Sub
```

15. Pressing *F5* will display the following message box:

Figure 13.9 – Values from cells

By changing the range to cell A3, A4, or A5, you will get different results every time.

16. We can even ask questions with a message box. Alter the code of the second procedure as follows:

```
Sub ConcatenateLines()
    MsgBox "The date is " & Date & "," & vbNewLine _
    & "week 32 of the year."

    MsgBox "Is this information correct?", vbQuestion _
    + vbYesNo, "Validate"
End Sub
```

17. Run the procedure and click **OK** to close the first message box. The second message box should look like this:

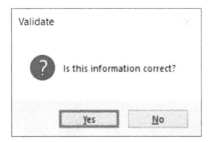

Figure 13.10 – Message box with Yes/No buttons

18. Since there is no way that we can store the choice, be it yes or no, we need to address that next. First, we need to create a variable to store the response. Add the following line of code to the procedure, before the first MsgBox function:

```
Dim ButtonChoice As VbMsgBoxResult
```

19. Assign the button choice to the variable by changing the second dialog box as follows:

```
ButtonChoice = MsgBox("Is this information correct?", _
    vbQuestion + vbYesNo, "Validate")
```

Take note of the parentheses that's been added to the message box prompt.

20. We now need to add an `If` statement to check which button was clicked. Add the following code after the previous line:

```
If ButtonChoice = vbYes Then
    MsgBox "Yes, it is correct."
Else
    MsgBox "No, it is incorrect."
End If
```

21. The final procedure should look like this:

```
Sub ConcatenateLines()
Dim ButtonChoice As VbMsgBoxResult

MsgBox "The date is " & Date & "," & vbNewLine _
& "week 32 of the year."

ButtonChoice = MsgBox("Is this information _
correct?", vbQuestion + vbYesNo, "Validate")

If ButtonChoice = vbYes Then
    MsgBox "Yes, it is correct."
Else
    MsgBox "No, it is incorrect."
End If
End Sub
```

22. Press *F5* to run the procedure. Click **OK** to close the first message box. When the second box appears, click **Yes**. The following message should appear:

Figure 13.11 – Confirmed as correct

23. Press *F5* to run the procedure one last time. After the first dialog box is closed, choose **No**. The following message should appear:

Figure 13.12 – Incorrect

Your imagination is the only limit when it comes to message boxes. These examples will give you a good starting point.

How it works...

Here is the explanation of what we did with message boxes:

1. The MsgBox function, in its simplest form, can be used to display a message box containing a text message of your choice.

2. To customize the MsgBox function, carefully read the IntelliSense guidelines. After the basic prompt, you can add symbols and a title for the message box.

3. The message that appears in the message box can also be enhanced. Use the ampersand (&) to combine strings of text or other functions.

4. If the line of text on the message box becomes too long, use the vbNewLine command in the Sub procedure to create a new line.

5. We sometimes need information from a specific cell or cells to be displayed in a message box. To achieve that, assign the MsgBox function to the cell.

6. There are more buttons than just the standard **OK** button available for use with message boxes. Use the buttons parameter to select, for instance, the **Yes/No** buttons.

7. Without some way of assigning the **Yes** or **No** choice to either a database or a variable, the buttons are not of much use.

8. Create a variable to store the choice. Then, use the If function to display either a **Yes** message box or a **No** message box.

Using the InputBox function

Input boxes are used to capture information from users. By its very nature, it obtains only one piece of information at a time, be it a value, date, or text information. It is the easiest, and also the most common way of gathering information from users.

Like message boxes, we can create and customize our own input boxes in VBA.

In this recipe, we will be using the `InputBox` function to create and manipulate input boxes to suit our needs.

Getting ready

Make sure that `DialogBoxes.xlsm` is still open. `Sheet1` should be active. Press *Alt + F11* to switch to the VBA Editor, then insert a new module.

How to do it...

Enter the following code to create an input box:

1. In **Module2**, create the following Sub procedure:

    ```
    Sub AskForName()
        InputBox "Please enter your name"
    End Sub
    ```

2. Press *F5* to run the code. The following input box will appear. Click on the **Cancel** button to close the dialog box:

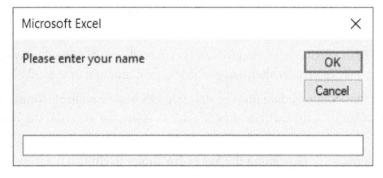

Figure 13.13 – A standard input box

3. To customize the input box, click at the end of the code line and enter a comma. The parameter list will appear. Take note that the last parameter specifies that the entry must be a string value:

```
Sub AskForName()

    InputBox "Please enter your name",|
     InputBox(Prompt, [Title], [Default], [XPos], [YPos], [HelpFile], [Context]) As String
End Sub
```

Figure 13.14 – Parameter list

4. Add a title for the input box by adding "Personal Details" after the comma:

```
Sub AskForName()

    InputBox "Please enter your name", "Personal Details"
    |
End Sub
```

Figure 13.15 – Title added in code

5. Press *F5* to run the code. The input box has a new title:

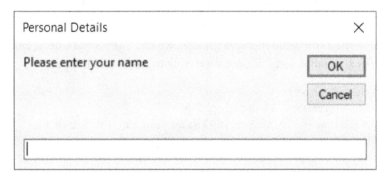

Figure 13.16 – New title in input box

6. We can even change the default value of the input box. Edit the text as follows:

```
Sub AskForName()
    InputBox "Please enter your name", "Personal _
    Details", "Enter first name here…"
End Sub
```

7. Press *F5*, and observe the resulting input box:

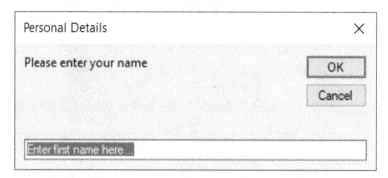

Figure 13.17 – Default value

8. Next, we want to capture what's been entered in the input box. Change the code as follows. Make sure that the arguments are put in parentheses:

```
Sub AskForName()
    Range("A2").Value = InputBox("Please enter your _
    name", "Personal Details")
End Sub
```

9. Press *F5* to run the code, enter your name in the input box, then click **OK**. Switch back to Excel to confirm that your name has been entered on cell A2.

10. Instead of writing the value to a specific cell, we can store what's been entered in the input box in a variable. Let's declare a variable to make this happen:

```
Sub AskForName()
    Dim YourName As String
    YourName = InputBox("Please enter your name", _
    "Personal Details")
End Sub
```

11. When you run the procedure, no entries or dialog boxes will be visible. Let's take care of that problem by adding a message box:

```
Sub AskForName()
    Dim YourName As String
    YourName = InputBox("Please enter your name", _
    "Personal Details")
    MsgBox "Hi " & YourName
End Sub
```

12. Run the code, enter your name, and click **OK**. The following dialog box will appear:

Figure 13.18 – Variable value displayed

13. When things go according to plan and users enter their names, as expected, we don't have any problems. When they cancel the input box without entering a name, the message box will not have any value to display. Let's take care of that.

14. Edit the procedure as follows:

```
Sub AskForName()
    Dim YourName As String
    YourName = InputBox("Please enter your name", _
    "Personal Details")
    If YourName = "" Then
        MsgBox "No entry was made"
    Else
        MsgBox "Hi " & YourName
    End If
End Sub
```

15. If you now run the procedure and cancel or close the input box, a message box will tell you that no entry was made. However, if you do enter a name, you will be greeted with the original message box.

How it works...

1. A convenient way to ask for information in Excel is to use an input box. It is the simplest way for users to interact and provide information.

2. Input boxes can be customized as far as the title, prompt, default value, and symbol are concerned. The parameter list serves as a guide to what can be added.

3. Values entered into an input box are often stored as a variable.

4. As in so many cases when programming in VBA, we need to plan for user errors. An example of this is **data validation**, which was covered in detail in *Chapter 12, Debugging*. Always add code to do data validation.

Knowing how to use the `InputBox` function is the first step of interacting with users.

Using the Application.InputBox method

The standard input box works well enough, until you try to capture data other than text. You're also limited to direct inputs, meaning that you cannot click on a value in the spreadsheet while the input box is active.

These are the two main limitations of the standard input box. The other one, *the absence of built-in error handling*, is also a drawback. There are, in other words, more than enough reasons to progress to the `Application.InputBox` method.

In this recipe, we will be using the `Application.InputBox` method to create input boxes with more functionality.

Getting ready

Make sure that `DialogBoxes.xlsm` is still open. Insert a new sheet and enter the following data on **Sheet2**:

	A	B	C
1	**Name**	**Age**	**Start Date**
2	Joe	25	01-Feb-17
3	Sue	35	01-Jun-15
4	Fred	28	01-Sep-13
5			

Figure 13.19 – Sample data

Now, switch to the VBA Editor and insert a new module.

How to do it...

Enter the following partial code to create an application input box:

1. In **Module3**, start creating the following Sub procedure:

```
Sub ApplicationInputBox()
    Dim Name As String
    Name = Application.InputBox(

End Sub
```

2. Before typing in the prompt, observe how the parameter list differs from the standard input box:

```
Sub ApplicationInputBox()

    Dim Name As String
    Dim StartDate As Date

    Name = Application.InputBox(|
                        InputBox(Prompt As String, [Title], [Default], [Left], [Top], [HelpFile], [HelpContextID], [Type])
```

Figure 13.20 – The parameter list for Application.InputBox

3. Complete the Sub procedure now. You do not have to specify a data type, because the default, namely `String`, will automatically be applied:

```
Sub ApplicationInputBox()
    Dim Name As String
    Name = Application.InputBox("Enter employee's name")
    Range("A1").End(xlDown).Offset(1, 0).Value = Name
End Sub
```

4. Press *F5* to run the code. The following input box will show. Enter a name, then click **OK**:

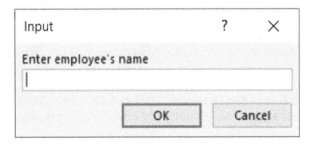

Figure 13.21 – An application input box

5. The data on **Sheet2** should be updated to include an extra name:

⊿	A	B	C
1	Name	Age	Start Date
2	Joe	25	01/02/2017
3	Sue	35	01/06/2015
4	Fred	28	01/09/2013
5	Mike		

Figure 13.22 – Updated data

6. For entering a number, there are two ways to handle the process required. The first is the following:

```
Sub ApplicationInputBox()
    Dim Name As String
    Dim Age As Integer

    Name = Application.InputBox("Enter employee's name")
    Age = Application.InputBox("Enter his/her age", , _
    , , , , 1)

    Range("A1").End(xlDown).Offset(1, 0).Value = Name
    Range("A1").End(xlDown).Offset(0, 1).Value = Age
End Sub
```

7. The second way is to use named parameters. This is a shorter and less complex technique. Entering all those commas in order to skip parameters to get to the Type parameter is confusing. Here is how we could do it differently:

```
Sub ApplicationInputBox()
    Dim Name As String
    Dim Age As Integer

    Name = Application.InputBox("Enter employee's name")
    Age = Application.InputBox(Prompt:="Enter his/her _
    age", Type:=1)

    Range("A1").End(xlDown).Offset(1, 0).Value = Name
    Range("A1").End(xlDown).Offset(0, 1).Value = Age
End Sub
```

8. When accidentally entering text, the following dialog box will appear:

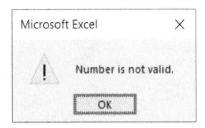

Figure 13.23 – Built-in validation

9. Run the procedure again, but instead of entering a name, click any cell with a name and press *Enter*. Next, choose a cell in column **B** to select an age value and press *Enter*:

◢	A	B	C	D
1	**Name**	**Age**	**Start Date**	
2	Joe	25	01/02/2017	
3	Sue	35	01/06/2015	
4	Fred	28	01/09/2013	
5	Mike			
6				
7				

Input   ?   ✕

Enter his/her age

= B2

OK   Cancel

Figure 13.24 – Clicking a cell to capture data

10. These values will be entered into the table:

◢	A	B	C
1	**Name**	**Age**	**Start Date**
2	Joe	25	01/02/2017
3	Sue	35	01/06/2015
4	Fred	28	01/09/2013
5	Mike		
6	Bill	25	

Figure 13.25 – Indirect entries

11. To capture dates, enter the following code:

```
Sub ApplicationInputBox()
    Dim Name As String
    Dim Age As Integer
    Dim StartDate As Date

    Name = Application.InputBox("Enter employee's name")
    Age = Application.InputBox(Prompt:="Enter his/her _
    age", Type:=1)
    StartDate = Application.InputBox(Prompt:="Enter _
    employment date dd/mm/yyyy", Type:=1)

    Range("A1").End(xlDown).Offset(1, 0).Value = Name
    Range("A1").End(xlDown).Offset(0, 1).Value = Age
    Range("A1").End(xlDown).Offset(0, 2).Value =
StartDate
End Sub
```

12. Run the code and enter values in the **Name** and **Age** boxes. For **Start Date**, you can enter anything that is recognizable as a full date, for example, 1/12/2015, or 1 December, 2015. See *Step 7* under the *How it works...* section on implicit datatype conversion.

	A	B	C
1	Name	Age	Start Date
2	Joe	25	01/02/2017
3	Sue	35	01/06/2015
4	Fred	28	01/09/2013
5	Mike		
6	Bill	25	
7	Anne	29	01/12/2015
8			

Figure 13.26 – Date displayed in the correct format

How it works...

1. The parameter list for the application input box differs from the standard input box. There are more options and, most importantly, we can assign a data type with the last parameter.

2. The following values should be used to indicate data types:

Value	Description
0	Formulas
1	Numbers
2	Text (a string)
4	Logical values (True or False)
8	Cell references, as a Range object
16	Error values, such as #N/A
64	Arrays of values

Table13.1 – Indicating data types

3. The application input box looks slightly different from the standard input box, but it fulfills the same function.

4. Specifying the return type is the most important factor distinguishing this input box from the standard input box. Using the Type 1 parameter, for example, will allow only numbers to be entered into the input box.

5. When entering the wrong data type, the built-in validation function will prevent the procedure from crashing. With a normal input box, you'd have a lot of work to write error-handling procedures.

6. Another valuable feature of the application input box is its ability to use existing values on the spreadsheet to fill the input box. Standard input boxes are of the modal type, meaning that nothing can be selected on the spreadsheet while the input box is open. That limitation means that you cannot click on a cell to read in that cell's value into the text box.

7. Dealing with dates is another challenge, because the application input box does not have a date type option. However, with the help of implicit datatype conversion, a string entry can be converted to a date, as long as the string is recognizable as a full date.

> **Note**
>
> For more detailed information on the `Application.InputBox` method, have a look at the Microsoft documentation, available at `https://docs.microsoft.com/en-us/office/vba/api/excel.application.inputbox`.

14
Creating UserForms

A macro is a wonderful time-saving tool in the Excel environment, but it has its limitations. When we want to run a macro, we have to click on ribbons and icons before choosing the desired macro from a list. Sure, we can use shortcuts, but you can only remember so many keyboard shortcuts.

Wouldn't it be wonderful if we could send data to a macro, and then watch as it populates a table for us?

So, welcome to UserForms, the interface between macros and spreadsheets. With UserForms, we can not only automate data capturing but also add buttons to activate macros on our spreadsheets. We are, in reality, going to create our own customized dialog boxes.

In this chapter, we will cover the following recipes:

- Inserting the form
- Changing properties
- Adding controls
- Using Frames

By the end of this chapter, you will be able to create your own UserForms.

Technical requirements

This cookbook was written and designed to be used with MS Office 2019 and MS Office 365, installed on either Windows 8, 8.1, or 10.

Demonstration files can be downloaded from `https://github.com/ PacktPublishing/VBA-Automation-for-Excel-2019-Cookbook`.

Please visit the following link to check out the CiA videos: `https://bit. ly/3jQRvVk`.

If your hardware and software meet these requirements, you are ready for this chapter.

Inserting the form

Unlike macros, UserForms are not created in newly inserted modules. They live elsewhere, which is what we're going to work on now.

In this recipe, we will be inserting a UserForm in the VBA Editor.

Getting ready

Open Excel and activate a new workbook. Save the file as a macro-enabled file on your desktop and call it `UserForms.xlsm`. **Sheet1** should be active.

How to do it...

Let's insert our first UserForm using the following steps:

1. Enter the following data into **Sheet1**. We will be creating a form to later add more data to this list:

	A	B	C	D	E	F
1	ID	Name	Dept	Age	Start Date	
2	1	Joe	HR	28	2015/06/01	
3	2	Sue	Sales	30	2017/02/01	
4						

Figure 14.1 – Data on Sheet1

2. Press *Alt + F11* to switch to the VBA Editor.
3. Right-click somewhere in the Project Explorer. From the pop-up menu that appears, select **Insert**, then click on **UserForm**:

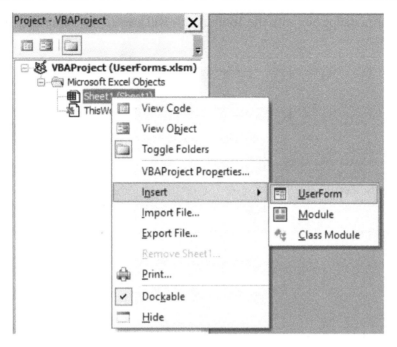

Figure 14.2 – Inserting a UserForm

4. A blank **UserForm1** window will appear to the right, and an icon for **UserForm1** will appear in the Project Explorer:

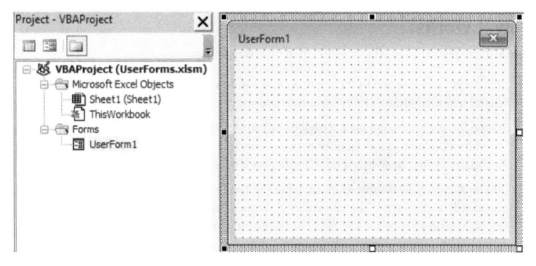

Figure 14.3 – Newly inserted UserForm1

5. By default, a dialog box with the **Toolbox** title will also appear somewhere in the VBA Editor:

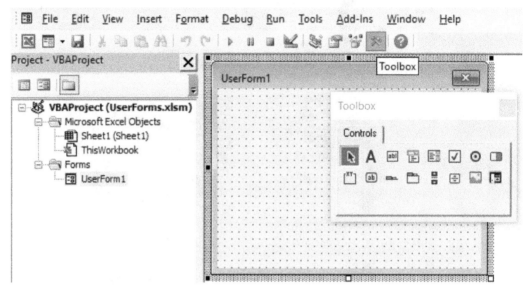

Figure 14.4 – The default Toolbox window for UserForms

That will take care of inserting a new form. Now that it's there, we can start working on the rest.

How it works...

Here is the explanation of what we did when inserting a form:

1. Forms are not inserted in the normal code window. Therefore, we do not have to insert a new module to insert or create a form.

2. Once the UserForm appears, a toolbox will appear by default. We will be using this toolbox a bit later in this chapter to insert controls. Click on the Toolbox icon in the standard toolbar to switch it off. Clicking on it again will make it reappear.

3. If you accidentally double-click anywhere in the form, the code window for the form will be displayed. You can either close the code window from the top right-hand corner or double-click on the Form icon in the Project Explorer.

Changing properties

The first thing we need to do after inserting a UserForm is to change certain properties. The **Properties** window displays a list of 35 different properties that can be changed, but we're going to start off slow. Once you know how to change one property, the rest will be easy.

In this recipe, we will be changing properties on a UserForm.

Getting ready

Make sure that UserForms.xlsm is still open. **UserForm1** should be visible, and both the Project Explorer and the **Properties** window should be visible on the left of the VBA Editor.

How to do it...

Let's start by changing the first property:

1. We need to give **UserForm1** a more appropriate name. In the **Properties** window, click on the first property of the form, and type in frmNewRecord:

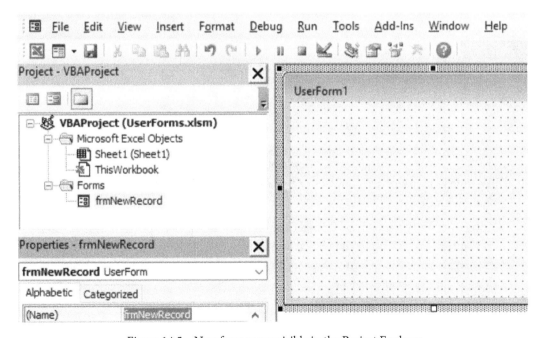

Figure 14.5 – New form name visible in the Project Explorer

> **Note**
>
> This recipe book uses Hungarian notation as standard. Read more about its origin here: https://en.wikipedia.org/wiki/Hungarian_notation.
>
> A list of prefixes can be found here: https://www.databasezone.com/techdocs/naming.html.

2.   Next, we're going to change the **Caption** property. Scroll down on the properties list until you see the **Caption** property. Type New Record Entry Form and press *Enter* when done:

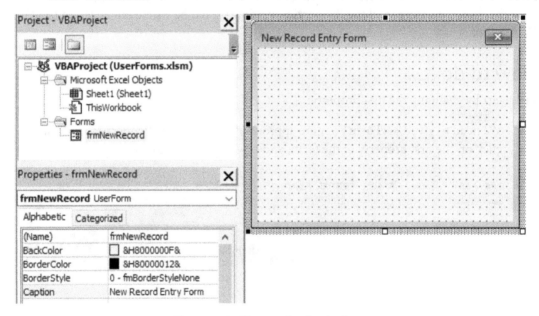

Figure 14.6 – New caption for the form

Take note that spaces are allowed for this property, while the **Name** property will not allow spaces.

3.   Another property that can be changed, although it is not as important as the **Name** and **Caption** properties, is the background property. Click on the drop-down arrow to the right of the **BackColor** property. Scroll up and down the list of available colors to choose an alternative:

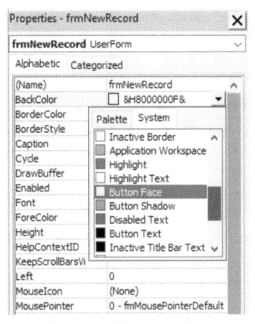

Figure 14.7 – The System colors

4. The **System** tab's colors are limited, so you can always choose from the **Palette** tab. Click on the **Palette** tab to display this somewhat more expansive range of colors:

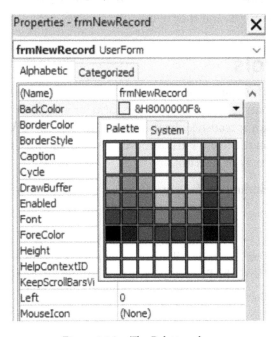

Figure 14.8 – The Palette colors

Changing properties on a UserForm is another way of saying changing the appearance of a form.

How it works...

Changing properties works as follows:

1. Whenever we need to change the property of an object, we need to make sure that the object is selected. Since the UserForm is the only object in our project, we can only change properties for the form.

2. By selecting a property in the **Properties** window, we can change that specific property by typing a new value to the right of the property.

3. In other cases, we change properties by selecting from a list of available colors, for instance.

4. Other properties still present options such as **True** or **False**, **Font Names**, and options **1** or **2**.

5. While changing the names and captions will make recognizing the form easier, we need to be careful when changing background colors. Too dark, and users won't be able to read the text on the form. At the same time, forms with colors that are too bright can be distracting, so it is better to keep to the standard Microsoft colors. Users don't like surprises, and they're used to tones of gray in forms.

Adding controls

UserForms with meaningful names and customized background colors are still not worth much. We need to add controls to bring life to the form, or at least to make it useful. After all, if we want to populate a spreadsheet by using a dialog box, there must be someplace for us to enter that data on the form. Furthermore, it would be nice to have some controls or buttons to cancel the entry or save it.

In this recipe, we will be adding controls to a UserForm.

Getting ready

Make sure that UserForms.xlsm is still open. **UserForm1** should be visible, and both the Project Explorer and the **Properties** window should be visible on the left of the VBA Editor.

How to do it...

Let's do the following exercise:

1. Make sure that the UserForm is selected, then click the Toolbox icon on the standard toolbar to open the **Toolbox** window.

2. On the **Toolbox** windows, click the Label control:

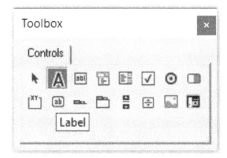

Figure 14.9 – The Label control in the Toolbox window

3. Click once in the top-left corner of the UserForm to add a label. Do not worry about the size for the moment, we will adjust that later:

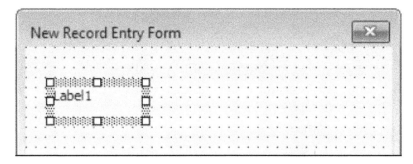

Figure 14.10 – Placing a label on the UserForm

4. In the **Properties** window, change the **name** property of this label to `lblName`. While there, you can also change the **caption** property to `Name:`

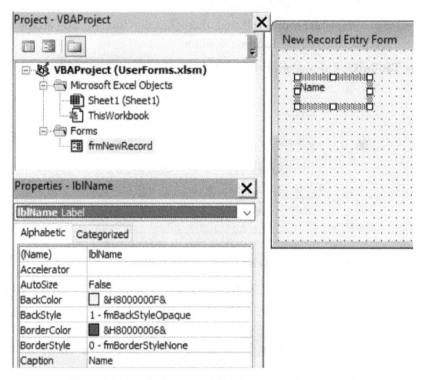

Figure 14.11 – The Name and Caption properties changed

5. Next, click on the TextBox control, and create a text box to the right of **Label1**:

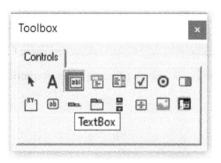

Figure 14.12 – The TextBox control

6. As with the label, you can click once or click and drag to create a textbox of a different size. For the moment, do not drag to place the text box, because we want all these items to be the same size to start with:

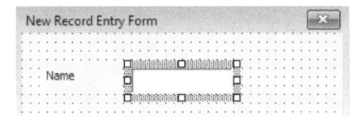

Figure 14.13 – Placing a text box

7. Change the **Name** property of the text box to txtName. Note that there is no caption property to change:

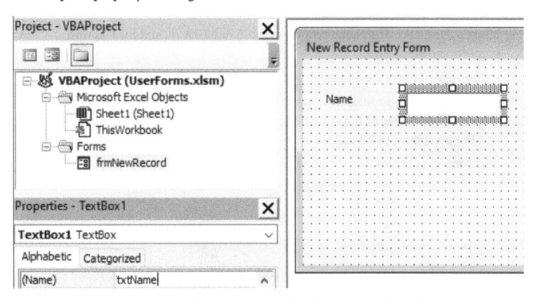

Figure 14.14 – The Name property for the text box is changed

8. Next, add a label for department, and change the **Name** property to lblDept and **Caption** to Department.

9.   Instead of a normal text box, we're going to add a combo box to the right of the **Department** label. Click on the Combo Box control in **Toolbox**, then click once to the right of the **Department** label. Our form should look like this now:

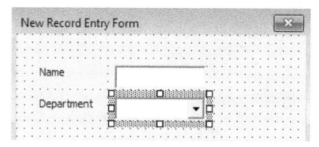

Figure 14.15 – Inserted combo box

10. Change the **Name** property of the Combo Box object to cboDept in the **Properties** window.

11. Insert a third label. The **Name** property should be lblAge, and the **Caption** property should be Age.

12. To the right of the preceding label, add a text box named txtAge.

13. Now, draw a spin button control to the right of this text box. Change the **Name** property to spnAge. At the same time, change the **Min** and **Max** values for the SpinButton control to 22 and 50, respectively.

14. Your form should look like this now:

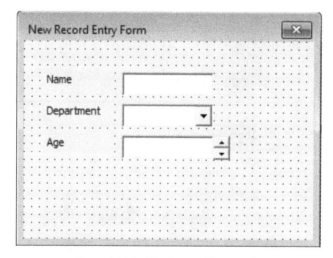

Figure 14.16 – The form with controls

15. The final label we need to insert is the **Start Date** label. Insert that below the **Age** label, and change the **Name** property to `lblStartD` and **Caption** to `Start Date`.

16. The text box that goes with this label will be named `txtStartD`. Insert that to the right of the last label. The form should look like this now:

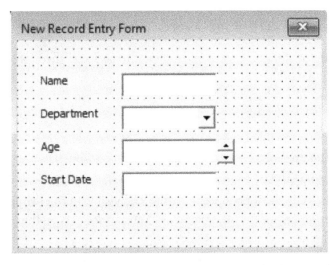

Figure 14.17 – The form with all the entry fields

17. To see what our form would look like in Excel, even if it's not complete, press *F5*, or click the Run button on the standard toolbar:

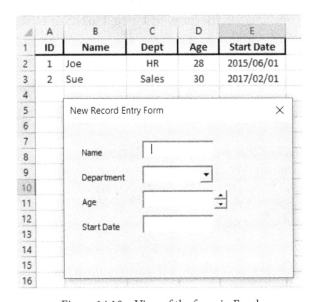

Figure 14.18 – View of the form in Excel

Spending time on the design and layout of a form will save us a lot of frustration during the process of creating the form. There should be a control to enter the date for each field in the spreadsheet.

How it works...

Let's take a look at what we did and how it works:

1. In order to capture data on a form and assign it to an Excel sheet, we need some way to capture that data. Therefore, we need to create a place, be it a text box, spinner control, or drop-down list, on a form that will correspond with each heading in the Excel sheet.

2. Placing objects on the form can be done in one of two ways: click once on the form to create a standard-sized object or drag to create a custom-sized one.

3. To change the properties of any object, that object must be selected. When you select the form, only the form's properties will be visible in the **Properties** window. The same goes for any of the other controls. You cannot change the properties of a text box if the specific item is not selected.

4. It is good practice to immediately change the **Name** property of each object as it is inserted. The **Caption** properties for labels should also be added the moment they're inserted.

5. Extra labels can be added the way we did it the first time, or we can copy an existing label and paste it anywhere in the form. Just drag it to the desired position, then change the **Name** and **Caption** properties.

6. Preview the form in Excel after inserting every label and textbox. It is better to make minor adjustments in the process of creating a form, than having to redo the entire form at the end of the process.

There's more...

1. Sometimes, the controls on our forms are not aligned or equally distributed. In this case, use the Select Objects tool in the **Toolbox** window to select the controls you want to align:

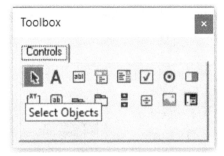

Figure 14.19 – The Select Objects tool

2. Drag the Select Objects tool over the controls you want to select, even if you are only partially selecting them:

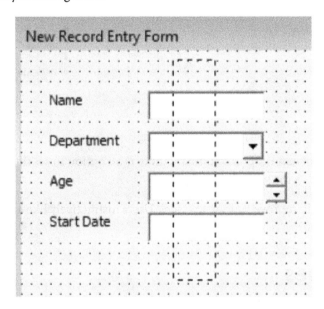

Figure 14.20 – Selecting controls with the Select Objects tool

3. Once selected, move to the standard toolbar and click **Align | Lefts**, should you want to align the boxes to the left:

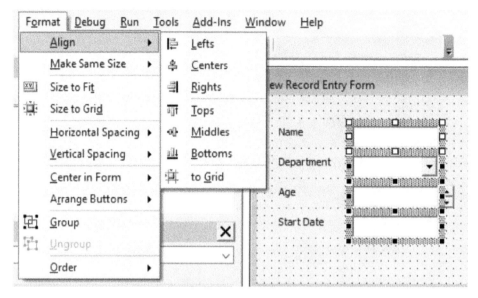

Figure 14.21 – Aligning controls

4. On the same **Format** drop-down menu, there is an option to set the horizontal spacing, as well as the vertical spacing.

Tidying up a form will improve its look and feel. Users instinctively like and trust well-designed, neat forms.

Using Frames

Not all forms are the same size or, said in another way, some forms display more controls than others. Having too many controls on a form can create confusion, hence the standard practice of organizing controls in groups. Just think of the **Alignment** dialog box in Excel or the **Page Setup** dialog box—not only are the controls separated in groups, but they also have several tabs to group related controls together.

The containers in which these clusters of controls are organized are known as **Frames**. In this recipe, we will be adding a Frame to our UserForm.

Getting ready

Make sure that UserForms.xlsm is still open. **UserForm1** should be visible, and both the Project Explorer and the **Properties** window should be visible on the left of the VBA Editor.

How to do it...

To insert a Frame, do the following:

1. Under normal circumstances, we would have inserted the Frame before creating any controls. Since we first had to understand the basic principles of controls, we will have to insert a Frame on another area of the UserForm, and then copy the existing controls in there.

2. Increase the size of the UserForm to double what it is currently. Activate the toolbox and select the Frame control. Click once on the open area of the UserForm to insert a Frame:

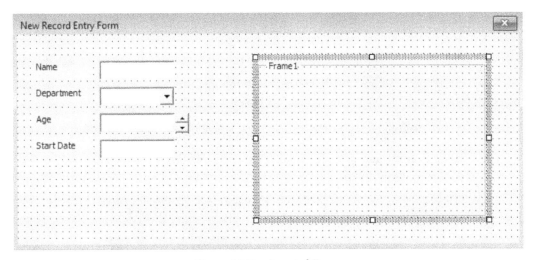

Figure 14.22 – Inserted Frame

3. Use the Select Objects tool on the **Toolbox** window to select all the existing controls. Press *Ctrl + X*, or right-click and select **Cut**:

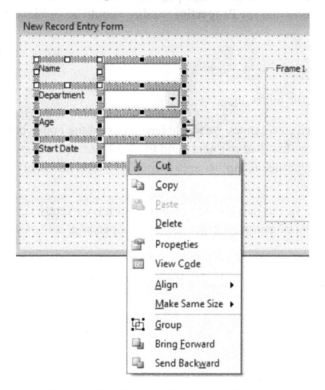

Figure 14.23 – Cut controls from the UserForm

4. Click inside **Frame1** and paste the objects by using the *Ctrl + V* shortcut, or right-click and select **Paste**:

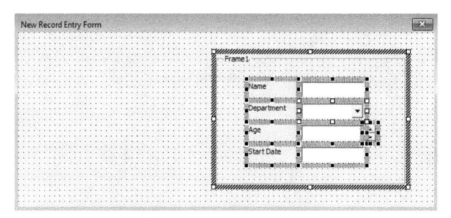

Figure 14.24 – Paste controls inside Frame1

5. Finally, click on the edge of the Frame and drag it to the top left-hand corner of the UserForm. All the controls inside the Frame should move with the Frame:

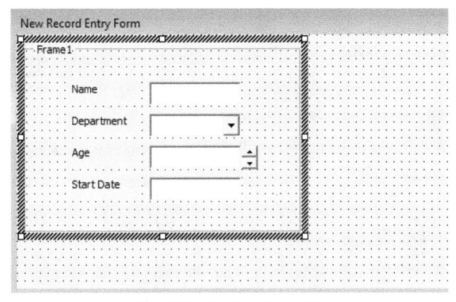

Figure 14.25 – Move Frame1 in position

6. With the Frame still selected, change the **Name** property to `fraNewRecordEntry` and **Caption** to `New Record Entry`.

There's more...

1. We should have added two command buttons when we inserted the other controls, yet we couldn't do this before knowing what the size of the Frame was. So, with the Frame in place, insert a command button outside the Frame, at the top right of the form.

2. Rename it cmdSaveEntry, and change the **Caption** property to Save this Entry:

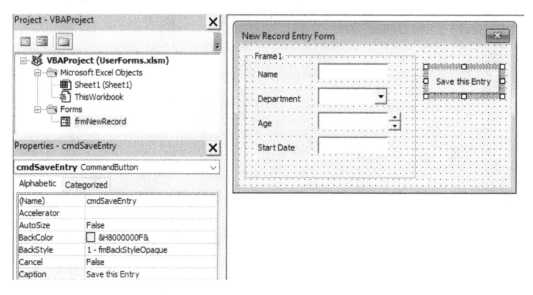

Figure 14.26 – The command button with changed properties

3. The second command button will fit directly below the **Save** button. Once inserted, change the **Name** property to cmdCancel and **Caption** to Cancel:

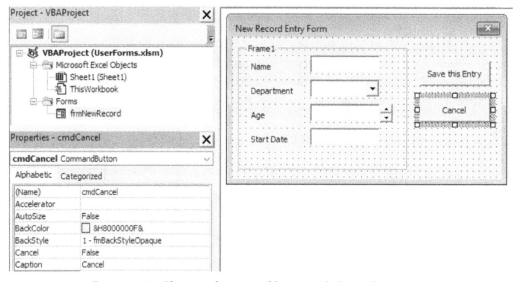

Figure 14.27 – The second command button with changed properties

Our form is complete, at least as far as buttons and controls are concerned.

15
UserForm Controls

UserForms are customized dialog boxes, and their purpose is to allow users various levels of interaction with Excel. These UserForms contain different controls, from obvious labels and textboxes, to more complex drop-down lists and combo boxes, to command buttons for saving, canceling, or closing the dialog box.

Behind each of these controls (buttons, lists, and so on) is a dedicated procedure, or VBA coding. This VBA code will determine which actions will follow when we click on a button, or select an option from a list, or where data will be stored if we enter information in a textbox.

In this chapter, we will cover the following recipes:

- Assigning controls
- Unloading a form
- Loading the form
- Using the Combo Box control
- Using the SpinButton control
- Setting the tab order

By the end of this chapter, you will be able to show a user form with working controls.

Technical requirements

This cookbook was written and designed to be used with MS Office 2019 and MS Office 365, installed on either Windows 8, 8.1, or 10.

If your hardware and software meet these requirements, you are good to go.

Demonstration files can be downloaded from `https://github.com/PacktPublishing/VBA-Automation-for-Excel-2019-Cookbook`.

Please visit the following link to check the CiA videos: `https://bit.ly/3jQRvVk`.

Assigning controls

We're finally ready to make a form do something. Adding controls to a form is only the first step in creating a working dialog box, or a UserForm. Adding data to a form where controls have not been assigned to certain actions and addresses in the spreadsheet will have no effect at all.

In this recipe, we will be assigning controls to specific fields and objects.

Getting ready

Make a copy of the file we used in *Chapter 14*, *Creating UserForms*, and save it as `Controls.xlsm`. Activate the VBA Editor. **New Record Entry Form** should be visible, and both the Project window and the Properties window should be visible on the left of the VBA Editor.

How to do it...

We will start with the **Save this Entry** button. Let's see how it's done:

1. On the **New Record Entry Form**, right-click the **Save this Entry** button and then choose **View Code** from the pop-up menu. Alternatively, double-click the button. The code window for the form itself will appear:

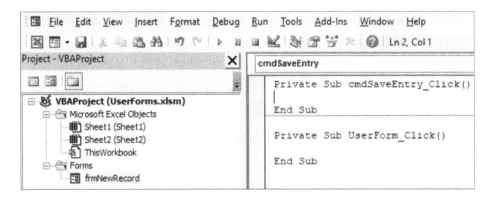

Figure 15.1 – The code window for frmNewRecord

2. Delete any redundant code (if any) in the window. Only the click event of the **Save this Entry** button must be available:

3. Add the following code to the command button's click event:

```
Private Sub cmdSaveEntry_Click()
    Sheet1.Activate
End Sub
```

4. To reach the first available blank cell in column A, enter the following code:

```
Private Sub cmdSaveEntry_Click()
    Sheet1.Activate
    Range("A1").End(xlDown).Offset(1, 0).Select
End Sub
```

5. Add the following line of code after the previous one to create a unique identifier:

```
ActiveCell.Value = ActiveCell.Offset(-1, 0).Value + 1
```

6. To move the focus one cell to the right and set that cell equal to the value of the first textbox in the form, enter the following line of code:

```
ActiveCell.Offset(0, 1).Value = txtName.Value
```

7. To search for the textbox reference, use the *Ctrl + spacebar* keyboard shortcut to activate the IntelliSense list. Start the search by typing `txt`. Thanks to the Hungarian naming convention, all the textboxes will appear in a group. All we need to do is select the appropriate textbox:

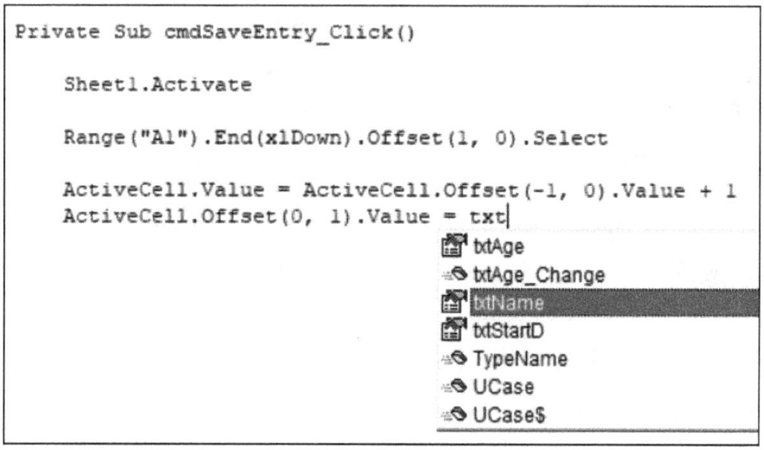

```
Private Sub cmdSaveEntry_Click()

    Sheet1.Activate

    Range("A1").End(xlDown).Offset(1, 0).Select

    ActiveCell.Value = ActiveCell.Offset(-1, 0).Value + 1
    ActiveCell.Offset(0, 1).Value = txt|
                                  txtAge
                                  txtAge_Change
                                  txtName
                                  txtStartD
                                  TypeName
                                  UCase
                                  UCase$
```

Figure 15.2 – Using IntelliSense

8. To reference the rest of the controls on our form, enter the following lines of code:

```
ActiveCell.Offset(0, 2).Value = cboDept.Value
ActiveCell.Offset(0, 3).Value = txtAge.Value
ActiveCell.Offset(0, 4).Value = txtStartD.Value
```

9. Confirm that entries to the form will be written to the correct cells in Excel by means of a test. Double-click the `frmNewRecord` object in the Project window to display the UserForm in the code window. Press *F5*, or click on the Run button on the standard toolbar to display the form in Excel.

10. Manually enter values in all the fields, since the Combo Box for **Department**, as well as the spin control for **Age**, has not been set up yet. Once these values have been entered, click on the **Save this Entry** button. Observe how the next row for ID 3 has been populated correctly:

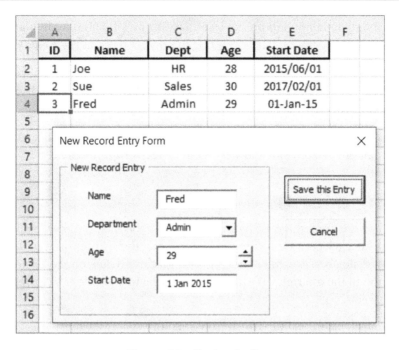

Figure 15.3 – Testing the form

11. Since we've not added any code to the **Cancel** button, close the form by clicking the close icon in the top-right corner of the dialog box.

How it works

Here is an explanation of what we did:

1. We had to access the code that sits behind the command button to assign actions to the button. It is important to note that we did not insert a new module. UserForms have their own code window.

2. The SaveEntry button will do much more than just save records, meaning that we will need to give extensive and exact instructions with our code. First, we need to make sure that we are in fact in **Sheet1**, hence that first code instruction.

3. Getting to the first available blank cell in column **A** was the next goal, which the next line of code did for us.

4. Reaching the end of the list was not enough. We needed a new, and also unique, identifier for the next record.

5. Being in the right position in our table, and with a new ID number in place, the rest of the code could be entered. First, we had to move one cell to the right. We then set that cell equal to the value of the first textbox in the form.

6. The other three controls on the form were assigned in much the same way, each with its own reference.

Testing the functionality of a UserForm while entering code is essential. This confirms the correct assignment of controls, and allow errors to be rectified immediately.

Unloading a form

Closing dialog boxes is something we hardly think about, because it either happens automatically, or we click on a **Cancel** button. That is exactly what we need to do with our custom dialog box, instead of having to ungracefully click on the Windows close down button in the top right. We need some coding to facilitate the closing, or unloading, process.

In this recipe, we will be unloading a form from memory.

Getting ready

Make sure that Controls.xlsm is still open. **New Record Entry Form** should be visible, and both the Project window and the Properties window should be visible on the left of the VBA Editor.

How to do it...

Let's see how to unload a form:

1. In the UserForm window, double-click the **Save this Entry** button, and then add the Unload method as the last line of code:

```
Private Sub cmdSaveEntry_Click()
    Sheet1.Activate
    Range("A1").End(xlDown).Offset(1, 0).Select

    ActiveCell.Value = ActiveCell.Offset(-1, 0).Value + 1
    ActiveCell.Offset(0, 1).Value = txtName.Value
    ActiveCell.Offset(0, 2).Value = cboDept.Value
    ActiveCell.Offset(0, 3).Value = txtAge.Value
    ActiveCell.Offset(0, 4).Value = txtStartD.Value
```

```
        Unload frmNewRecord
    End Sub
```

2. Test this by switching to the form, and then press *F5* to run it. Add values in every field, and observe how the form will close and return to the VBA Editor the moment you click the **Save this Entry** button.

3. Double-click on the **Cancel** button on the form (in the VBA Editor), and then add the following code in the click event for the button:

```
    Private Sub cmdCancel_Click()
        Unload frmNewRecord
    End Sub
```

4. Switch to the UserForm view, click on the form background, and press *F5* to run it. Clicking on the **Cancel** button will now close the form (and return to the VBA Editor) without any issues.

How it works...

Here is an explanation of what we did:

1. We need to clear the memory of the PC we're working on when exiting an application, or closing a dialog box. Unloading is, therefore, the last action executed in our UserForm code.

2. The **Save** button can be used to unload a form, although this is not always the case.

3. The **Cancel** button normally closes a form, hence the reason for our instruction to that effect in the code.

Loading the form

Every time we wanted to use the form so far, we had to run it from the VBA Editor. This is not ideal for users, you might agree. We need some way of making the form available from within the spreadsheet itself. The most effective way of achieving that is to create a button in the spreadsheet, which will launch the dialog box.

In this recipe, we will be loading a form.

Getting ready

Make sure that `Controls.xlsm` is still open. **New Record Entry Form** should be visible, and both the Project window and the Properties window should be visible on the left of the VBA Editor.

How to do it...

We need to do the following:

1. Switch back to Excel and make sure that **Sheet1** is active. Click on **Developer | Controls | Insert | ActiveX Controls | Command Button**:

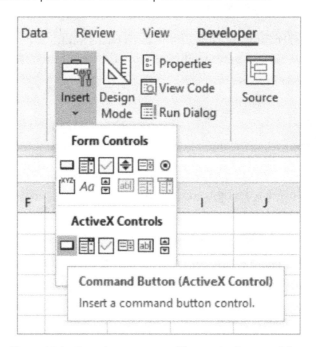

Figure 15.4 – Inserting a command button in the spreadsheet

2. Click to the right of the table to insert a command button of default size. Instead of returning to the VBA Editor to edit its properties, click on **Developer | Controls | Properties**. The familiar **Properties** window will appear in Excel. Change the **Name** and **Caption** properties to `cmdShowForm` and **Add New Record**:

Figure 15.5 – The Properties window in Excel

3. Once done, close the **Properties** window and activate the code window for the button. Take note that the **Properties** window in the VBA Editor has also been closed, so press *F4* to reactivate it. Add the following code in the code window:

```
Private Sub cmdShowForm_Click()
    frmNewRecord.Show
End Sub
```

4. Switch back to Excel again and deactivate **Design Mode** by clicking on the icon:

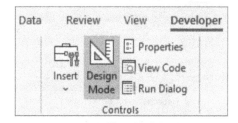

Figure 15.6 – Switching off Design Mode

5. Click on the newly added **Add New Record** button to display our custom dialog box, this time from within Excel. Close the form.

How it works...

Here is an explanation of what we did:

1. Placing a command button on a spreadsheet makes it possible for users to access the UserForm without having to open the VBA Editor.

2. Setting the **Caption** property will determine whether users understand the command button.

3. As with other controls, it is the coding behind the command button that does the work. We assigned Show command to the button in this case.

Using the Combo Box control

We still need to create a list of values for the Combo Box. Users must select a department from a pre-defined list, rather than being unsure about the possible options. To populate the Combo Box, we first need to create that lookup list.

In this recipe, we will be using the Combo Box control.

Getting ready

Make sure that Controls.xlsm is still open. **New Record Entry Form** should be visible, and both the project window and the properties window should be visible on the left of the VBA Editor.

How to do it...

We need to do the following:

1. Before configuring the Combo Box, we need to create a lookup list. Switch to Excel and insert a new sheet. In **Sheet2**, create the following list:

Figure 15.7 – Lookup list for the Combo Box

2. Once done, select the list and save it as a range, (click in the Name Box, then type the word `Department`, and press *Enter*), calling it **Department**.

3. Switch back to the UserForm and select the **Department** Combo Box. In its **Properties** window, look for the **RowSource** property and type in the name of the range, Department, we've just created. Press *Enter*:

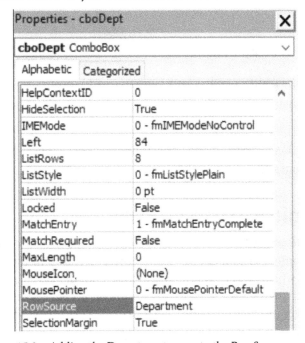

Figure 15.8 – Adding the Department range to the RowSource property

4. Now, click on the drop-down arrow of the Combo Box to test whether the list will appear when we click on the drop-down list:

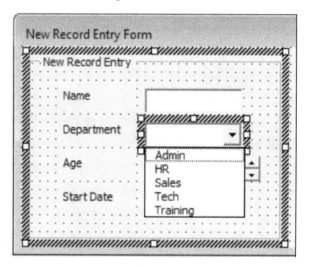

Figure 15.9 – Testing the Combo Box

Combo boxes can be used for almost any situation where a selection must be made from pre-defined options.

How it works...

Here is an explanation of what we did:

1. A lookup list is the source needed for a Combo Box to display its options.

2. The **Properties** window of the Combo Box determines which Named Range will be used.

3. Using a Combo Box gives users the opportunity to choose input from a list. It saves time, and eliminates spelling mistakes.

Using the SpinButton control

We also need to make changes to the SpinButton control for the **Age** textbox, since it is currently not functioning, or so it appears. The arrows on the SpinButton control do actually change values when we click on them, but this is not displayed anywhere. We can, therefore, not see the changing values. What we need to do is code an event for the spin button, so that whenever its value changes, it also changes the value of the textbox.

In this recipe, we will be using the SpinButton control.

Getting ready

Make sure that `Controls.xlsm` is still open. **New Record Entry Form** should be visible, and both the project window and the properties window should be visible on the left of the VBA Editor.

How to do it...

We need to do the following:

1. Double-click on the SpinButton control to open the code for the control. Add the following code:

    ```
    Private Sub spnAge_Change()
        txtAge.Value = spnAge.Value
    End Sub
    ```

2. Set parameters for the SpinButton control. Let's say the maximum age for people working in our company is 60. To set that value, go to the **Properties** window of the SpinButton control and set the **Max** value to 60 and **Min** to 0. Finally, change the **Value** property to 26, which will be the default value that appears in the **Age** textbox when we load the form:

Figure 15.10 – Values for the Spin control

3. Display the UserForm by double clicking the **frmNewRecord** object in the Project window.

4. Double-click on the background of the form to get to its code window. By default, the `Click` event will appear, which is not what we need. Click on the drop-down list (top right) to list all the events for the UserForm, and select the `Initialize` event:

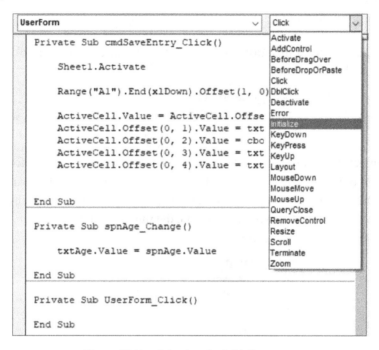

Figure 15.11 – Selecting the Initialize event

5. Delete the code for the `Click` event, and then add the following code to the `Initialize` event:

```
Private Sub UserForm_Initialize()
    txtAge.Value = spnAge.Value
End Sub
```

6. Switch to Excel , **Sheet 1**, and click the **Add New Record** command button. The default value in the **Age** textbox will be 26, and clicking on the arrows will increase or decrease the values from the value 26, to a maximum of 60.

7. And yet this is still not the end. Let's say we add the value 35 to the **Age** textbox when the form is loaded, and then click on the spin buttons. Instead of counting from 35 up or down, the value will jump back to the default, 26, and increase or decrease from there. Here's how to resolve this issue—link the textbox to the spin button by entering the following code. Close the dialogue box, then switch to the VBA Editor. Add the following Sub procedure:

```
Private Sub txtAge_Change()
    spnAge.Value = txtAge.Value
End Sub
```

Run the form one last time to confirm that the spin buttons will respond correctly to changes in the textbox.

How it works...

Here is an explanation of what we did:

1. The SpinButton control cannot display its own value, hence the need to assign those values to a textbox where it can be displayed.

2. Setting parameters on the SpinButton control limits the range of the numbers through which it can scroll. Be careful not to set a lower level limit, since this can cause unexpected runtime errors that must be handled with extra coding.

3. The **Value** property of the SpinButton control will set the default value for the control.

4. To display the spin button's default value of 26 in the **Age** textbox whenever the form is loaded, we need to change the `Initialize` event of the UserForm. That will set the **Age** textbox to the initial value of the spin button.

5. We also need to link the textbox back to the spin button in such a way that values entered in the textbox will update the SpinButton control.

There's more...

The SpinButton control might be working fine, but there is always the potential danger of a user typing text into that textbox, or deleting the value. In both these cases, an error would spoil our fun. Add the following line of code:

```
Private Sub txtAge_Change()
    If IsNumeric(txtAge.Value) Then
        spnAge.Value = txtAge.Value
    End If
End Sub
```

More testing will surely reveal other potential errors, but for the moment, things are working fine.

Setting the tab order

Setting the tab order in our form is the last thing we need to do. The correct tab order will ensure that the focus will be on the **Name** textbox when the form is loaded. Furthermore, every time we press *Tab*, the focus will move in an orderly manner from one control to the next; from the **Name** box to **Department**, then **Age**, **Start Date**, the **Save Button**, and finally the **Cancel** button. It makes the form user friendly, in the sense that you can complete the form by pressing the *Tab* key, jumping from field to field, without using the mouse.

In this recipe, we will be setting the tab order.

Getting ready

Make sure that Controls.xlsm is still open. **New Record Entry Form** should be visible, and both the Project window and the Properties window should be visible on the left of the VBA Editor.

How to do it...

We need to do the following:

1. Select the Frame object on the form. If the UserForm is selected, we wouldn't be able to set the tab order for the items inside the frame.

2. Click on the **View** menu, and then select the **Tab Order** option:

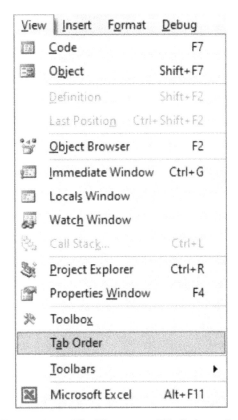

Figure 15.12 – The View menu, Tab Order option

3. If you click on the **Tab Order** option, the **Tab Order** dialog box will appear:

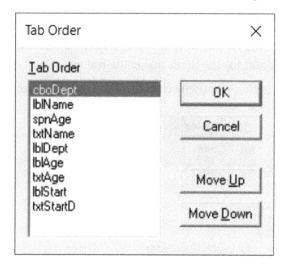

Figure 15.13 – The Tab Order dialog box

4. Click on **lblName**, and then click on the **Move Up** button to move it to the top. Repeat the process for all the other controls. The **Tab Order** should be as follows:

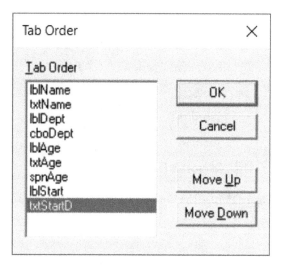

Figure 15.14 – New tab order

5. Click on **OK** to close the dialog box:

6. Switch to Excel, and then launch the dialog box. Press *Tab* repeatedly, and observe how the focus moves from top to bottom, in sequence.

How it works

This is how setting the tab order works:

1. Make sure that the frame inside the UserForm is selected, otherwise we wouldn't be able to set the tab order for the items inside the frame.

2. All the controls displayed in the frame can be moved up and down—either to the top or bottom of the list. The first item in the **Tab Order** list will be the active control when the UserForm is loaded.

3. The **Tab Order** doesn't influence label controls, but we prefer to keep it with its corresponding textbox control.

16
Creating Custom Functions

Chapter 8, Using Functions, covered the basic principles of functions. In this chapter, we will take it to a different level altogether.

By definition, functions only return values, as you may know by now. What might surprise you is that Excel already has approximately 470 built-in functions.

Generally speaking, we hardly use more than 10 Excel functions at any given time. Granted, some advanced or specialist users may need more than that to get their work done, but even they would hardly utilize more than 25% of the total functions available.

If this is the case, then why would we go to the trouble of creating extra functions? The short answer is *automation* and *increased productivity*. Instead of building highly complex nested functions from scratch every time the need arises, you can embed and save the entire group of arguments as a single custom function. Imagine how much time you'll save for yourself!

In this chapter, we will cover the following recipes:

- Writing functions
- Calling functions

- Adding function arguments
- Displaying function and argument descriptions

By the end of this chapter, you will be able to create your own custom functions.

Technical requirements

This cookbook was written and designed to be used with MS Office 2019 and MS Office 365, installed on either Windows 8, 8.1, or 10.

If your hardware and software meet these requirements, you are ready for action.

Demonstration files can be downloaded from `https://github.com/ PacktPublishing/VBA-Automation-for-Excel-2019-Cookbook`.

Please visit the following link to check the CiA videos: `https://bit.ly/3jQRvVk`.

Writing functions

Writing a function is similar to writing a procedure, in the sense that both are created in the VBA Editor. That is where the similarities end, though.

Apart from the fact that functions only return values, and cannot be executed independently like `Sub` procedures, there is also a difference in structure, headings, code structure, and then the all-important arguments.

Once you understand these principles, creating your own functions will become an important part of your VBA journey.

In this recipe, we will be creating and writing several functions.

Getting ready

Open Excel and activate a new workbook. Save the file as a macro-enabled file on your desktop and call it `CustomFunctions.xlsm`. **Sheet1** should be active. Press *Alt + F11* to switch to the VBA Editor, then insert a new module.

How to do it...

Here is how to write a function:

1. As in so many other cases in the Microsoft environment, there is more than one way of achieving the same result. Starting a new function is no different. The first way to initiate the process is to click on **Insert | Procedure**. The **Add Procedure** dialog box will appear:

Figure 16.1 – The Add Procedure dialog box

2. Enter the name of the function in the **Name:** text box of the dialog box. In this case, we want to call it CurrentDate. Next, select the **Function** option under **Type**. Click **OK** once done:

Figure 16.2 – Completed dialog box

3. Without typing a word, you've created the start of a new custom function. Add the following code to complete the process. Essentially, assign the built-in `Date` function to the `CurrentDate` custom function:

```
Public Function CurrentDate() As String
    CurrentDate = Date
End Function
```

4. Switch to Excel to test the function. In cell A1, or any open cell, enter the equals sign, as you would with all functions. Now type the first letters of the function name, and wait for the auto-complete list to display the function:

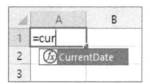

Figure 16.3 – Inserting the function in Excel

5. Double-click the name on the presented list and press *Enter*. The current date will appear in the cell. Note that if the serial number for this date (44061) appears in the cell, change the data type from general to date:

	A	B
1	18/08/2020	
2		
3		

Figure 16.4 – The current date, inserted by using a custom function

6. The second way of writing a function is to type everything manually. Switch back to the VBA Editor. Click in the code window, in an open space under the `CurrentDate` function, then type the first part of the code:

```
Function CustomDate As String
```

7. Once done, press *Enter*. The rest of the code will autocomplete, including the parentheses after the function name:

```
Function CustomDate() As String

End Function
```

8. Complete the function by adding a line between the opening and closing statements. In this case, we're using the `Format` built-in function to change the appearance of the `Date` built-in function, finally assigning all that to the custom function:

```
Function CustomDate() As String
    CustomDate = Format(Date, "dddd dd mmmm yyyy")
End Function
```

9. Switch to Excel to test the custom function. The result should look similar to this:

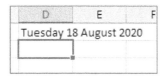

Figure 16.5 – The result after running a custom function

Following these steps will enable you to write a custom function Click on cell D1, then use the `CustomDate` function. without problems.

How it works...

Here is an explanation of what we did:

1. In some cases, Excel doesn't have a function that suits our special needs, hence the reason why it will allow us to create custom functions in VBA.

2. The code for a custom function must be written in the VBA Editor. Code can be entered by inserting a function procedure, or by manually typing it in.

3. Testing the function can be done in the Excel spreadsheet.

Calling functions

Using a custom function from within Excel, the way we did just now, has some value. If nothing else, it's an effective way of testing whether the function works or not. However, the point of writing VBA code is to automate your work. In other words, ideally, we want to run custom functions like a standard `Sub` procedure, either by pressing *F5* in the VBA Editor or by pressing a command button in Excel.

The only way to do that is to write an extra `Sub` procedure, which we know can be executed, and then call the function. By *calling*, we mean calling up the non-executable function to do its work via the `Sub` procedure.

In this recipe, we will be calling a function.

Getting ready

Make sure that `CustomFuntions.xlsm` is still open and the VBA Editor is active.

How to do it...

These are the steps to call a function:

1. Add the following `Sub` procedure below the two custom functions in `Module1`:

```
Sub InsertNewSheet()
    Worksheets.Add
    Range("A1").Value = CustomDate
End Sub
```

2. Instead of running the function, press *F8* to step into the code.

3. The next instruction, highlighted in the `Sub` procedure, is to set cell A1 equal to the `CustomDate` function. In simple English, this is an instruction to call the function to action:

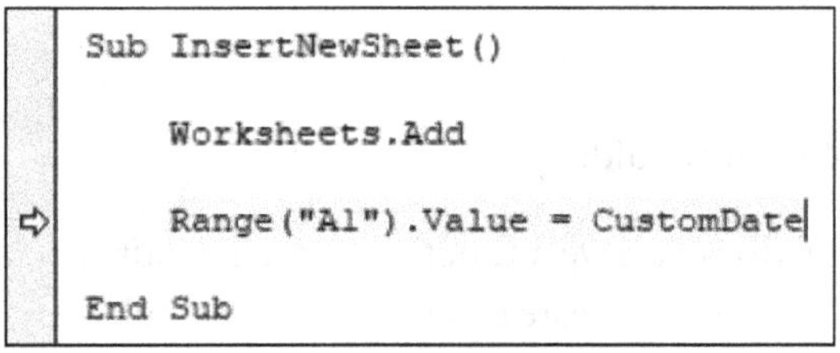

```
Sub InsertNewSheet()

    Worksheets.Add

⇨   Range("A1").Value = CustomDate

End Sub
```

Figure 16.6 – Calling the CustomDate function

4. Press *F8* again. The focus now jumps from the `Sub` procedure to the custom function:

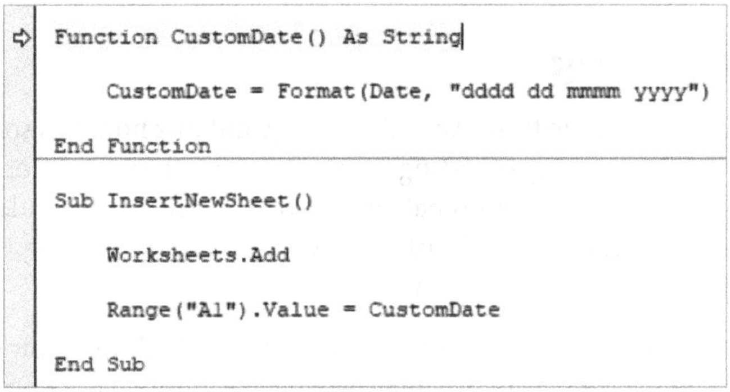

```
⇨ Function CustomDate() As String

      CustomDate = Format(Date, "dddd dd mmmm yyyy")

  End Function

  Sub InsertNewSheet()

      Worksheets.Add

      Range("A1").Value = CustomDate

  End Sub
```

Figure 16.7 – Activating the CustomDate function

5. Press *F8* three more times to execute the custom function, step by step. Because the

focus was set on cell A1, the formatted date will be inserted there.

6. Pressing *F8* a fourth time will end the function and transfer the focus back to the current Sub procedure.

7. Press *F8* one last time to end the Sub procedure.

8. Switch to Excel and observe the newly inserted **Sheet2**, as well as the custom date in cell A1 of that sheet:

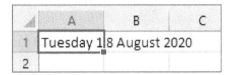

Figure 16.8 – Result of calling a custom function

These instructions will enable you to call any function from a Sub procedure.

How it works...

Here is an explanation of what we did:

1. Because functions cannot be executed independently, we had to create a Sub procedure to call our custom function.

2. When running the Sub procedure, it will call the function to do what it was designed for, and then present the result in a spreadsheet.

Adding function arguments

In VBA terms, when referring to an argument within a function, we refer to information that needs to be passed to the function in order to present us with a sensible answer.

The functions we have written so far haven't had any arguments, meaning that there was no need to pass any information to it. It simply presented us with the result of a built-in VBA function.

Although VBA will let you add as many as 60 arguments to a function, we hardly ever use more than three or four. In many cases, we get along fine with a single argument.

In this recipe, we will be adding function arguments to a custom function.

Getting ready

Make sure that `CustomFuntions.xlsm` is still open. Activate **Sheet1**, and enter the following data:

	A	B
1	**Mark**	**Pass/Fail**
2	45	
3	55	
4	39	
5	72	
6	65	

Figure 16.9 – Data on Sheet1

Once done, switch to the VBA Editor.

How to do it...

Follow these steps to add a function argument:

1. We need a function that can tell us which students passed or failed a test, where they needed a 50% or higher mark to pass.

    A simple `If` function in Excel will do just fine, but you still need to set it up every time you need it. A custom function can be saved and reused with much greater ease.

2. In the open space below the last procedure, enter the following code:

    ```
    Function PassFail(Mark As Integer) As String
        If Mark >= 50 Then
            PassFail = "Pass"
        Else
            PassFail = "Fail"
        End If
    End Function
    ```

3. Switch to Excel and click in cell B2 of **Sheet1**. Press =, and then start typing `PassFail`:

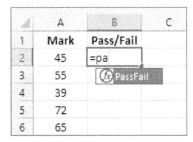

Figure 16.10 – Using the PassFail custom function

4. Double-click on the function prompt, then click on cell A2 to enter the argument:

	A	B
1	**Mark**	**Pass/Fail**
2	45	=PassFail(A2
3	55	
4	39	
5	72	
6	65	

Figure 16.11 – Entering the argument

5. Close the parenthesis, then press *Enter* to complete the function. The result will appear on cell B2. Use autofill to apply the function to the rest of the values in column **A**:

	A	B	C
1	**Mark**	**Pass/Fail**	
2	45	Fail	
3	55	Pass	
4	39	Fail	
5	72	Pass	
6	65	Pass	
7			
8			

Figure 16.12 – Using the custom function on all cells

6. Delete the results on cells B2:B6 and switch to the VBA Editor. Now enter the following Sub procedure to call the function:

```
Sub InsertSymbol()
    Sheet1.Activate
    Range("A2").Select
    Do Until ActiveCell.Value = ""
    ActiveCell.Offset(0, 1).Value =  _
    PassFail(ActiveCell.Value)
    ActiveCell.Offset(1, 0).Select
    Loop
End Sub
```

7. Run the InsertSymbol procedure, and confirm that the results have been inserted in column **B**.

These instructions will help you set up function arguments where needed.

How it works...

Here is an explanation of what we did:

1. Not all functions depend on functions to present a value – for example, Date functions.

2. Some functions do need some input, which will differ every time the function is invoked.

3. Users can supply those values by clicking on data in cells, or by manually typing in values.

4. Each part of such a function is called an argument.

There's more...

Some custom functions need more than one argument, by their very nature. The technique discussed here can be applied to add a third and fourth argument too:

1. To create a custom function with two arguments, enter the following code:

```
Function Exponent(x As Integer, y As Integer) As Integer
    Exponent = x ^ y
End Function
```

2. Switch to Excel and click in any open cell on **Sheet1**. Press =, and then start typing Exponent.

3. Double-click on the function prompt. Let's say you want to raise 5 to the power of 2. You now need to *Enter* the base value, 5, then enter a comma, and then enter the exponent, 2. Press *Enter*.

4. The result of the calculation will appear in the selected cell.

Displaying function and argument descriptions

Adding descriptions to the components of your custom functions is the final finishing touch. It's a nice way of refreshing your memory if you haven't used the function in a while, and it will also be of help to users that are not familiar with your custom functions.

If you use the **Insert Function** dialog box to insert the **PassFail** custom function at this stage, no help will be available:

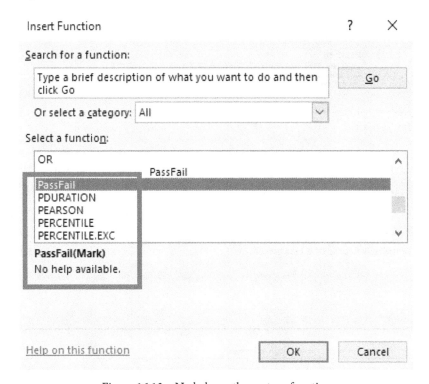

Figure 16.13 – No help on the custom function

In this recipe, we will be adding function and argument descriptions to be displayed in the **Insert Functions** dialog box.

Getting ready

Make sure that `CustomFuntions.xlsm` is still open. Activate **Sheet1**.

How to do it...

What we need to do is the following:

1. To add a description to a custom function, open the **Macro** dialog box: **Developer | Code | Macros**. The **Macro** dialog box will appear.

2. Click on the **Macro name** text box and enter the name of the custom function. It is important to note that the names of custom functions will not appear among the listed macros, hence the need to enter it manually:

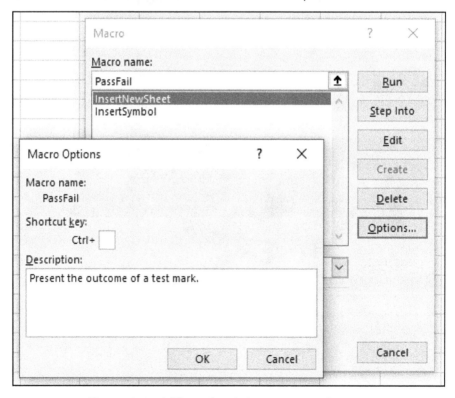

Figure 16.14 – Adding a description to a custom function

3. Click the **Options** button, then enter a short description of what the custom function does. Click **OK**. When the **Macro Options** dialog box is closed, click **Cancel** on the **Macro** dialog box.

4. To check how the description is displayed for users, open the **Insert Function** dialog box by clicking **Formulas | Insert Function.**

5. Scroll down the list of functions until the **PassFail** function is visible. Click once to select it. The description will appear below the box with the list of functions:

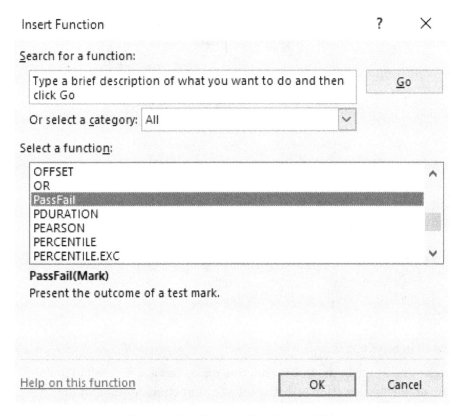

Figure 16.15 – Function description visible

6. After selecting the **PassFail** custom function from the **Insert Function** dialog box, no argument description will be visible. Click on Cancel to close the dialogue box:

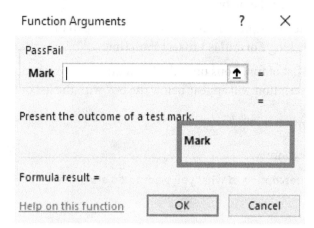

Figure 16.16 – No argument description visible

7. To add argument descriptions, you need to add the following Sub procedure in the code window. You only need to run it once to display the argument description for the function. Each custom function will need a similar Sub procedure, with dedicated coding:

```
Sub AddArgumentDescriptions()
    Application.MacroOptions Macro:="PassFail", _
    ArgumentDescriptions:=Array( _
    "Range that contains the mark")
End Sub
```

8. Press *F5* to run the code.

9. Switch to Excel. Open the **Insert Function** dialog box again. Scroll to find the **PassFail** function, select it, and click **OK**. The **Function Arguments** dialog box will appear, displaying the description of the **Mark** argument:

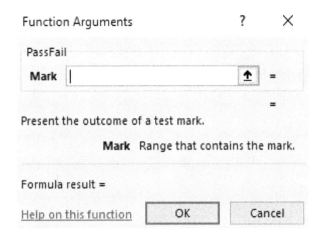

Figure 16.17 – Displaying the argument description

10. Now that we've confirmed that the argument description is displayed the way it should, you can click **Cancel** to close the dialog box.

By following and implementing these steps, you will be able to display function and argument descriptions for your custom functions. By adding function and argument descriptions in the **Functions** dialog box, we make it easier for users to use the function effectively.

17
Creating Word Documents with Excel VBA

When dealing with VBA for Excel, you'd be forgiven for thinking that your coding would limit you to working within Excel only. However, if you think carefully about the role of VBA within Office Suite, you'd realize that it is common to all the applications within the suite.

Knowing this, a new set of possibilities opens up. You can, for instance, capture data in Excel via a user form, and then automatically export it to a Word document. The beauty of this is that everything is executed in the background. In other words, you don't need to manually copy data from Excel, search for the correct Word document to paste this information, save the file, and then close Word again.

In this chapter, we will cover the following recipes:

- Creating a new instance of Word
- Writing and formatting text
- Copying data into Word
- Using templates and bookmarks

By the end of this chapter, you will be able to create Word documents from within Excel.

Technical requirements

This cookbook was written and designed to be used with MS Office 2019 and MS Office 365, installed on either Windows 8, 8.1, or 10.

If your hardware and software meet these requirements, you are good to go.

Demonstration files can be downloaded from `https://github.com/PacktPublishing/VBA-Automation-for-Excel-2019-Cookbook`.

Please visit the following link to check the CiA videos: `https://bit.ly/3jQRvVk`.

Creating a new instance of Word

The first step in the process of creating a Word document from within Excel requires some changes to the available references. To be exact, we'll have to set a reference to Word's object library in the VBA Editor. Without this step, Excel cannot communicate with Word at all, let alone create documents and paragraphs.

In this recipe, we will be creating a new instance of Word from within Excel.

Getting ready

Open Excel, and activate a new workbook. Save the file as a macro-enabled file on your desktop and call it `Word_Interaction.xlsm`. **Sheet1** should be active. Press *Alt + F11* to switch to the VBA Editor, and then insert a new module.

It goes without saying that MS Word must also be installed on your computer in order for the instructions in this recipe to work effectively.

How to do it...

Here is how to link Word to Excel:

1. In the VBA Editor, click on **Tools | References**. The **References - VBAProject** dialog box will open:

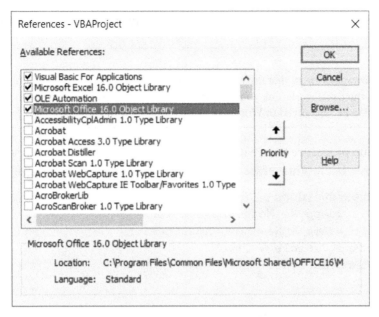

Figure 17.1 – The References - VBAProject dialog box

2. Scroll down the list of available references until you find **Microsoft Word 16.0 Object Library**. Earlier versions of Word will have a different number, but will still refer to the Word object library:

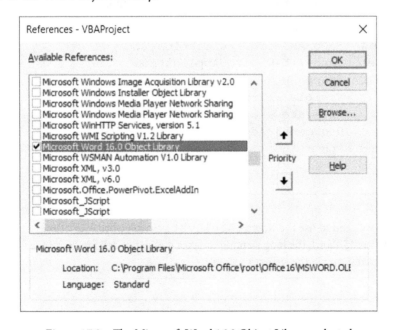

Figure 17.2 – The Microsoft Word 16.0 Object Library selected

3. Once selected, click on **OK** to save the selection and also to close the dialog box.

> **Note**
>
> It is important to know that the reference to the Word object library is only valid for the Excel workbook you're working in currently. Every new workbook will have to be referenced to Word in exactly the same way.

4. Create a Sub procedure to initiate Word from within Excel. There are several ways of doing this, but for this recipe, we will be using this specific technique:

```
Sub CreateWordDoc()
    Dim wdApp As Word.Application
    Set wdApp = New Word.Application
    wdApp.Visible = True
    wdApp.Activate
End Sub
```

5. Press *F5* to run the procedure, or to test it, if you will. A new instance of Word will appear on your screen. Close the Word application once you know that the Sub procedure is working.

6. Opening Word without opening a new document is not very useful. Add the next lines of code to the Sub procedure to open a new document:

```
Sub CreateWordDoc()
    Dim wdApp As Word.Application
    Set wdApp = New Word.Application
    With wdApp
        .Visible = True
        .Activate
        .Documents.Add
    End With
End Sub
```

> **Note**
>
> Because we need to use the Word.Application keyword every time we refer to MS Word, the loop structure makes it easier to refer to Word.Application via the wdApp variable.

7. If you now run the procedure, Word will open again, this time displaying a new document, **Document1**.

8. Close Word, but don't save the document. Return to the VBA Editor in Excel.

These steps will enable you to create a new instance of Word from within Excel, using VBA for Excel.

How it works...

Enabling the Microsoft Word object library for this Excel workbook made it possible to use Word keywords and methods within Excel. These keywords can open an instance of Word, as well as a new Word document, all from within Excel.

Writing and formatting text

It's all very well to know how to open Word with a new document available. However, we need more than this. A heading for the new document would be a good start, but that is still not enough. Formatting the heading is also necessary, and will round it off professionally.

In this recipe, we will be writing and formatting text.

Getting ready

Make sure `Word_Interaction.xlsm` is still open, and that the VBA Editor is active.

How to do it...

These are the steps to enter and format text in Word:

1. To add text to a Word document via Excel, add the following line of code:

```
Sub CreateWordDoc()
    Dim wdApp As Word.Application
    Set wdApp = New Word.Application
    With wdApp
        .Visible = True
        .Activate
        .Documents.Add
        .Selection.TypeText "Employee Information"
    End With
End Sub
```

2. Press *F5*. Running the Sub procedure will now result in a new instance of Word, with a new document open, and the line of text in the Sub procedure at the top of the page. Close Word without saving, since there is more code to add to our procedure in Excel:

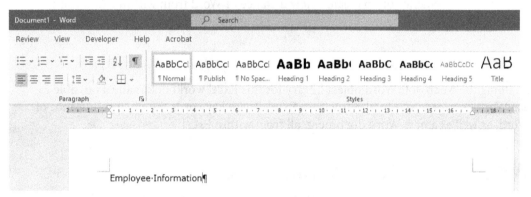

Figure 17.3 – New instance of Word, with document and text

3. It is quite clear that we need to do some formatting here. By starting a nested loop structure, this will save us repeating the keywords. Furthermore, if you haven't done it so far, you can use IntelliSense to assist you with all the Word keywords.
   Add the following lines of code to the VBA Editor:

```
Sub CreateWordDoc()
    Dim wdApp As Word.Application
    Set wdApp = New Word.Application
    With wdApp
        .Visible = True
        .Activate

        .Documents.Add

        With .Selection
            .ParagraphFormat.Alignment = _
            wdAlignParagraphCenter
            .BoldRun    'Switch Bold on
            .Font.Size = 16
            .TypeText "Employee Information"
            .BoldRun    'Switch Bold off
            .TypeParagraph    'Enter a new line
            .Font.Size = 11
            .ParagraphFormat.Alignment = _
            wdAlignParagraphLeft
```

```
            .TypeParagraph
        End With
    End With
End Sub
```

4. When you run the Sub procedure now, there will be a marked improvement in appearance:

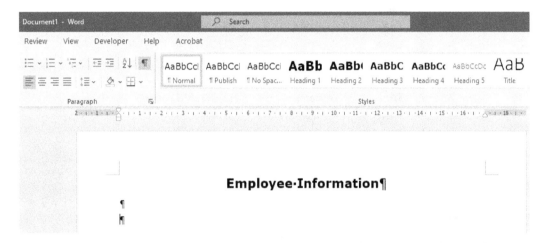

Figure 17.4 – Formatting done via VBA in Excel

Using these principles, users will be able to format a Word document with VBA coding in Excel.

Copying data into Word

We could have opened Word manually and achieved what we've just done, but the whole purpose of the exercise is to do it from Excel, so that data in a spreadsheet can be written to the Word document automatically.

What we need to do now is select data, copy it, and then paste that as part of the opening and formatting process.

In this recipe, we will be copying data into Word.

Getting ready

Make sure that `Word_Interaction.xlsm` is still open. Activate **Sheet1**, and enter the following data:

	A	B	C	D	E
1	ID	Name	Department	D.O.B.	Age
2	1	Joe	Admin	01/03/1988	32
3	2	Sue	Sales	25/10/1992	28
4	3	Dave	Projects	11/06/1996	24
5	4	Anne	HR	15/04/1989	31
6	5	Bill	Sales	20/01/1990	30
7	6	Tom	Sales	21/08/1993	27
8	7	Fred	Training	07/07/1995	25
9	8	Bob	Technical	09/05/1991	29
10	9	Jane	Admin	14/02/1994	27

Figure 17.5 – Working data

How to do it...

Follow these steps to copy text from Excel to Word:

1. Create code to automatically select whatever range is on a sheet:

```
Sub CreateWordDoc()
    Dim wdApp As Word.Application
    Set wdApp = New Word.Application
    With wdApp
        .Visible = True
        .Activate

        .Documents.Add

        With .Selection
            .ParagraphFormat.Alignment =  _
            wdAlignParagraphCenter
            .BoldRun    'Switch Bold on
            .Font.Size = 16
            .TypeText "Employee Information"
            .BoldRun    'Switch Bold off
            .TypeParagraph    'Enter a new line
            .Font.Size = 11
```

```
            .ParagraphFormat.Alignment =  _
            wdAlignParagraphLeft
            .TypeParagraph
        End With
    End With

    Range("A1", Range("A2").End(xlDown) _
    .End(xlToRight)).Copy
    wdApp.Selection.Paste
End Sub
```

2. Run the Sub procedure to check your coding. We know that the first part will work, but in this case, we need to see whether the data on our spreadsheet was copied into Word:

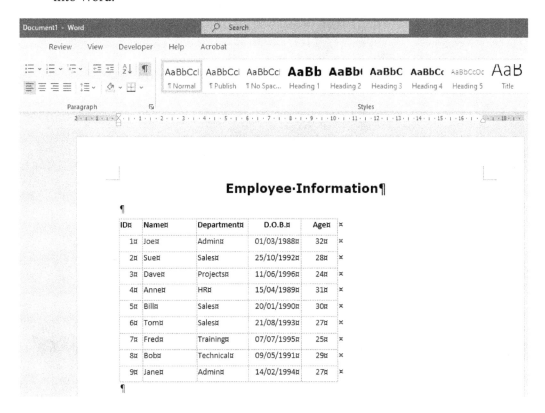

Figure 17.6 – Excel data copied and pasted into Word

3. Saving the Word document is what we need to do next. When you add these lines of code, pay attention to the changes in the `With` statement:

```vba
Sub CreateWordDoc()
    Dim wdApp As Word.Application
    Set wdApp = New Word.Application
    With wdApp
        .Visible = True
        .Activate
        .Documents.Add

        With .Selection
            .ParagraphFormat.Alignment =  _
            wdAlignParagraphCenter
            .BoldRun     'Switch Bold on
            .Font.Size = 16
            .TypeText "Employee Information"
            .BoldRun    'Switch Bold off
            .TypeParagraph    'Enter a new line
            .Font.Size = 11
            .ParagraphFormat.Alignment =  _
            wdAlignParagraphLeft
            .TypeParagraph
        End With

        Range("A1", Range("A2").End(xlDown) _
        .End(xlToRight)).Copy

        .Selection.Paste
        .ActiveDocument.SaveAs2 Environ("UserProfile") _
        & "\Desktop\EmployeeReport.docx"
    End With
End Sub
```

4. The last thing we need to do is close down the document, and finally, Word itself. Just add the following two lines in a new line after the filename:

```vba
.ActiveDocument.Close
.Quit
```

5. When you run the procedure now, you will see Word open briefly, and immediately close again. If you want to eliminate that, simply comment the following two lines out:

```
'.Visible = True
'.Activate
```

6. We're still not done, because every time we run the procedure, the file is replaced without giving us the option of saving it under a new name. We need to add code to create a unique filename every time we run the procedure. By declaring a new variable, SaveAsName, and then assigning a formatted version of the Now function, we can create a unique name for the file every time it is saved. Add these two lines after .Selection.Paste:

```
SaveAsName = Environ("UserProfile") _
& "\Desktop\EmployeeReport " _
& Format(Now, "yyyy-mm-dd hh-mm-ss") & ".docx"
.ActiveDocument.SaveAs2 SaveAsName
```

7. Every time you run the procedure now, a new file with a unique name will be saved.

Following these instructions will enable you to automatically copy data from Excel into Word.

How it works...

Here is an explanation of what we did.

Selecting data in Excel is not a new concept, and neither is copying. Saving it in a Word document with Excel VBA requires making use of the Environ function, as well as formatting of the filename. This will ensure that a new file is created every time the Excel VBA procedure is executed.

See also

Visit https://bettersolutions.com/vba/functions/environ-function.htm for more information on the Environ function and keywords.

Using templates and bookmarks

To copy an entire Excel spreadsheet and paste it into Word doesn't make sense. You could rather have done everything in Word from the beginning, saving you the whole effort of copying from Excel and pasting in Word.

The point is, if you have an existing Word document or even a Word template, and you regularly need to export selected information from a spreadsheet in Excel to this template, this is the way to do it. The word *automation* acquires new meaning if you can link Excel with Word in this manner.

In this recipe, we will be pasting Excel data into a Word document at a specific bookmark.

Getting ready

Make sure that `Word_Interaction.xlsm` is still open, and that the VBA Editor is active.

How to do it...

We need to do the following:

1. Open the Word document that was saved to the desktop. Delete the inserted table, (select only the entire table – no lines before or after, click the **Layout** contextual tab, and then **Rows & Columns | Delete | Delete Table**)

2. Enter the short sentence `Latest information on employees` in the open space.

3. Insert a bookmark in the first open line after this sentence. Click on **Insert | Bookmark**. The **Bookmark** dialog box will appear. Enter a name in the **Bookmark name** textbox, and then click on **Add** to close the dialog box:

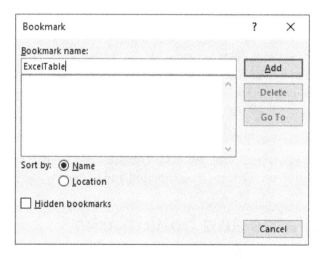

Figure 17.7 – Bookmark name

4. Click on **File** | **Save As**, and save the file as a Word template. The file extension is
    .dotx. Call the file EmployeeReportTemplate.

5. Depending on the operating system and the version of MS Office on your PC, the
    file will be saved in a specific folder, dedicated to template files:

C:\Users\User\Documents\Custom Office Templates

Figure 17.8 – Folder for template files

6. Close the file and return to the VBA Editor in Excel.

7. Add the following line of text in the code window to open a specific file, and not just
    a blank document:

```
Sub CreateWordDoc()
    Dim wdApp As Word.Application
    Set wdApp = New Word.Application
    With wdApp
        .Visible = True
        .Activate
        .Documents.Add "C:\Users\User\Documents\Custom _
        Office Templates\EmployeeReportTemplate.dotx"
```

8. Because we're making use of a template, we do not need any of the formatting
    we did for the previous document. Delete the following lines of code:

```
With .Selection
    .ParagraphFormat.Alignment = _
    wdAlignParagraphCenter
    .BoldRun    'Switch Bold on
    .Font.Size = 16
    .TypeText "Employee Information"
    .BoldRun    'Switch Bold off
    .TypeParagraph    'Enter a new line
    .Font.Size = 11
    .ParagraphFormat.Alignment = _
    wdAlignParagraphLeft
    .TypeParagraph
End With
```

9. Use the `GoTo` method to instruct Word exactly where the copied data from Excel must be inserted. That's why we created a bookmark in the Word template. The final coding for the entire procedure should look like this:

```
Sub CreateWordDoc()
    Dim wdApp As Word.Application
    Dim SaveAsName As String

    Set wdApp = New Word.Application

    With wdApp
        '.Visible = True
        '.Activate

        .Documents.Add "C:\Users\User\Documents\Custom _
        Office Templates\EmployeeReportTemplate.dotx"

        Range("A1", Range("A2").End(xlDown) _
        .End(xlToRight)).Copy

        .Selection.Goto wdGoToBookmark, , , "ExcelTable"
        .Selection.Paste

        SaveAsName = Environ("UserProfile")   _
        & "\Desktop\EmployeeReport "   _
        & Format(Now, "yyyy-mm-dd hh-mm-ss") & ".docx"

        .ActiveDocument.SaveAs2 SaveAsName
        .ActiveDocument.Close
        .Quit
    End With
End Sub
```

These instructions will enable you to create a template in Word, and then automatically place content from Excel into the Word document at specific bookmarks.

Inserting Excel data into a Word template can be done with Excel VBA. Inserting a bookmark in the Word template enables Excel to send data to a specific insertion point for the data to be pasted.

See also

Visit `https://docs.microsoft.com/en-us/office/vba/api/word.selection.goto` for more information on the `GoTo` method.

18
Working with PowerPoint in Excel VBA

Experience has shown by now that VBA is common to all the applications within the Office Suite. This means that data in an Excel spreadsheet can be automatically exported to PowerPoint as well.

The advantage of knowing how to use VBA to automate these tasks saves a lot of time. Instead of manually copying from Excel and pasting into PowerPoint, everything can be automated, using the appropriate procedures in VBA.

In this chapter, we will cover the following recipes:

- Creating a new instance of PowerPoint
- Creating presentations and slides
- Adding text to textboxes
- Copying Excel content into PowerPoint

By the end of this chapter, you will be able to initiate a PowerPoint slideshow from within Excel.

Technical requirements

This cookbook was written and designed to be used with MS Office 2019 and MS Office 365, installed on either Windows 8, 8.1, or 10.

If your hardware and software meet these requirements, you are good to go.

The code for this book is stored at the following link: `https://github.com/PacktPublishing/VBA-Automation-for-Excel-2019-Cookbook`.

Please visit the following link to check the CiA videos: `https://bit.ly/3jQRvVk`.

Creating a new instance of PowerPoint

The process of setting a reference to the object library with Word is similar to that of PowerPoint. Hence, the same must be done with PowerPoint, or else Excel cannot communicate with PowerPoint at all.

In this recipe, we will be creating a new instance of PowerPoint from within Excel.

Getting ready

Open Excel, and activate a new workbook. Save the file as a macro-enabled file on your desktop and call it `PPoint_Interaction.xlsm`. **Sheet1** should be active. Press *Alt + F11* to switch to the VBA Editor, and then insert a new module.

It is a prerequisite that MS PowerPoint must also be installed on your computer in order for the instructions in this recipe to work effectively.

> **Note**
> In this chapter, we will only cater to the latest version of MS Office. Coding for previous or legacy versions is not covered.

How to do it...

Here is how to link PowerPoint to Excel:

1. In the VBA Editor, click on **Tools | References**. The **References - VBAProject** dialog box will open:

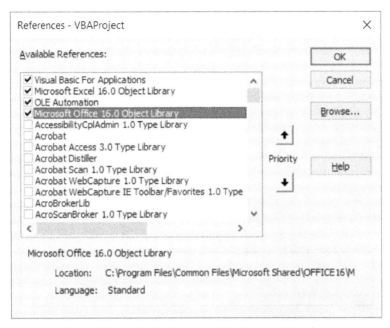

Figure 18.1 – The References - VBAProject dialog box

2. Scroll down the list of available references until you find **Microsoft PowerPoint 16.0 Object Library**:

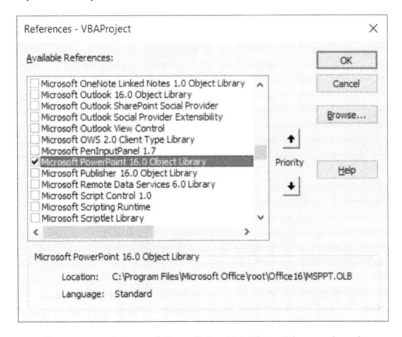

Figure 18.2 – Microsoft PowerPoint 16.0 Object Library selected

3. Once selected, click on **OK** to save the selection and also to close the dialog box.

> **Note**
>
> It is important to know that the reference to the PowerPoint object library is only valid for the Excel workbook you're working in currently. Every new workbook will have to be referenced to PowerPoint in exactly the same way.

4. With the object library in place, we can initiate PowerPoint from within Excel. There are several ways of doing this, but for this recipe, we will be using this specific technique:

```
Sub CreatePPointSlides()
    Dim PowPntApp As PowerPOint.Application
    Set PowPntApp = New PowerPoint.Application
    PowPntApp.Visible = True
    PowPntApp.Activate
End Sub
```

5. Test the Sub procedure by pressing *F5*. A new instance of PowerPoint will appear on your screen, with no presentation or slide active. Close the application once you know that the Sub procedure is working:

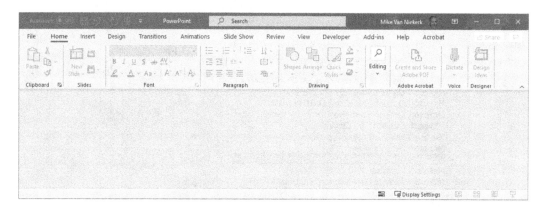

Figure 18.3 – New PowerPoint instance

With the Microsoft PowerPoint object library enabled, it is possible to use PowerPoint keywords and methods within Excel.

Actions such as opening an instance of PowerPoint, which was previously not possible, can now be done.

Creating presentations and slides

Opening PowerPoint without opening a new presentation is not very useful. It stands to reason that a new presentation, with at least one slide, should be initiated together with the application.

Getting ready

With Excel still open, make sure that PPoint_Interaction.xlsm is available. **Module1** in the VBA Editor must be visible.

How to do it...

Here are the steps to follow:

1. Add the next lines of code to the Sub procedure to open a new presentation with a new slide:

```
Sub CreatePPointSlides()
    Dim PowPntApp As PowerPoint.Application
    Dim PowPntPrsnt As PowerPoint.Presentation
    Dim PowPntSlide As PowerPoint.Slide

    Set PowPntApp = New PowerPoint.Application

    PowPntApp.Visible = True
    PowPntApp.Activate

    Set PowPntPrsnt = PowPntApp.Presentations.Add

    Set PowPntSlide = _
    PowPntPrsnt.Slides.Add(1, ppLayoutTitle)
End Sub
```

2. If you now run the procedure, PowerPoint will open again, this time displaying not only a new presentation, but also a new slide.

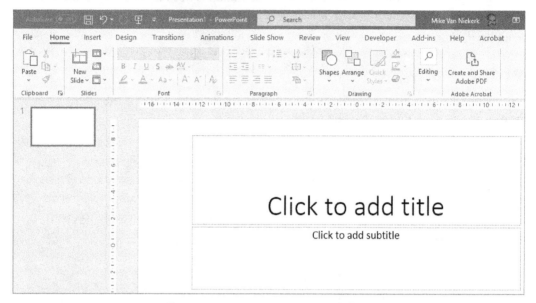

Figure 18.4 – New presentation and slide

3. Close PowerPoint, but don't save anything. Return to the VBA Editor in Excel.

Opening a new instance of PowerPoint creates a new presentation as well as a new, empty slide. By using the appropriate VBA coding in Excel, the process can be automated.

Adding text to textboxes

It's all very well to know how to open PowerPoint, create presentations, and make a slide available. The next objective is to add text to the two available textboxes on **Slide1**.

In this recipe, we will be adding text to the textboxes on **Slide1**.

Getting ready

Make sure `PPoint_Interaction.xlsm` is still open, and that the VBA Editor is active.

How to do it...

These are the steps to enter and format text in PowerPoint:

1. To add text to a PowerPoint presentation via Excel, add the following line of code:

```
Sub CreatePPointSlides()
    Dim PowPntApp As PowerPoint.Application
    Dim PowPntPrsnt As PowerPoint.Presentation
    Dim PowPntSlide As PowerPoint.Slide

    Set PowPntApp = New PowerPoint.Application

    PowPntApp.Visible = True
    PowPntApp.Activate

    Set PowPntPrsnt = PowPntApp.Presentations.Add

    Set PowPntSlide = _
    PowPntPrsnt.Slides.Add(1, ppLayoutTitle)

    PowPntSlide.Shapes(1).TextFrame.TextRange = _
    "Employee Information Slide"
    PowPntSlide.Shapes(2).TextFrame.TextRange = _
    "by Presenter"
End Sub
```

2. Press *F5*. Running the Sub procedure will now result in a new instance of PowerPoint, with a new presentation and slide open:

Figure 18.5 – New instance of PowerPoint, with a presentation, slide, and text

3. Each textbox will have its own line of text. Close PowerPoint without saving, since there is more code to add to our procedure in Excel.

Using the appropriate code will enable you to add customized text to individual textboxes on a slide.

Copying Excel content into PowerPoint

Automatically copying content from Excel to PowerPoint saves a lot of time. What we need to do now is select data, copy it, and then paste that into yet another newly inserted slide.

In this recipe, we will be copying a table into PowerPoint.

Getting ready

Make sure that `PPoint_Interaction.xlsm` is still open. Activate **Sheet1**, and enter the following data:

	A	B	C	D	E
1	ID	Name	Department	D.O.B.	Age
2	1	Joe	Admin	01/03/1988	32
3	2	Sue	Sales	25/10/1992	28
4	3	Dave	Projects	11/06/1996	24
5	4	Anne	HR	15/04/1989	31
6	5	Bill	Sales	20/01/1990	30
7	6	Tom	Sales	21/08/1993	27
8	7	Fred	Training	07/07/1995	25
9	8	Bob	Technical	09/05/1991	29
10	9	Jane	Admin	14/02/1994	27

Figure 18.6 – Working data

How to do it...

Follow these steps to copy text from Excel to PowerPoint:

1. Before selecting anything in Excel, we need to insert a new blank slide in PowerPoint. Add the following lines of code:

```
Sub CreatePowPntShow()
    Dim PowPntApp As PowerPoint.Application
    Dim PowPntPrsnt As PowerPoint.Presentation
```

```
        Dim PowPntSlide As PowerPoint.Slide

        Set PowPntApp = New PowerPoint.Application

        PowPntApp.Visible = True
        PowPntApp.Activate

        Set PowPntPrsnt = PowPntApp.Presentations.Add

        Set PowPntSlide = _
        PowPntPrsnt.Slides.Add(1, ppLayoutTitle)

        PowPntSlide.Shapes(1).TextFrame.TextRange = _
        "Employee Information"
        PowPntSlide.Shapes(2).TextFrame.TextRange = _
        "by Presenter"

        Set PowPntSlide = _
        PowPntPrsnt.Slides.Add(2, ppLayoutBlank)
        PowPntSlide.Select

    End Sub
```

2. Run the Sub procedure to check your coding. We know that the first part will work, but in this case, we need to check whether a second slide was inserted:

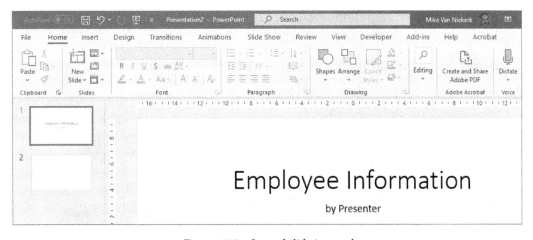

Figure 18.7 – Second slide inserted

3. To select the data in Excel, add the following line of code, directly below the previous entry. This will select the data on **Sheet1** and then copy it:

    ```
    Range("A1").CurrentRegion.Copy
    ```

4. Once the data has been copied, it must be pasted into the current slide. Enter the next line of code, once again directly below the previous line of code:

    ```
    PowPntSlide.Shapes.Paste
    ```

5. The last thing we need to do is close down the document, and finally, PowerPoint itself. Just add the following two lines in a new line after the filename:

    ```
    PowPntPrsnt.Close
    PowPntApp.Quit
    ```

Selecting data in Excel, copying it, and then pasting it into PowerPoint can all be automated with VBA in Excel.

There's more...

As a finishing touch, we can add code to create a unique filename for each PowerPoint presentation:

1. We can create a unique name for the file every time it is saved. Add the following lines after .Shapes.Paste:

    ```
    PowPntPrsnt.SaveAs Environ("UserProfile")       _
        & "\Desktop\EmployeeInformation "       _
        & Format(Now, "yyyy-mm-dd hh-mm-ss") & ".pptx"
    ```

2. Every time you run the procedure now, a new file with a unique name will be saved.

3. The complete Sub procedure should look like this:

    ```
    Sub CreatePPointSlides()
        Dim PowPntApp As PowerPoint.Application
        Dim PowPntPrsnt As PowerPoint.Presentation
        Dim PowPntSlide As PowerPoint.Slide

        Set PowPntApp = New PowerPoint.Application
        PowPntApp.Visible = True
        PowPntApp.Activate

        Set PowPntPrsnt = PowPntApp.Presentations.Add
    ```

```
        Set PowPntSlide = _
        PowPntPrsnt.Slides.Add(1, ppLayoutTitle)
        PowPntSlide.Shapes(1).TextFrame.TextRange = _
        "Employee Information"
        PowPntSlide.Shapes(2).TextFrame.TextRange = _
        "by Presenter"
        Set PowPntSlide = _
        PowPntPrsnt.Slides.Add(2, ppLayoutBlank)
        PowPntSlide.Select
        Range("A1").CurrentRegion.Copy
        PowPntSlide.Shapes.Paste
        PowPntPrsnt.SaveAs Environ("UserProfile") _
        & "\Desktop\EmployeeInformation " _
        & Format(Now, "yyyy-mm-dd hh-mm-ss") & ".pptx"

        PowPntPrsnt.Close
        PowPntApp.Quit
    End Sub
```

Following the instructions in this recipe will enable you to select information in Excel, copy it there, and then paste it into a specific slide in PowerPoint.

Other Books You May Enjoy

If you enjoyed this book, you may be interested in these other books by Packt:

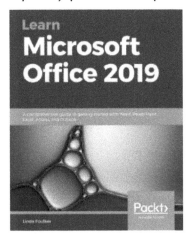

Learn Microsoft Office 2019

Linda Foulkes

ISBN: 978-1-83921-725-8

- Use PowerPoint 2019 effectively to create engaging presentations
- Gain working knowledge of Excel formulas and functions
- Collaborate using Word 2019 tools, and create and format tables and professional documents
- Organize emails, calendars, meetings, contacts, and tasks with Outlook 2019
- Store information for reference, reporting, and analysis using Access 2019
- Discover new functionalities such as Translator, Read Aloud, Scalable Vector Graphics (SVG), and data analysis tools that are useful for working professionals

Learn Power Query

Linda Foulkes, Warren Sparrow

ISBN: 978-1-83921-971-9

- Convert worksheet data into a table format ready for query output
- Create a dynamic connection between an Access database and Excel workbook
- Reshape tabular data by altering rows, columns, and tables using various Power Query tools
- Create new columns automatically from filenames and sheet tabs, along with multiple Excel data files
- Streamline and automate reports from multiple sources
- Explore different customization options to get the most out of your dashboards
- Understand the difference between the DAX language and Power Query's M language

Leave a review - let other readers know what you think

Please share your thoughts on this book with others by leaving a review on the site that you bought it from. If you purchased the book from Amazon, please leave us an honest review on this book's Amazon page. This is vital so that other potential readers can see and use your unbiased opinion to make purchasing decisions, we can understand what our customers think about our products, and our authors can see your feedback on the title that they have worked with Packt to create. It will only take a few minutes of your time, but is valuable to other potential customers, our authors, and Packt. Thank you!

Index

W